DO NOT REMOVE
CARDS FROM POCKET

ALLEN COUNTY PUBLIC LIBRARY
FORT WAYNE, INDIANA 46802

You may return this book to any agency, branch,
or bookmobile of the Allen County Public Library.

DEMCO

GAINSHARING
and
EMPLOYEE
INVOLVEMENT

GAINSHARING and EMPLOYEE INVOLVEMENT

Brian Graham-Moore
Timothy L. Ross

with contributions by
Ruth Ann Ross
Paul S. Goodman
James E. Jarrett
James W. Dean, Jr.
Larry L. Hatcher

The Bureau of National Affairs, Inc., Washington, D.C. 20037

Library of Congress Cataloging-in-Publication Data

Graham-Moore, Brian E., 1935–
    Gainsharing and employee involvement / Brian Graham-Moore, Timothy
L. Ross, with contribution by Ruth Ann Ross ... [et al.].
        p.   cm.
    Updated ed. of: Gainsharing. 1990.
    Includes bibiliographical references and index.
    ISBN 0-87179-875-1
        1. Gainsharing.   2. Gainsharing—United States.   I. Ross,
Timothy L., 1938–   .   II. Ross, Ruth Ann.   III. Title.
HD4928.G34G69   1995
658.3′225—dc20   94-49405
                                                            CIP

Published by BNA Books, 1231 25th St., N.W.
Washington, D.C. 20037

Printed in the United States of America
International Standard Book Number: 0-87179-875-1

Foreword

An acquaintance once described an uncle of his as the essence of the traditional, the unchanging. The uncle would urge his nephew to hold fast to the old, tried, and true ways of life and thought and to shun deviations from established custom and practice. "Take me, for instance," the uncle would say, "My father and grandfather were cabinet makers and, as you know, so am I. That's tradition. My father and grandfather always voted conservative and so do I. That's tradition. My father and grandfather always bowed before the wisdom of their superiors, and so do I. That's sound tradition. And my father and grandfather were bachelors, and, as you know, so am I!"

Obviously, not all tradition is worthy of rigid preservation!

It is heartening to witness the changes, the departure from tradition, which are spreading gradually within the field of labor-management relations.

The Tayloristic concept of the authoritarian work organization is losing its luster as, increasingly, it is recognized that employees as individuals and in groups often put management and engineers to shame, once afforded the opportunity to apply their knowledge, their experience, and their bent for innovation. Experimentation in participative management processes has taken many different forms, with varying degrees of success. When emphasis has been directed toward enhancing the role of the employees in the decision-making process, and toward creating the climate for improved job satisfaction, the workplace traditions that inhibit creativity become discarded. New approaches to solving old problems displace the tired habits of the past. An excitement runs through the organization as it enjoys renewed vitality. When the emphasis, however, is directed essentially toward producing more for the sake of increased profit, this process becomes a management gimmick, co-opted to its advantage with but limited benefit to the work force that makes improvement possible.

Gainsharing plans have a unique role to play in bringing about rational change in the organization of work—and even in the management of enterprises. It is all the more urgent that they not become a gimmick designed just to fulfill management's objectives, but that they represent a mutually beneficial pact in a joint action process. True, gainsharing programs are anchored in the opportunity to win larger paychecks and enhance profitability. The driving force, nevertheless, should be based on producing a work climate that will advance the dignity of the employees as the adult human beings they are and ensure that they will not be treated as mere cogs in a machine.

In the final analysis, the most potent protection against management co-optation of gainsharing programs is the co-equal status with management of the employees' collective bargaining representative in planning, designing, implementing, and administering the program. The joint union-management structure promises assurance against undue advantage being taken by management. It provides a necessary voice for the work force in promoting the most desirable qualities of gainsharing. It guarantees joint effort in all aspects of its operation—in a genuine mode of cooperative endeavor.

Whether the gainsharing takes the form of Scanlon as its initiator originally envisaged its implementation, or of Rucker® or Improshare®, which are more directly related to production standards as the base for reward, the ultimate test is whether the work force will be recognized as true co-partners in the operation.

This vital point is incorporated, although not outrightly expressed, in the authors' finding that institutionalization of gainsharing programs is best achieved when there are common goals. Fulfillment of common goals is best accomplished when the factors leading to institutionalization are jointly managed. Joint commitment, joint training, jointly devised allocation of reward, joint examination of feedback, joint diffusion of the process throughout the organization, joint alteration of the program as the need for change becomes evident—these are the elements for a sound initiative and continuing success. And, success within this scenario makes absolutely imperative the commitment to depart from tradition and create a mind-set, a culture which "thinks anew and acts anew."

The authors' study of gainsharing judiciously analyzes the features that more likely assure success for gainsharing plans and the overall enhancement of job satisfaction. While their treatment does not dwell on the importance of union involvement as I would view it, the basic elements that are the firm foundation for gainsharing as an instrument for the economic viability of organizations are carefully explored and are presented with clarity. Their work should give added impetus to the expansion of the use of gainsharing programs, with the studied explanation of the procedures for success and the reasons for failure. Management and unions alike would do well to note the findings and give heed to the recommendations.

Irving Bluestone
University Professor of Labor Studies
Wayne State University
Retired Vice President, UAW

Introduction

There is ample evidence that gainsharing continues to grow at an accelerating rate. Large scale studies by the American Compensation Association in 1992 and 1994 indicate increases in gainsharing programs across many industries. Articles on pay for performance and contingent/variable compensation are commonly found in a wide range of publications. Major sectors of the economy now have broad forms of gainsharing from private to public and nonprofit. The integration of gainsharing into regular pay systems has been achieved by organizations that, five years ago, never contemplated compensation beyond fixed rates of pay. Why this increasing interest? What is the best fit of a gainsharing plan into an organization's culture? Where are the pitfalls? The answers to these questions are the reasons for this book.

Although traditional gainsharing practitioners may be disturbed by current trends, gainsharing is meeting the strategic needs of many different kinds of organizations. For example, one firm may use it to help save itself from bankruptcy; another may use it to phase out an obsolete individual incentive system; others may use gainsharing to improve labor relations, whereas still others may install gainsharing as a substitute for normal wage increases. Even if purists may find these trends disturbing, they occur nevertheless.

More ideal applications are also found in very successful organizations that see gainsharing as just an expansion of already successful techniques. These firms use gainsharing for integrating improved communications and cooperation, enhancing existing employee involvement, and increasing their competitiveness. Cost control, quality, and customer service combined with the shared financial benefits of gainsharing help to mutually reinforce existing systems of quality organizations. Also, these organizations see sharing financial gains as a fair practice. One thing is certain, adding financial rewards adds a powerful ingredient to the change and identity variables of organizational success.

In this book, we attempt to explain why gainsharing works and why it sometimes does not. Theoretical underpinnings are discussed in Chapter 1 with the understanding that no one model is likely to explain gainsharing success. It may lead to organizational change in one situation, or it may reinforce positive organizational change in another. In these situations, different and appropriate models are needed to match organizational requirements with their environments. This edition emphasizes employee involvement gainsharing as opposed to just organization-wide bonus plans.

Other conceptual issues are discussed in the remainder of Part One. Chapter 2 discusses the extensive literature on gainsharing; Chapter 3 is totally new and covers typical involvement systems; Chapters 4 and 5 cover most of the important measurement issues that, without becoming overly complex, must be considered; and Chapters 6 and 7 delve into why plans fail or succeed in the long run.

Part Two provides much practical experience, starting with a 19-year case study. In fact, companies with as many as 40 years of gainsharing experience exist. From this we know that gainsharing can last a long time. One problem is the lack of appropriate information on long-term gainsharing success. A variety of other issues are covered in subsequent chapters. Some issues regarding government sector applications are covered in Chapter 9, and current union trends are outlined in Chapter 10. Chapter 11 focuses primarily on current quality and customer service issues.

Research studies of apprehensions and change processes underlying gainsharing are presented in Chapters 12 and 15. If an organization is planning a major change process with much employee involvement, Chapter 13 provides some useful educational outlines. The growing area of service sector organizations is reviewed in Chapter 14. Most good professionally oriented books should also provide some predictions of future expectations. This is done in our Chapter 16.

No book is solely the result of the author's efforts. This is particularly true in our case since the fruits of this book would have been impossible without the tremendous support of numerous firms and individuals who allowed us to learn at their expense. Without this cooperation, certainly this book would never have been written. Fortunately, this is the great thing about gainsharing— companies that successfully practice it really do believe in the concept. This makes our research and writing activities immeasurably easier because these firms want to share their knowledge and experience.

A special acknowledgement is due to our students and colleagues at The University of Texas at Austin and at The Ross Institute in Chapel Hill, North Carolina. They have listened to our ideas many times and provided much useful criticism. While we are responsible for our expression here, they have helped in the continual process of improving those ideas that make employee involvement gainsharing more accessible. The communication of our ideas has been further enhanced by the editing contributions of Robin Graham-Moore and by Bookmark for BNA.

We sincerely appreciate the contributions of our colleagues James W. Dean, Jr., Paul S. Goodman, Larry Hatcher, James E. Jarrett, and Ruth Ann Ross.

September, 1994   Brian Graham-Moore
                                        Timothy L. Ross

Contents

**3. Employee Involvement—The Key Link to Successful
Long-Run Gainsharing** ....
Timothy L. Ross and Ruth Ann Ross

**4. Formulas for Developing a Reward Structure to Further
Organizational Goals** ....
Brian Graham-Moore

Part Two. Cases and Applications

List of Exhibits

Part One

Theory, Measurement, and
Conceptual Issues

Chapter 1

Understanding Gainsharing

Brian Graham-Moore and Timothy L. Ross

INTRODUCTION

Gainsharing is a formal reward system that has existed in a variety of forms for over 50 years. Sometimes gainsharing is known as the Scanlon Plan, the Rucker Plan,® or Improshare.® The generic term, however, is gainsharing, and its definition usually is made up of these three components:

1. the philosophy of cooperation,
2. the involvement system,
3. the financial bonus.

This book will continually define these components and provide examples, but a brief discussion of each of these terms follows. The philosophy of cooperation refers to an organizational climate wherein high levels of trust, two-way communication, participation, and harmonious industrial relations exist. Positive values supporting these behaviors are held by most, if not all organizational members at good installations.

The second component, the involvement system, refers to the structure and process whereby organizational productivity is improved. Most typically it is a broadly based suggestion system implemented by an employee-staffed team or group structure that usually reaches all areas of the organization. The teams may be vertical, department oriented, or cross-functional, and often they may be a combination of the three. Sometimes this structure involves work teams, but it usually includes an employee-based improvement system. The employees involved develop and implement ideas related to productivity or quality improvement.

The third component is the financial bonus. Historically, this bonus is determined by a calculation that measures the difference between expected costs and actual costs during a bonus period. Indeed, the very word gainsharing was probably coined by F. Taylor in 1886 to refer to the payment of bonuses out of these differences. Some firms use expected versus actual time as their bonus calculation and others use profit improvement. Many varieties of calculations are found in practice, and most firms today custom design calculations that best meet their needs. As Chapters 4, 5, 9, 11, and 14 point out, many calculations are no longer strictly based on cost savings.

These three definitional components mutually reinforce each other. Higher levels of cooperation lead to information sharing, which, in turn, leads to employee involvement. Typically, this employee involvement leads to new behaviors, such as the offering of suggestions, which improve organizational performance. This increase in performance then results in a financial bonus (based on the amount of the performance increase) that rewards or reinforces the philosophy of cooperation. While some forms of gainsharing may emphasize one component of this definition over the other two, or even delete one or more of these components, most long-term, successful gainsharing examples employ all three components while reflecting significant employee involvement.

Descriptive Model

Defining and describing gainsharing is an easier task than predicting its success. For example, developing a theory for gainsharing is very difficult because it exists in so many variations and in so many different environments. While theoretical development is a desirable goal, few comprehensive efforts have been made in this direction. Nevertheless, decision makers within organizations wish to know where and how gainsharing has failed. Presumably, they would like to avoid similar pitfalls. While this approach would imply that failure avoidance is a safe strategy, this framework doesn't predict success, just the avoidance of sure failure. This position is, in effect, only partial theory and begs for a more complete answer. Obviously, gainsharing needs more and better predictive theory.

Our approach in this chapter is to present a description of gainsharing along with some predictions as to how well it can work under various conditions. First, we present a descriptive model that describes, in part, how gainsharing works for contingent compensation strategies or the traditional gainsharing strategy, i.e., the self-directed work force[1] (see Exhibit 1.1). This model permits us to list and defend what we do know about gainsharing. While this is useful in the same way as failure avoidance, the descriptive model doesn't permit full prediction and validation of those propositions that make gainsharing success possible. Later in the chapter, some elements of predictive gainsharing theory will be introduced. For now, let's turn to Exhibit 1.1 and the descriptive model.

Exhibit 1.1 Gainsharing Descriptive Model

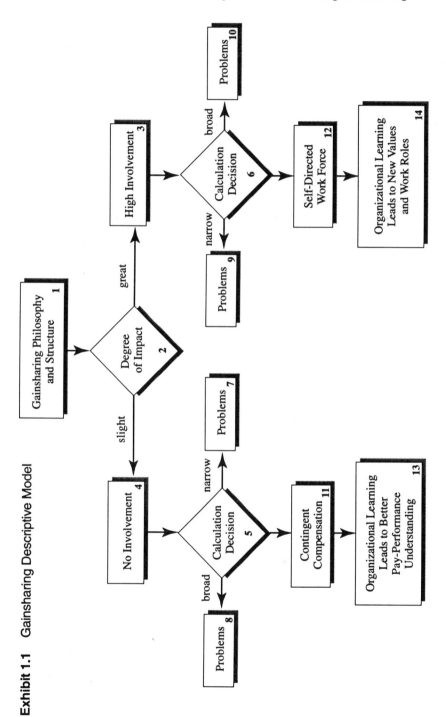

As we can see, box 1 refers to all of the knowledge that goes into and supports what we perceive to be true concerning gainsharing. The first decision diamond (no. 2) raises the question concerning the degree of impact gainsharing is intended to have on the organization. In cases in which the intended impact is slight, no involvement (no. 4), then it is honest to say that some organizations use gainsharing in a fashion contrary to what the literature reveals in Chapter 2. Very clearly, the past has seen concessionary bargaining and take-aways of pay and fringe benefits. As compensation experts re-design their reward packages, they wish to avoid those policies that tend to feed inflation. Also, they are drawn toward innovative reward systems that adjust for economic realities, i.e., variable pay, two-tiered pay, pay for performance, and, even, gainsharing.

Decision diamond (no. 5) could lead to a broad gainsharing calculation or a narrow gainsharing calculation. Boxes 7 and 8 indicate that each choice will represent a different set of problems. Narrow calculations have the advantage of simplicity. If they are targeted in unambiguous ways, then employees may understand and accept management's message to work harder. Broad calculations, at box 8, without an involvement system, run the risk of overloading employees with a calculation too great in scope. As a result they may feel powerless to influence performance even by attempting to work harder and smarter because there are no mechanisms for problem solving.

Box 11 of Exhibit 1.1 states that contingent compensation is one gainsharing strategy. In this instance, base pay may be slightly lower than the market, but bonuses are employed to meet or exceed prevailing rates when they are justified by commensurate human performance. The most significant outcome is organizational learning. That is, better knowledge of pay-performance relationships may occur, as indicated at box 13. The work force can learn that high quantity leads to high bonuses. This outcome differs from that created by individual incentives because the gainsharing bonus is typically contingent on the quantity produced by *all* employees, not just one person.

Looking at Exhibit 1.1 again, if the degree-of-impact decision is to adopt high involvement and the calculation decision is to develop a broad or narrow calculation, then successful gainsharing may be associated with a more self-directed work force (box 12) or at least many activities. The organizational learning includes new work values and work roles, and the organizational culture is markedly changed as indicated by box 14. Chapter 3 explores the involvement issues in some detail. Chapters 4 and 5 delve into the intricacies of calculation development. These chapters specify the trade-offs required in the use of various calculations to reinforce appropriate organizational strategies. The degree of impact desired does not always produce the predictable results seen in Exhibit 1.1. For example, decision makers could offer a narrow calculation to employees in combination with a high involvement system. That is, high involvement with a narrow calculation could lead to feelings of frustration and inequity as indicated by box 9. Why does this occur? Successful gainsharing culture shows the human resource how to work smarter, cooperate, and partici-pate in ways that lead to a self-directed work force. A narrow calculation rein-forces only part of those behavioral changes. True self-management isn't partial. It is a real commitment to influence *all* of the factors associated with an organ-ization's success—if they are under the control of the work force. A narrow calculation excludes many factors that are under work force control to at least some degree.

It is clear that gainsharing exists in a variety of forms and stages of devel-opment. Virtually all of the literature reviewed in Chapter 2 is concerned with traditional gainsharing. The traditional view suggests that the only long-term goal of gainsharing is a self-directed work force. Obviously, there are other strategies, such as contingent compensation, and numerous examples exist where gainsharing has been used to further this compensation strategy. It is possible an organization could evolve from no involvement gainsharing to high involvement gainsharing, but probably not the converse.

TRADITIONAL GAINSHARING AND ORGANIZATIONAL FIT

The conditions that favor traditional gainsharing have been "known" for some time.[2] We say known because recognition of these conditions has been achieved through various types of research. Exhibit 1.2 lists four broad cate-gories of conditions and variables that affect the success of gainsharing. For example, Exhibit 1.2 denotes organizational size, as measured by total number employed at one location, as an important factor. Since part of the gainsharing philosophy is to share information, cooperate, and have an influence on one's working environment, it is not surprising that increasing organizational size works against gainsharing. A national survey of gainsharing companies taken

Exhibit 1.2 Conditions That Affect the Success of Gainsharing Plans

Organizational Factors	**Financial/Market Factors**
Size	Financial measures
Climate	Market for output
Communication	Product stability
	Seasonal nature
	Capital investment
Technological Factors	**Labor Force Factors**
Type	Work force characteristics
Technological uncertainty	Union relations
Work flow/cycle	Supportive services
	Overtime history

in 1987 reported that gainsharing companies ranged in size from fewer than 250 employees (22 percent of the gainsharing companies) to more than 20,000 employees (6 percent of the gainsharing companies). The reported median was a surprisingly high 954 employees.[3] However, 60 percent of the organizations reported 500 or fewer employees. Size is perhaps a factor, yet it would appear that larger organizations are attempting gainsharing than has been previously thought. The 1992 and 1994 American Compensation Association (ACA) studies found similar results.[4]

Organizational climate and communication must be conducive to the acceptance of traditional gainsharing philosophy. That is, sufficient trust and open communication must exist within an organization before gainsharing can have an impact. If there are no norms and values reinforcing the sharing of information, the institution of a gainsharing plan alone probably would not effect this change.

Exhibit 1.2 lists technological factors as impacting on gainsharing success. For example, if there is a high degree of task interdependency, then sharing and rapid movement of information is needed to achieve task success. Thus, the way work is organized can help or hinder gainsharing success. If each work station is only concerned with its own output, then gainsharing may not have general appeal. In the same way, if the technology is well understood, highly programmed, tightly controlled by the machine process with few variances, then opportunities to "work smarter" are limited. Reciprocal workflows and longer work cycles help gainsharing because they require sharing information, teamwork, and coordination. Indeed, these are new sources of intrinsic satisfaction that can lead to higher levels of participation.

Financial and market factors should not be overlooked. As will be explained in Chapters 2 through 6, the degree of sophistication of financial information systems will either work for or against gainsharing. Organizations that cannot assemble accurate historical cost data should not entertain the idea of traditional gainsharing. In addition, a series of economic factors needs to be assessed. For example, will there be a market for increased output? Is product stability likely or will there be many changes to the product line that change the accuracy of historical costs? Does the seasonal nature of the production cycle influence the measure of productivity? Do very long runs reflect the same patterns of efficiency? In reference to financial-market factors, will planned capital investments change the amount of value added by labor? Chapters 4 and 5 explore some of these questions.

The last category on the list of conditions affecting gainsharing (Exhibit 1.2) regards the characteristics of the labor force. For instance, levels of job satisfaction and employee motivation must be sufficiently high for gainsharing to be perceived as an instrumental link to even higher levels of human performance. Chapters 2 and 3 will provide insights into appropriate employee characteristics. In addition, if union relations with management are poor, gainsharing would be expected, as a structure, to lead to better levels of industrial relations. It should be obvious that gainsharing can reinforce harmonious relations more easily than it can change an adversarial climate. Also, an organization's supportive services (for example, engineering, maintenance, supply, etc.) will be strained under a gainsharing program because new demands will be placed upon them from the involvement system. Therefore, these supportive services should be flexible and capable of expansion.

The last condition of Exhibit 1.2 is overtime history. Case studies discussed in Chapter 2 have indicated how overtime practices, if poor, can undermine a gainsharing program. For example, in a case in which overtime is not justified, a gainsharing bonus will make this unfair difference in pay even larger. Therefore, overtime practices perceived as fair are a favorable condition for gainsharing because dollars earned is typically used as the basis for calculating a gainsharing bonus, although other options are sometimes possible and still comply with the Fair Labor Standards Act.

Nontraditional Gainsharing and Organizational Fit

All the same variables must be considered in a nontraditional gainsharing plan, but calculations are much more flexible. Nontraditional, then, really means that a firm does not use one of the more traditional calculations. Today, a whole range or family of measures can be in practice and the plan can still be called gainsharing. These may heavily emphasize quality and customer service variables or be goal-oriented by not being based on historical performance at all. Gainsharing today is being installed in new company or plant start-ups and large departments and about anywhere an organizational pay-for-performance is desired.

ORGANIZATIONAL VARIABLES: THE DEGREE OF FIT

Our ability to predict how well gainsharing will fit into organizations with favorable conditions comes from understanding what the research has told us so far. Chapters 4 and 5 outline many of these relationships as they affect the gainsharing calculation. Most typically, decision makers who have opted for gainsharing plans in the past 50 years have had to consider conditions associated with success and failure and then compare them to their own situation. The patterns of conditions that have emerged are listed in Exhibit 1.2. Throughout this book, these conditions are explored theoretically and then tested empirically with survey and case study data. For example, in Chapter 2, "Review of the Literature", early literature on the subject is separated from more current studies and clear patterns of contemporary conditions that favor gainsharing begin to emerge. These clear results are obtained partly from the use of theory driven research, but mostly because of the improvement of research techniques in recent years.

One contemporary approach to considering a gainsharing program is to immerse oneself in the literature, compare the characteristics of one's organization to the characteristics known to favor gainsharing, and then begin a task-oriented assessment. Exhibit 1.3 depicts this process and presents the five steps involved. The first is to review the available literature and to make a judgment, perhaps based on many of the conditions listed in Exhibit 1.2, as to whether to assemble people for staff meetings.

The second step would be to develop a task force and pursue an educational effort to see if a consensus on gainsharing can be reached. If the employees of the organization have a union, union representatives should become involved early in the process. Also, employee surveys may be useful in acquiring more information on the chances of gainsharing success. Step 3 marks the assessment of the calculations that may be used for gainsharing. At some point the committee or task force must decide on the best calculation formula for the organization. This decision and the review of the organization's climate (via survey data) leads to the formulation of a gainsharing plan. After one year, the system is typically evaluated. If the plan is deemed a success and if conditions remain favorable, gainsharing is usually retained for a much longer period of time.

This sequence of 5 steps represents the prototypical stages of development for traditional gainsharing. At every step, rejection of gainsharing is clearly possible. Most of the people who are involved in the gainsharing program should want it to continue as a measure of their commitment to the value of gainsharing. It is better to reject the program rather than force the philosophy and structure on all concerned. This notion expresses the idea that gainsharing *lags* the organization's particular profile of conditions. If gainsharing is to *lead* the organization to better conditions, rather than lag behind, then it must serve to build higher levels of trust and cooperation. A pattern of strong bonuses, which must be perceived as fair,[5] will gradually create a change in attitude. Either way, lag or lead, gainsharing is new to the organization and represents organizational change. The organizational learning required in adopting traditional gainsharing will be less if it assumes a lagging role and considerably more if it leads. This is probably true of a nontraditional plan as well.

Our concern in this chapter has been to raise the issues involved in understanding gainsharing. One approach has been to separate contingent gainsharing from traditional gainsharing. To improve our understanding of how gainsharing might fit into any particular organization, we specified those conditions (Exhibit 1.2) which influence gainsharing success. Then, we introduced the prototypical steps involved in installing a gainsharing plan. Most organizations deliberately go through these steps while comparing themselves to the conditions known to bring about success in gainsharing. While this is prudent posture, we cannot be satisfied with it alone. We believe decision makers and all interested readers would want a clear way to predict gainsharing success—not merely a way to avoid failure.

Exhibit 1.3 Steps of Gainsharing Assessment

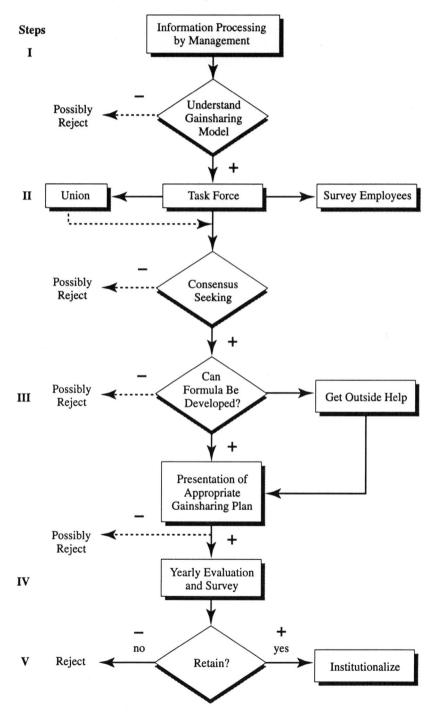

PREDICTIVE GAINSHARING

Why does gainsharing work? It is a fair question to raise. Somehow, *ex post facto* analyses of successful case studies as a way of understanding the "why" of gainsharing seems inappropriate in today's scientific world. As will be discussed in Chapter 2, there have been very few theoretical specifications which predict gainsharing success or failure.

Frost, Wakely, and Ruh[6] attempted to explain increased worker effort by the assumed intrinsic value of participation as reinforced by gainsharing bonuses and the perception of fair reward. Goodman and Moore[7] carefully assessed the psychological processes associated with gainsharing by employing expectancy motivation theory. They attempted to predict learning of organizational members as explained by their beliefs, their new roles in production committees, and their contributions of suggestions. During the six-month period of their organizational experiment Goodman and Moore were unable to predict changes in beliefs as a function of individual, interpersonal, and organizational level variables. They did report relatively high levels of positive beliefs as being conducive to gainsharing success, but these were unexplained by the theory they employed.

Perhaps the most interesting development at the individual and role level of analysis is by Tove Hammer.[8] She hypothesizes that both bonus payments and participation are important for gainsharing success and has stated that much previous research has stressed intrinsic factors such as participation more than the use of bonuses. As indicated by Hammer (see Exhibit 1.4), bonuses reinforce participation twice—once when they are promised and again when they are regularly received. Given this, participation has three hypothesized outcomes:

1. identification of and solutions to productivity problems,
2. intrinsic motivation increases due to changes in job design,
3. information sharing and feelings of employee empowerment.

Each of these outcomes follows participation which is in turn reinforced by the gainsharing bonus. Trust in management and commitment to gainsharing are also strengthened. As we asserted at the beginning of the chapter in Exhibit 1.1, a more self-directed work force then emerges when gainsharing conditions are ideal.

The advantage to Hammer's model is, of course, the ability to specify variables in advance and then assess them as Goodman and Moore attempted. If the relationships are validated, then we can more fully understand gainsharing as a form of organizational learning.

CONCLUSION

This chapter introduces the reader to the philosophy and structure of gainsharing. Gainsharing has been a part of the incentive and industrial relations field for 50 years, yet full understanding of why it works has eluded

Exhibit 1.4   Worker Role Outcomes Under Bonus Conditions

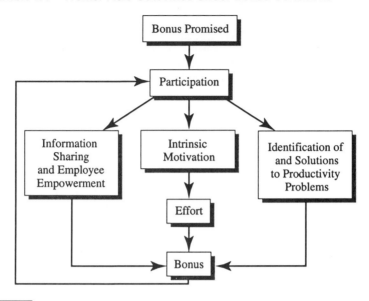

Adapted from T. Hammer, "New Developments in Profit Sharing," in J. Campbell, R. Campbell, and Associates, *Productivity in Organizations* (San Francisco: Jossey-Bass, 1988).

behavioral science. How gainsharing works in certain situations has, however, been adequately researched. Indeed, the following chapters will demonstrate these accomplishments well.

Contingent, traditional, and nontraditional gainsharing reinforce organizational learning. The result of this learning may be a sharpening of the pay/performance relationship. That is, all employees begin to recognize that a portion of their pay is clearly connected to the performance of the organization they work for. In traditional and nontraditional gainsharing, this learning process is more complex. We want to understand its dynamics more fully because of the immense value of the new organizational culture that evolves from it. Employees begin the process by working harder and smarter. Later they reach higher levels of cooperation and identification with organizational goals, eventually becoming self-directed. While it is true that employers become more competitive, mature gainsharing organizations are known to be good places to work. That is, these organizations appear to be leaders in their industries for many reasons—not simply for their gainsharing philosophy.

Of all the conditions associated with success in gainsharing, perhaps a positive organizational climate and a strong network for communication stand out as most important. Climate is a catch-all word referring to virtually all the behavioral aspects of work. However, the level of trust in management, the perceptions of the quality of supervision, the overall level of job satisfaction, to name but a few climate factors, are critical to the adoption of new ways exemplified by gainsharing. Communication is equally basic to the success of the process. For example, some organizations have no system for communicating to all of their employees except through the supervisory structure and, maybe, through the use of a public address system. It's not surprising that messages with any content become distorted in transmission when they move down the hierarchy. It's nothing short of miraculous when messages are accurately transmitted up through the same system! Traditional gainsharing adds an additional structure for communication to the organization, and underlying this structure is the increased value of performance information. Because communication now benefits all concerned, cost and performance information flows rapidly up and down the hierarchy.

The remaining chapters review what is known about gainsharing. Chapter 3 discusses typical involvement systems. Chapters 4 and 5 provide excellent insight into the method of gainsharing calculations, the area that is initially of greatest interest to employees. Over time, the bonus calculation diminishes in importance because gainsharing, if it succeeds, becomes a way of organizational life. One visit to a traditional gainsharing company proves this point to even the most disinterested observer. The long-term effect of traditional gainsharing is a strong change in behavior and values concerning organizational performance and a commitment to organizational learning.

Notes

1. Contingent gainsharing is a form of variable compensation since the fixed rate of pay is less than the fair value for any given job. This fixed rate *plus* the gainsharing bonus brings the total pay up to a competitive pay level. Traditional gainsharing computes bonuses on top of the fair rate of pay. Nonbonus months are not perceived as inequitable because the fixed rate of pay reflects the organization's compensation strategy to lead or meet the market in terms of pay.

2. R.J. Bullock and E.E. Lawler III, "Gainsharing: A Few Questions and Fewer Answers," *Human Resource Management* (1984) 5, 197–212.

3. C. O'Dell and J. McAdams, *People, Performance, and Pay* (Houston: American Productivity Center, 1987).

4. J.E. McAdams and E.J. Hawk, *Capitalizing on Human Assets: The Benchmark Study* (Scottsdale, Arizona: American Compensation Association, 1992) and J.E. McAdams and E.J. Hawk, *Organizational Performance Rewards* (Scottsdale: American Compensation Association, 1994).

5. E.E. Lawler III, "Gainsharing Theory and Research: Findings and Future Directions," Technical Report no. 85-1(67), CEO, University of Southern California, 1985.

6. C.F. Frost, J.H. Wakely, and R.A. Ruh, *The Scanlon Plan for Organizational Development: Identity, Participation, and Equity* (East Lansing: Michigan State University Press, 1974).

7. P. Goodman and B. Moore, "Factors Affecting Acquisition of Beliefs About a New Reward System," *Human Relations*, June 1976, 571–588.

8. T. Hammer, "New Developments in Profit Sharing" in J. Campbell, R. Campbell, and Associates, *Productivity in Organizations*, (San Francisco: Jossey-Bass, 1988).

Chapter 2

Review of the Literature

Brian Graham-Moore

Interest in gainsharing appears to have increased significantly if the number of publications is used as an indicator. Exhibit 2.1 tabulates all known U.S. publications of gainsharing books, articles, and magazine stories on gainsharing. Granted, archival retrieval has been greatly enhanced by electronic library information systems. Nevertheless, the sheer number of books and academic articles has doubled in the last four years.

This chapter reviews the significant gainsharing literature from two perspectives—historically and in terms of significance. We believe that the yield to knowledge and brevity is served by using these two perspectives. All publications on gainsharing were reviewed. Their citations and sources are available from the author.

In the management literature of the 1930s, the name Joseph Scanlon immediately surfaces. A former cost accountant, steelworker, union official, and, finally, lecturer at the Massachusetts Institute of Technology, Scanlon has been so important to the gainsharing movement that it was suggested that a generic term for gainsharing be the "Scanlon Plan".[1] Scanlon himself never attempted to put his name to the plan, but his support of gainsharing had a strong influence on a generation of managers, labor leaders, consultants, and academicians. These individuals have kept gainsharing alive to this day, even to the point of institutionalizing it in the form of the Scanlon Plan Association.

WHAT IS GAINSHARING?

Gainsharing involves a measurement of productivity combined with the calculation of a bonus designed to offer employees a mutual share of any increases in total organizational productivity. Usually all those responsible for

15

Exhibit 2.1   Gainsharing Publications: 1937–1993

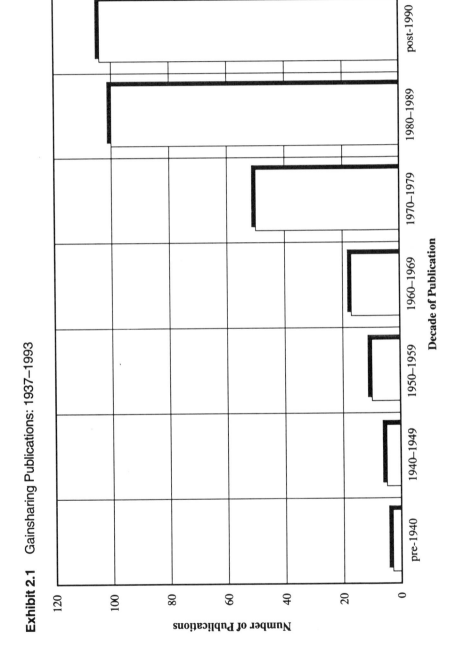

the increase receive the bonus. Total productivity is an all-encompassing term when we consider that outside forces also affect a firm's productivity. For example, the lack of financial productivity can eliminate the gains of performance productivity. Nationally, productivity has been defined by most economists as output per hour of all persons. As this ratio of output to input increases, real economic growth occurs. With such a broad definition of productivity, many factors could be considered influences on it, not the least of which could be the level of technology, the quality of the workforce, and the amount of capital investments. With so many forces influencing productivity, our understanding of aggregate economic behavior does not elucidate the behavior of specific firms. Each firm must study its own economic behavior. The relationship between sales value of production and the labor cost required to produce the product or service can be remarkably stable for many industries.[2] Any company can refer to the U.S. Department of Commerce for reports on its industry's average value added per dollar of plant payroll.

Of the many variables used to measure total productivity, one significant variable is labor productivity. Thus, the term gainsharing is sometimes more easily understood when it is described as labor gainsharing. Although nonlabor factors influence labor costs, many firms probably will base their bonus sharing on gains in productivity out of the decrease in expected labor cost.

Requirements of Gainsharing Formulas

Whatever the particular gainsharing plan, most plans require that a historical standard of expected labor costs be computed. Any increase in output combined with the same or lower actual labor cost creates a bonus. Most gainsharing plans split this bonus between the company and the total workforce.[3] The mechanics of establishing the historical standard are not necessarily simple. How to construct the bonus calculation denotes the variant of gainsharing—be it Improshare,® Rucker,® or a Scanlon plan. However, the keys to all successful gainsharing formulas are:

1. that the normal, average, or standard labor cost is measurable,
2. that the ratio of either sales value of production or units of production value to labor cost is relatively stable, and
3. that the policy established for sharing true increases in labor productivity is fair.[4]

There is little question that there is some confusion in the literature of gainsharing concerning its definition. For some authors it is nothing more than a bonus calculation. For others, it is an organizational transformation. *The Blackwell Dictionary of Organization Behavior* (1995) provides this definition

Gainsharing, maximally defined, is an organization-wide *involvement system* that focuses attention on problem solving while sharing financial gains in cost reduction, improvements in quality and productivity in the form of a variable cash bonus paid weekly, monthly, or quarterly. Historically, its philosophy is one of *industrial cooperation.* In 1937, Joseph Scanlon, a local union president, was instrumental in helping the Empire Steel Company of Mansfield, Ohio become more competitive by reducing costs via collaboration between workers and management. Minimally defined, gainsharing is just a financial formula for paying broadly-based cash bonuses for increases to productivity.

Broadly-based bonuses are distinguished from individual bonuses (piece-rate) because bonuses are usually distributed as a percent of earned salaries and wages for a particular time period. Everyone receives the same percent which is then multiplied times individual earnings to equal the bonus amount. Individual high and low producers in the same wage grade receive the same bonus. Gainsharing philosophy reinforces cooperation and the sharing of information among workers rather than competition and the pursuit of narrow self-interest between workers.

Gainsharing is a generic term. It is variously known by a variety of proprietary and proprietary-sounding names, e.g., Improshare,® Rucker Plan, Scanlon Plan. The key distinctions between gainsharing plans resides in the type of financial formula and the extent of the involvement system (c.f., Graham-Moore and Ross, 1990:48- 80). For example, Scanlon Plans always have a system of production and screening committees to process suggestions. Rucker Plans may have suggestion systems. Originally, Improshare® plans did not have involvement systems since its financial formula reinforced quantity and not problem solving. However, contemporary organizations draw from any aspect of gainsharing to create their own programs. Indeed, there is no one gainsharing plan as empirical literature indicates that a successful plan is adapted to fit a particular *organization's culture* and objectives (Doyle, 1983).[5]

The Human Side of Gainsharing

A complete definition of gainsharing requires introduction to the rest of the description of gainsharing—the behavioral and philosophical elements. Here, the literature has been extensive. One of the best sources is *The Scanlon Plan for Organizational Development* by Frost, Wakely, and Ruh.[6] Carl Frost capped many years of successful Scanlon experience by collaborating with former students to produce this book, which undertakes a comprehensive exposition of the philosophy of Scanlonism. For example, they delineate what they call the three conditions for a Scanlon plan—identity, participation, and equity.

By identity, Frost and his associates mean a clear statement of organizational goals and intended achievements. Furthermore, this identity of organizational goals and intended achievements should meld with personal goals that each employee would like to achieve through his or her role in the organization. If organizational and personal goals are congruent, then the perceived identity of both is a very powerful form of organizational development. While organizations may strive to communicate their objectives, clarifying *how* the individual can match personal goals with these objectives requires a constant educational process.

The second condition is participation. Frost and his associates quite simply assert that participation is defined as the opportunity provided to the employee to be involved while exercising responsibility. Increasing the employee's awareness of his or her responsibility for achieving a fiscally sound and competitive organization is essential if both the employee and firm are to fulfill themselves. Clearly, increased participation reinforces individual commitment to and identification with the firm.

The third condition is the mutual commitment to equity—by both the employee and the firm. In effect, the firm strives to create a return to all employees in exchange for their participation and increased responsibility. The financial basis for this return is expressed by the gainsharing formula. Thus, the investment of all employees in identity and participation is enhanced by a fair method for sharing the value of increases in productivity. The increased interest in the firm and its reliable performance, as well as mutual trust, are exchanged via a formula for sharing that is equitable according to Frost, et al.

Initial interest in gainsharing often focuses on the formula, the payout, or the bonus because managers do not want to create a giveaway. Once the exercise of researching, constructing, and testing a gainsharing formula is completed, however, it becomes apparent that many gainsharing formulas may work, but not optimally, as Chapters 4 and 5 explain. The philosophical and behavioral differences associated with the varying gainsharing formulas need careful understanding as they become more important. While it fails to deal with the philosophical issues surrounding all gainsharing formulas, the Frost book is quite useful because it delves into the behavioral issues more than any other source. Frost's book is unique in that it does reveal so well the human side of gainsharing. The only other book dealing with gainsharing before this time was edited by F.G. Lesieur in 1958. Both books are hard to find except in good libraries. Neither of these books, however, explained how to develop a gainsharing plan, test the formula, install the involvement system, and maintain gainsharing over time.

Moore and Ross addressed this area in 1978 in *The Scanlon Way to Improved Productivity*. R. Doyle's book, *Gainsharing and Productivity*, which appeared in 1983 is also a detailed and orderly accounting of how to implement a gainsharing plan. In 1991, *Gain Sharing* by J. Belcher and in 1992, *Gain Management* by R. Doyle were added to the growing literature on gainsharing. The many articles and books by E. Lawler and associates in the area of using reward systems to lead organizational change have kept gainsharing solidly in view. All of the books on gainsharing tend to be organized around the central themes of the gainsharing literature—industrial cooperation, employee involvement, and empowerment as reinforced by a particular gainsharing formula. This chapter will employ those themes as part of its organizational structure in order to unfold the early literature. Later in the chapter, the emphasis shifts to the burgeoning new literature that focuses on organizational goals, union issues, service industry issues, and issues of variable compensation. To begin, we will look at some generic types of gainsharing plans: (1) Scanlon-simple, (2) Scanlon-complex, (3) Rucker,® and (4) Improshare.®

Scanlon Calculation—Simple

The original Scanlon plan was developed by Joseph Scanlon. Through his leadership, management and labor made a strong effort to improve labor-management cooperation. Scanlon believed that the average worker was a great reservoir of untapped information concerning labor-saving methods. Workers needed a mechanism permitting them "to work smarter, not harder." This following excerpt epitomizes Joe Scanlon's belief in labor-management cooperation:

> One of the greatest advantages of this kind of collective bargaining from the worker's point of view is the knowledge that it gives him of the business. When a slump is coming, he knows it. He is even given a chance to combat it, in the sense that if he can devise a cheaper way of turning out his product, perhaps the company will be able to take away business from somebody else. In a number of instances the Lapointe workers have actually done this, the most spectacular example being that of an order from a big automotive concern in December, 1942. The workers had been pressing management to accept orders even at the break-even point so as to tide over a bad period. Mr. Prindiville, who sometimes sits in on the screening-committee meetings, had given in to the pressure some months previously to the extent of taking an order from this firm for 100 broaches at $83 per broach. But Lapointe had lost 10 percent on the deal, and Mr. Prindiville now put his foot down. If this business was to be taken again the price would have to be raised. In view of new competition, it meant that Lapointe almost certainly would not get the business—at a time when work was scarce. The gloomy gathering that listened to Mr. Prindiville's pronouncement was then electrified by a question from Jimmie McQuade, skilled grinder and one of the most outspoken members of the screening committee. Who says we can't make those broaches at that price for a profit? Mr. McQuade wanted to know. If you'd give the men in the shop a chance to go over over the blueprints before production starts and to help plan the job, there are lots of ways of cutting costs without cutting quality. The idea grew, and the next day the suggestion ran around the shop like wildfire. The order was taken at the old price, this time with a profit of 10 percent—a total gain in efficiency of 20 percent. The truth is that the Scanlon Plan has generated a competitive spirit throughout the factory: one hears as much about competition from the workers as from management itself. If there is a question of struggling for existence the whole company struggles collectively, and all the brains available are focused on the fight. The worker is no longer a pawn in a game he does not understand. He is a player. He enjoys it. And his contribution is worth money to all concerned.[7]

This kind of story is common to most contemporary Scanlon companies. Such companies enjoy a very high degree of employee involvement. In a word, they have teamwork. One measure of this involvement is the high percentage of suggestions received that are put into use.[8]

While sentiments about cooperation, participation, teamwork, and unleashing the knowledge of the worker depicted the original Scanlon plan, the first plan had no bonus calculation.[9] Joe Scanlon ultimately designed a bonus system to reinforce these philosophies. By that time he was working for the production-engineering department of United Steel Workers. The Adamson Company in East Palestine, Ohio, was perhaps the first company to try a bonus calculation constructed by Scanlon. This calculation is the most imitated gainsharing calculation. The most commonly applied Scanlon formula is generalized as:

$$\text{Base ratio} = \frac{\text{Labor costs}}{\text{Sales value of production}}$$

Scanlon's idea was to focus the attention of everyone on those variables within the control of the firm and its human resources. Because of its apparent simplicity, the calculation was quickly adopted into use. At the same time, the Scanlon plan became the darling of the industrial relations literature focusing on labor-management cooperation. Most industrial relations personnel textbooks of the time include a section on the Scanlon plan.[10]

Scanlon Calculations—Complex

In instances in which Scanlon plans have failed, this failure has been attributed to the formula.[11] In almost all cases, simple Scanlon formulas, i.e., the single ratio, were used. Multiple products create a complex situation that may render the simple ratio inaccurate. Firms with many product lines that vary in labor content, such as produced labor or buy-out labor, were either over-valuing or under-valuing the expected labor cost. Early research and publications focussed on this. As a consequence, the split ratio formula was developed. Controllers designed a base ratio for each product line which could more accurately reflect a fair measure of labor input.[12] The split ratio formula deals more equitably with problems of product mix. The single ratio formula mentioned in Chapter 4, Exhibit 4-6, Assumed Bonus Under Single and Split Ratios, for example, overpays by $40,000 when there is no true increase in productivity. The allowed labor calculation also evolved in response to some Scanlon formula problems. A crucial difference between allowed labor calculations and the original Scanlon formula is the exclusion of sales value. Measurement is based on labor only.[13] The rationale is to decrease problems associated with product mix *and* variations in selling price. This formula assumes that accounting data or engineered time standards are available for all or most direct hours. Then, allowed times are based on actual past performance. The allowed hour formula can be seen as antithetical to the Scanlon philosophy of teamwork and cooperation because it can easily become a management tool. Since allowed labor can be calculated for product line and department, this split ratio calculation could isolate problem areas for corrective action by management. Clearly, this is a goal of gainsharing, but only mature gainsharing firms can take advantage of this kind of information—for example, Lincoln Electric has the kind of human resource that actively uses cost information in order to solve problems.[14]

A more useful, sophisticated formula is the multicost ratio.[15] This formula could approach some aspects of profit sharing—which, of course, is not technically gainsharing. Incidentally, it is reported that many profit-sharing firms are inclined to have other incentives, including gainsharing.[16] Some cash profit-sharing plans take their place alongside Improshare,® Scanlon, and Rucker® plans as alternate or complementary ways to bring about more productivity as well as a mutually beneficial relationship between management and employees.

Except for its timing, cash profit sharing is held by some to be the ultimate in the total system incentive approach because it links motivation and reward to the final measure of corporate performance—profits.[17] Profit sharing rewards or penalizes all those who contribute to the growth of the enterprise in relation to the firm's economic productivity—as accepted by and paid for by the market place.

The idea behind the multicost ratio, however, is to include most or all costs in the formula. It does not directly share profits or economic productivity. Instead, it shares improvements to the value of production and, of course, pays much more frequently than any profit sharing plan. The base ratio becomes:

$$\text{Base ratio} = \frac{\text{Labor} + \text{other costs}}{\text{Value of production}}$$

Assuming a firm has a comprehensive, sophisticated accounting system, this calculation can be made monthly—which, of course, makes its timing better than that of profit sharing. Most of the problems of product mix and inflation reported in case studies of Scanlon failures[18] are considerably decreased with the use of the multicost calculation.

Trying the multicost calculation should be discouraged because of the behavioral considerations. The objectives of gainsharing are to involve everyone, at some level, with the overall goal of improving productivity.[19] If employees find the complex gainsharing formula difficult to understand, they may react with distrust or perceive it as a gimmick. Obviously acceptance and learning may be thwarted.

Rucker® Plan

Using studies of data collected by the U.S. Census and Surveys of Manufacturers, Allan W. Rucker showed in the early 1930s that economic productivity had been extremely stable from 1899 to 1929.[20] A parallel analysis for the years 1964 to 1968 was conducted by P. J. Loftus, Director of the Statistical Office of the United Nations.[21] The results were the same. While each industry has its own pattern, there was a stable relationship between production value and value added by labor.

The concept of value added for pay systems is well known in accounting circles.[22] As with all gainsharing plans, this formula can be tailored to include only workers with a very close connection to the production process or all personnel in an organization. Thus, value added is defined as the difference between the value of production (sales ± various adjustments) less outside purchases, such as materials and supplies.

The following example is offered in Exhibit 2.2, The Rucker®/Value Added Formula. Step 1 reflects the difference between the selling price and price adjustments for seasonality. Step 2 reflects subtractions for outside purchases such as materials, supplies, and energy. Step 3 is value added of $340,000, or 34 percent of the selling price. Now, Step 4 applies the historical average of labor value added to the product. This is called the Rucker® Standard. In this example, 41.17 percent, or $140,000, is the allowed (or expected) labor costs. Step 5 shows that the actual labor cost was $130,000. Thus, Step 6 reflects a bonus pool of $10,000. A 50/50 split is a common policy (as in Improshare®), and Steps 7 and 8 reflect this. Steps 9 and 10 reflect a policy of a reserve for deficit months (as in the case of many Scanlon companies). Since the participating payroll is $80,000 (Step 11), then the bonus percentage becomes 5 percent in Step 12.[23]

Exhibit 2.2   The Rucker Value-Added Formula

Value-Added Calculation Method—Month X

1. Value of production (sales ± various adjustments)		$1,000,000
2. Less outside purchases (materials, supplies, energy)		
Materials and supplies	$500,000	
Other outside purchases, nonlabor costs	160,000	660,000
3. Value added (#1–#2)		340,000
4. Allowed employee costs (from diagnostic		
historical analysis) #3 × 41.17%		139,978
5. Actual labor (employee costs)		129,978
6. Bonus pool (#4 – #5)		10,000
7. Company share (#6 – #7)		5,000
8. Employee share		5,000
9. Reserve for deficit months (20% × #8)		1,000
10. Bonus pool (#8 – #9)		4,000
11. Participating payroll		80,000
12. Bonus percentage (#10/#11)		5%

Adapted from B. E. Moore and T. L. Ross, *The Scanlon Way to Improved Productivity* (New York: Wiley-Interscience, 1978), 81.

Many similarities exist between Rucker® and Scanlon—and these are both similar to some extent to Improshare.® In principle, the early gainsharing plan formulas vary in subtle yet profound ways. Subtle, because the measurements all attempt to capture the ratio of labor input to production outputs. Profound, because the sensitivity of the measurements can be magnified by environmental and product mix factors in ways that could be a problem if left unchecked. More importantly, the differences in the formulas can result in behavioral differences that must be considered when choosing a formula. That is, no gainsharing plan will work without acceptance and some level of trust. With this in mind, it should be remembered that Rucker® Plans can share many similarities with Scanlon plans, therefore, much of the behavioral information to be reviewed concerning Scanlon plans can be generalized to include the Rucker® Plans.

Improshare®

Improshare® means *imp*roved *pro*ductivity through *shar*ing. This plan is relatively new to the field of gainsharing. Invented in 1973, it is the creation of Mitchell Fein, an educator, consultant, and industrial engineer. Because of its overall simplicity and lack of emphasis on employee involvement, Improshare® is relatively easy to install. The plan focuses on the number of work hours saved for a given number of units produced in much the same way the allowed labor calculation does. The actual hours taken to produce a given number of units are subtracted from hours required (or expected) to produce the same number of units. Savings realized by producing a given number of units in a reduced number of hours are shared equally by the firm and the worker. There are three key factors to Improshare®:

1. the work-hour standard;
2. the base productivity factor (BPF);
3. the understanding by most workers of the relationship of hours worked to units produced.

By definition, a work-hour standard is the total production hours worked divided by the units produced. The acceptable standard could be produced by the use of engineered standards (e.g., time studies) and/or through the use of previously generated accounting data. Either way—it is the agreed or expected hours required to produce an accepted level of output.

The base productivity factor, or BPF, is the total production and non-production hours divided by the value of work in work hours. For an example, see Exhibit 2.3, The Improshare® Calculation. While there is a more complete discussion on the Allowed Labor/Improshare® calculation in Chapter 4, Exhibit 2.3 shows how the U.S. General Accounting Office publication presents principal ideas of this calculation:

Exhibit 2.3 Allowed Labor/Improshare® Calculation

Base Period of Acceptable Productivity

Facts: 40 direct and 20 indirect employees

$$\text{Work hour standard} = \frac{\text{total production work hours}}{\text{units produced}}$$

$$\text{Product A} = \frac{20 \text{ employees} \times 40 \text{ hours}}{1000 \text{ pieces}} = 0.8 \text{ per piece or } .8 \times 1000 = 800$$

$$\text{Product B} = \frac{20 \text{ employees} \times 40 \text{ hours}}{500 \text{ pieces}} = 1.6 \text{ per piece or } 1.6 \times 500 = 800$$

Total standard value hours 1,600 in Base Period

$$\text{Base Productivity Factor (BPF)} = \frac{\text{total production and nonproduction hours}}{\text{total standard value hours}}$$

$$\text{BPF} = \frac{\begin{array}{c}(40 \text{ direct employees} \times 40 \text{ hours})\\(20 \text{ indirect employees} \times 40 \text{ hours})\end{array}}{\text{actual hours}}$$

$$= \frac{2400 \text{ production hours}}{1600 \text{ standard value hours}} = 1.5$$

Bonus Calculation for Month X

Product A = 0.8 hours × 600 units × 1.5 BPF	= 720
Product B = 1.6 hours × 900 units × 1.5 BPT	= 2,160
Improshare hours (standard hours for actual units produced)	= 2,880
Less actual hours (assumed)	= 2,280
Gained hours	600

$$\text{Employee share} \left(50\% \text{ of } 600 = \frac{300}{2280} = 13.158\% \right) \qquad = 13.2\%$$

Adapted from *Productivity Sharing Programs: Can They Contribute to Productivity Improvement?* U.S. General Accounting Office, AFMD-81-22 (March 3, 1981), 11.

1. work hour standards are total production hours of "good production,"
2. work hour standards are normally computed for each product line, and
3. the base productivity factor (BPF) is the ratio of actual human resource hours to standard hours.

Each product line's output, at its own standard, is multiplied by the BPF to compute the expected number of total hours required to produce that output. Then, actual hours are calculated and subtracted from the expected hours (sometimes called Improshare® hours). The difference, positive in this example, is 600 hours. These hours can be converted at average wage rates to create a cash value.

Simplicity of Improshare® Formula

Another key factor associated with Improshare® is the simplicity of the formula and, thus, its ready comprehension by the work force. While Fein has stated that many elements of the Improshare® formula have been in use for twenty years,[24] he has assembled a formula that avoids some problems of Scanlon-type formulas. Fein's formula offers the concept of productivity to the worker in a psychologically accessible form. Americans probably think in terms of so many hours to produce so many units of work. Indeed, we are a time-conscious culture.

There is some evidence to suggest that workers in Scanlon firms fail to understand the bonus formula. Many Scanlon firms spend a great deal of time educating the work force about the formula—often to little avail. Conversely, one study of an Improshare® firm shows that line supervisors can readily explain what factors influence the formula to their subordinates.[25]

Fein has incorporated elements of the Halsey premium plan (which dates from 1890) into an organizationwide formula. By pooling all production and nonproduction hours from a selected base period, Fein created the BPF. This is a significant contribution. The BPF, while based on standards, is a composite measure of direct and indirect work. That is, it is assumed that indirect labor co-varies with direct labor in a stable manner. The BPF, therefore, is constructed with data from an average period of productivity, or one that management recognizes as acceptable. This differs from a Scanlon analysis, which looks at the total budget period. Clearly, the Improshare® plan seeks to increase quantity. The calculation is constructed to "beat yesterday's performance" if yesterday was a representative day. Once the BPF is computed it "represents the relationship in the base period between actual hours worked by all employees in the group and the value of the work in (work hours) produced by these employees."[26]

Aside from product mix problems cited in the literature, Fein has argued (in a similar fashion as the Value Added/Rucker® Plan) that volatility in the inputs and outputs of doing business such as raw materials prices and the fluctuating prices of sales, hurts the Scanlon gainsharing calculation. In effect, allowed labor/Improshare® calculations exclude these ingredients from their formulas, only hours to produce are being used.

Acceptance of Improshare®

The timing of Improshare® with the general acceptance of gainsharing has been impressive. The adoption of Improshare® has been extensive.

While a series of educators, consultants, managers, and labor leaders have contributed to the development of Scanlon-type plans, Mitchell Fein is unique in his singular contribution to gainsharing. The following is an excerpt from "An Alternative to Traditional Managing."

> Traditional work measurement established the time "it should take" to perform a given task under prescribed conditions, not how long it took to perform the work in the past. Such normal or fair day's work standards are established through performance rating with stop watch time study or predetermined standards, against a defined measurement base. This leveling or normalizing of observed data is the keystone of traditional work measurement; it must be employed.
>
> The arguments that arise in setting traditional time standards are avoided by measuring productivity against the average level of an agreed base period. Using a method called measurement by parameters, standards are set at the average of the past, using historical data within a place of work, with no need to performance rate the work performance data. The rationale for this approach is that "yesterday's" performance is established as the Accepted Productivity Level (AFL). Measurements in the future will be made against this APL base.[27]

Traditional work measurement may seem antithetical to some of the assumptions of gainsharing—namely, it might remind one of the individual incentives. However, a measure of labor productivity must start somewhere. Fein has blended many older ingredients into a newer, more successful package. However, there is no set philosophy associated with Improshare.®

Mentioned earlier, for example, was the fact that no employee involvement is required to install Improshare.® Technically this is true, but in practice Improshare® may have almost the same advance build-up as a Scanlon plan, including, perhaps, the installation of labor-management committees. That is, an outside consultant may prepare management with a program and training so that employees have sufficient information about the plan. However, *there is no particular structure to Improshare®* as there is with Scanlon. Fein, who favors a good communications network, believes that labor-management committees under Scanlon plans are too structured.[28]

In point of fact, Improshare® can be installed in firms with either autocratic or participative management styles. Labor-management committees, suggestion systems, and other examples of employee involvement may or may not be a part of Improshare.® Gainsharing exists in many forms and can become a way of life in any of them. For example, Lincoln Electric has the nation's most successful incentive system and there is no commitment to a sophisticated management philosophy. Instead, Lincoln strives to maximize every day in every way the shared gains in increased productivity. There aren't enough publications about Lincoln Electric,[29] and the inference to be drawn from these works is that the firm's personnel are highly motivated by pay and have a highly rational view towards productivity.

In many ways, Improshare® spans the gap between those firms with no interest in participative management and concepts like the quality of work, and those firms that do espouse those management philosophies. Therefore, Improshare® is, above all, a formula that can be applied to many situations. As a formula, however, Fein argues it is a "way of life" because management obligates itself to a set of rules, yet places no limitations on the workers.[30] No memo of understanding, vote, or commitment is sought in advance from the employees. The purpose of Improshare® is to make workers "bottom-line oriented."

GAINSHARING INVOLVEMENT PROCESSES

While other gainsharing plans may or may not have a structure to achieve labor-management cooperation and participation, all known Scanlon organizations have a commitment to an interlocking system of committees to process suggestions that require much involvement from employees. Predating Quality Control Circles, Scanlon committees have strived to produce productivity-related suggestions. This aspect of Scanlonism has been generally impressive.

Graham-Moore (see Chapter 8) has analyzed suggestion-making. The pattern of results reported is similar to many other Scanlon companies. For example, over a five year period, Schuster reports 2,477 suggestions made from 890 union employees of a large aircraft engine manufacturer.[31] The acceptance rate was 70 percent, i.e., percent in use. An additional 5 percent were under investigation and had not been rejected. This case's experience indicates that most employees find quantity–improving suggestions easiest to make, and, thus, this type forms the majority. Suggestions regarding quality and cost-reduction suggestions are far fewer in number.

Ideally, suggestions unrelated to productivity should disappear after the first year of a Scanlon program. Apparently, this channel of communication, once opened, will always incur some suggestions motivated by irritation within the organization. Since the involvement system is not by definition a grievance procedure, these suggestions normally are referred to the appropriate channels by most firms.

Two critiques of the involvement system are a part of the literature. Gray[32] maintains that in a large English automobile body-stamping plant, production committees used more work hours than was cost effective. Fein, speaking for Improshare,® favors labor-management committees or Quality Control Circles because he has less confidence in the structural committees of Scanlon Plans.[33]

One fact is irrefutable. Scanlon production and screening committees produce more accepted and implemented suggestions than are produced by individual suggestion systems. Scanlon case studies reveal that from 46 to 95 people out of each 100 employees make at least one suggestion a year. Conversely, individual suggestion systems (pay for suggestion) report a rate of only 26 people out of 100.[34] Again, percent acceptance and rapid implementation of suggestions is much higher in Scanlon companies (see Chapter 8). By rotating personnel through the Scanlon committee system, workers are brought into close contact with management, as both pursue problem solving. Scanlon managers clearly identify with participative management philosophies.[35] The structure of the involvement system makes these rotating assignments routine, and guarantees representation and exposure of all employees to the involvement system. Mature Scanlon companies have had virtually all employees serving at some time in the committee system. Peer review of suggestions makes reinforcement of suggestion-making behavior easier—whether suggestions are accepted or rejected.[36] The Scanlon involvement system serves as a form of organization development since it becomes a new communication structure for many firms.[37] Most literature on the Scanlon plan cites not only participation and communication but also willingness, cooperation, and acceptance of change that occur because of the structure and process of the suggestion system.[38]

Evaluation Studies

For years, the only evaluation studies of Scanlon plans came from MIT, because of its historical connection with Joe Scanlon. In the Midwest, Carl Frost has been directly responsible for the direction and leadership of the Scanlon Plan Association, originally based at Michigan State University. This association has had considerable impact on firms generally in Michigan, Ohio, Indiana, Illinois, and elsewhere. Occasional studies by the association are published as reports but these are generally available only for association members.

In general, evaluation case studies are the type of evidence modern managers wish to see. Older literature is replete with testimonials and anecdotes, but today's decision makers and behavioral scientists want more quantitative information and they want it collected rigorously within a theoretical framework. This anecdotal, less rigorous type of case study was the predominant method of Scanlon and gainsharing study until the late 1960s. It is possible to review older case studies and newer empirical studies by organizing them around their principle findings—regardless of their methodology. The following are organizational or environmental conditions associated with early Scanlon plan research:

- Front-line supervisors may feel threatened by the suggestion system because they feel they are no longer bosses or because a high rate of suggestions makes their past behavior look autocratic.[39]
- The performance norm is difficult to adjust in the face of changing conditions.[40]
- A fair measurement of an organization's performance may be impossible.[41]
- Managerial attitudes must either favor participative management or be disposed to change.[42]
- Previous wage structures, such as individual incentive-suggestion systems, must be phased out. Compromises here are common and lead to transitional (protected) rates.[43]

- The plan can focus too intently on labor savings while not providing sufficient attention to other sources of savings.[44]
- The characteristics of the firm, such as size, management philosophy, climate, technology, sophistication of accounting systems require matching gainsharing to optimize on these factors.[45]
- The plan enhances coordination, teamwork, and sharing knowledge at lower levels.[46]
- Social needs are recognized via participation and mutually reinforcing group behavior.[47]
- Attention is focused on cost savings—not just quantity.[48]
- Acceptance of change due to technology, market, and new methods is greater since higher efficiency leads to bonus.[49]
- Attitudinal change of workers occurs and they demand more efficient management and better planning.[50]
- Workers try to reduce overtime; to work smarter, not harder or faster.[51]
- Workers produce ideas as well as effort.[52]
- More flexible administration of union-management relationship occurs, including rational of competence.[53]

WHAT DO WE KNOW?

In the periodical literature there are hundreds of anecdotal pieces which were written on gainsharing from 1935 to 1994. Also, there have been many published case studies, some more rigorous than others, that evaluate the impact of gainsharing on a single organization. Chapter 1 points out that describing gainsharing is relatively easy. Predicting its success from the results of carefully controlled, theory-driven research is more difficult, but controlled studies are appearing in the literature.[54] We now know, for example, that of the 104 organizations that implemented Improshare® since 1981, success was claimed by 80. Success is measured by the existence of Improshare® after three years and the fact it continues to pay bonuses.[55] An estimated 273 organizations have attempted the plan according to Fein. Kaufman's evaluation study of the 104 respondents reflects a sample of 44 percent. During the study period of 1981 to 1988, the median productivity rose about 8 percent in the first year. After three years, productivity gains rose to about 17.5 percent and reached a plateau. Clearly, some increases to productivity were associated with declines in absentee, defect, and downtime rates. Bonuses ranged from 4 percent to 11 percent and the average bonus over six years was 7.3 percent. However, the plateau of bonus performance appears achieved at the third year for most companies and then sustained at that level. As a purely financial incentive, devoid of the traditional gainsharing definition, the Improshare®'s allowed labor calculation has demonstrated its usefulness to some organizations.

Organizational Size

Using available case studies of small organizations, researchers originally thought that organizational size influenced success in gainsharing. It probably does, but not to the extent once thought. In their review of the literature, Moore and Goodman reported that the median size of gainsharing organizations was 250 employees. Bullock and Lawler reviewed unpublished master's theses and doctoral dissertations of the Massachusetts Institute of Technology (where Joseph Scanlon finished his career as lecturer), as well as other sources and fixed the median at 500. The national survey conducted by the American Productivity Center (1987) is a better indication of size.[56]

Number of Employees	Percent Responding (*n* = 55)
1– 250	38%
251– 500	22
501– 1,000	13
1,001– 5,000	22
5,001–10,000	5
	100%

The median size of 500 was once thought to be correct. However, it is surprising to see larger organizations with greater than 5,000 employees using gainsharing. Markham, et al.'s[57] survey indicates that the average size of gainsharing organizations reflected large differences by industry. For example, the smallest plans were found in healthcare organizations with 652 employees on average. Mining plans average 1,443 employees, and manufacturing averaged 1,770. Wholesale/retail firms reported more than 10,000 employees covered by gainsharing. In all instances, hourly and salary were covered by the gainsharing plan. The key factor seems to be that at some point organization-wide incentives lose impact. The larger the group the greater the difficulty workers encounter in seeing what effect a change in their performance can have on production.

The diffusion of gainsharing from manufacturing to other industries took a relatively long time as there were few reported studies prior to 1986. Conceptual articles by Ross and Hauck[58] and Graham-Moore,[59] argued in favor of this diffusion. In 1990, Jarrett[60] reviewed the experimentation of gainsharing in the public sector beginning, for the most part, in the mid 1980s. Now, we have case studies, such as Bowie-McCoy, et al.[61] that report on traditional gainsharing in public accounting. Over the first three years of the plan, suggestions numbered 148 with 76 percent accepted. Suggestions fell by 46 percent (31 suggestions) in the third year, but suggestion quality remained high. The analysis of the content of the suggestions indicates support for working smarter, not harder. Using controlled measurements, overtime was reduced after gainsharing was introduced. So, while gainsharing has spread from its historical base in manufacturing slightly over half of all plans are still in manufacturing. Markham, et al.[62]

surveyed a national sample of 219 active plans. The breakdown is similar to other sample surveys in that combined manufacturing sectors were 51 percent of their total sample of gainsharing plans. However, transportation (8 percent), wholesale/retail (9 percent), financial institutions (4 percent), services (9 percent), and healthcare institutions (9 percent) reflect widespread movement from manufacturing to other sectors. Perhaps more revealing was the percent actively considering gainsharing. It ranged from 53 percent to 94 percent of respondents in all industries (sample reflected responses from 1,639 human resources directors, managers, and vice-presidents).

The mix of different gainsharing plans, as measured by the type of calculation employed, is diverse. Markham, et al.[63] report about the same mix of plans that the American Productivity and Quality Center did in 1987 with custom designed gainsharing reflecting 44 percent of total plans. Profit sharing were 26 percent, Scanlon 10 percent, Improshare® 9 percent, and Rucker® 2 percent. Average bonuses in 1991 ranged from .01 percent to 13 percent of annual pay with manufacturing and financial services industries doing the best. Healthcare organizations averaged 8 percent bonuses.

Union and Nonunion Organizations

One institutional variable that has been examined empirically is union-management cooperation. Since the philosophy of gainsharing stresses increased cooperation, one might be surprised that this factor needs assessment; however, Schuster, in a longitudinal study, assessed the impact of union-management cooperation in nine manufacturing firms over a four to five year period. Six of the nine manufacturers had either Scanlon or Rucker® Plans. Time series analysis in unionized gainsharing companies showed that four organizations experienced statistically significant positive changes in productivity and two others had positive trends. Employment remained stable in eight of the nine organizations. Only one gainsharing firm fared poorly in his sample. Larger samples and longer time frames are always preferred, but Schuster drew these conclusions from this study:

> Cooperation requires a stimulus to change a traditional bargaining relationship; in the present study, cooperation was stimulated by the dire financial position of one company and by adverse competitive conditions in several others. Additional stimuli were provided by factors internal to the firm, including a desire to upgrade the workplace environment, improve communication, and replace or supplement an existing compensation program.[64]

Graham-Moore and Rodgers surveyed gainsharing organizations to assess the relationship between institutional/organizational factors and type of gainsharing calculation. They found no difference in bonus history between union and nonunion organizations. Even though gainsharing began in the union environment, its greatest growth recently has been in nonunion environments.[65]

The union/nonunion variable appears to offer no explanatory power in their study. This is an important finding when one considers the strategy of contingent gainsharing mentioned in Chapter 1. That is, even when organizations use gainsharing in a mode different from that called traditional gainsharing, certain basic principles still apply. That is, equity must be preserved if the mutually reinforcing components of the gainsharing definition are expected to work.

As a result of the strong interest in worker participation strategies, such as quality of work life, quality circles, and employee involvement programs, some industrial relations researchers have characterized worker participation programs as a "mixed bag" full of risks for union members and union leaders. Indeed, stand-alone employee involvement programs seem to have a poor chance of becoming permanent parts of the organizational structure. Schuster's research offers some true support for gainsharing's ability to reinforce organizational cooperation with equitable bonuses. Other ideas that support the institutionalization of employee involvement systems can also be found in Chapter 6, "Making Productivity Programs Last." The research indicated that process is more important than institutions or structures. That is, the way in which gainsharing is introduced and whether it is perceived as an equitable program are greater determinants of long range success than the existence of a union or nonunion environment.

Motivation and Learning Theory

More rigorous research has looked at variables other than organizational size. Goodman and Moore assessed these variables and studied the process wherein all employees developed new beliefs concerning a Scanlon Plan. The chance of making a productivity suggestion was associated with group attitudes and supervisory acceptance. Since researchers have focused their attention on the involvement system of gainsharing, the variables listed above are assessed in order to understand how they influence or moderate the processes of learning and change that have been the reported outcomes of successful gainsharing organizations. Group and supervisory approval seem to influence appropriate gainsharing beliefs.

Lawler's review of the same research led him to hypothesize that we know a fair amount of motivation and learning theory, an important component in the formulation of gainsharing programs. Therefore, gainsharing plans will increase organizational performance if:

1. beliefs are established that rewards are based on organizational performance,
2. communication of organizational performance is provided to everyone,
3. ways or mechanisms are established for employers to influence organizational performance contingently measured by the reward system, and

4. opportunities to learn how to contribute to organizational performance are provided along with interpreting measures of performance.[66]

Participative Management

As has always been argued in the literature of gainsharing, participative management is crucial to traditional gainsharing success. Often misstated by others, the exact contribution of participative management is to clarify the connection between individual contribution and organizational performance—not just to require more effort. Lawler and Mohrman hypothesize that participative management refers to those behaviors and actions that build trust during the process of improving organizational performance, a necessary precedent to the bonus.[67] This idea is echoed in older case studies that state how important it is for the work force to understand how the gainsharing calculation works. Participative management shifts power, knowledge, and information down into the organization. If managers ask employees for intelligent input, in exchange they must offer some power, knowledge, and information.

COMMON SOURCES OF
GAINSHARING FAILURES

According to the literature reviewed, the most common causes of gainsharing failures were economic—the existence of wage inequities or the inability to provide bonuses. Also, the formulas used did not adequately reflect rapid changes in product mix. Those studies noting failures are Gilson and Lefcowitz,[68] Gray,[69] Helfgott,[70] Johnson,[71] Jehring,[72] and Ruh, et al.[73] Gilson and Lefcowitz report poor plan installation, poor understanding of the formula, and a high component of secondary wage earners who preferred individual incentives. Most compelling is the fact that the product mix greatly affected the ratio of the formula. To counteract this, more complex and exhaustive methods of formula construction are now in use.[74] Gray reports large inequities in pay between departments of an English auto body manufacturer. In this case, as with other plan failures, the formula was too narrow and did not adequately reflect changes in the market (see Chapter 5). The results were usually no bonus or bonuses were paid with no increase in true productivity. Work practices apparently conflicted with the need for reassigning workers, and conflict rather than cooperation ensued. Gray challenged the motivational role of the suggestion system. He states that since the suggestion system is to be learned as an instrumental way to increase productivity, why wouldn't it work without a bonus? In another case study, however, Lesieur cites workers actually searching for ways to improve business (by suggestion making) during hard times with no bonuses.[75] Then, too, management attitudes can greatly affect the commitment to gainsharing (see Chapter 6). In Jehring's study, management decided to shift its emphasis to a profit-sharing plan when keeping the gain-sharing formula accurate was perceived as too difficult.

Goodman identified 72 coal companies using various forms of gain-sharing since 1982. While these plans appear to be in use today, their inception was caused by a general intent to use gainsharing to lead the human resource to increase productivity, reduce costs, and, in some plans, to reduce accidents. According to Goodman, the typical coal company is a poor choice for gain-sharing. That is, their pay system values are characterized by:

1. secretive behavior,
2. decision making concentrated in top management,
3. centralized structures,
4. organizationwide performance practices for rewards,
5. standardized pay systems,
6. job-based versus skill-based pay,
7. hierarchical versus egalitarian orientation,
8. reliance on a tradition driven system.[76]

One wonders why so many leaders from the United Mine Workers signed off on these plans. As Goodman points out, a secretive communication system runs counter to traditional gainsharing philosophy. His technical report makes clear that gainsharing, though existing, is a poor fit for the typical coal company. Apparently, most coal companies are poor choices for systems that require a high level of commitment, even though other reward system alternatives could be employed in coal companies. For this reason, the ideas surrounding the interaction of gainsharing calculations and organizational goals presented in Chapter 4 take on special relevance if decision makers are to avoid failure.

GAINSHARING MODIFICATIONS

Obviously, defining gainsharing, as we have, as not just a productivity inventive system might exclude Improshare®—if it is solely an incentive sys-tem. Also, traditional gainsharing focuses heavily on cost savings as a way to pay bonuses and this often doesn't exist in some organizational settings. For example, public sector gainsharing plans avoid costs, they rarely save money. Nevertheless, modified gainsharing occurs when it is adapted to new settings and organizational goals, as Chapters 4 and 5 will point out. One of the preva-lent adaptations is goal sharing. Belcher[77] and Doherty, et al.[78] provide ample examples wherein goals of organizations are quantified, then monetized. For example, many organizations are interested in quality and safety. The dollar value of quality and safety are calculated based on historical costs. Then, "savings" based on these expected costs are reduced by the cost of conducting the goal sharing program. The return on investment (of the goal sharing pro-gram) is calculated to produce total net "savings." Goal sharing writers still view the plan as self-funding. Now, the cost savings of at, say, Donnelly Mirrors, increases the value of its products under traditional gainsharing. Goal sharing pays bonuses on improvements in quality goals. In a service industry, this might be customer satisfaction, possibly measured by a decrease in complaints—a negative measure. While a service organization would not dispute the importance of customer satisfaction for repeat business, the dollar amount of reduced complaints is hard to value. Chapters 4, 5, and 14 deal with some of these issues of valuing increases in physical performance and financial performance. Perhaps a better term than goal sharing is modified gainsharing. Goal sharing grew out of gainsharing and in some settings, the calculation is a hybrid, but the total plan meets the definition of gainsharing.

GAINSHARING AS A WAY OF LIFE

Gainsharing can become a way of life. A firm successfully embarking on the route to gainsharing begins a form of organizational development. One of the forces that drives gainsharing is the unleashing of the worker's intelligence.[79] It is not surprising that a Firestone manager experienced with Improshare® states, "No one knows the job better than the one doing it."[80]

Given that a job incumbent knows his or her job better than anyone else, just how does an organization unleash this knowledge? The conditions stated in Chapter 1 come quickly to mind because levels of involvement and trust, and the quality of managerial philosophy become crucial. Does an organization possess the characteristics to a sufficient extent so that employees can perceive their individual growth as congruent with organizational objectives? Within the framework of the involvement system, many of the steps of a gainsharing trial year are analogous to the steps of organizational development (OD).

OD Structure and Process

French and Bell[81] have listed eight common steps or factors of the OD structure and process which are described in Exhibit 2.4. Step 1, diagnostic activities, frequently includes measurement of opinions and attitudes. Gainsharing trial years often use the same approach in order to gauge whether to begin or to develop a baseline measure with which to compare growth. Interestingly, problem identification for OD refers to process consulting wherein basic learning situations are presented to clarify perception and understanding. These learning situations are usually handled in special training sessions. Conversely, these opportunities to learn are created within involvement systems. For example, a worker may be a member of a committee to research the usefulness of a suggestion. The particular suggestion may not truly be acceptable, yet the worker will search for ways to make it acceptable through modification and improvement rather than dismissing the suggestion. The result is that the

Exhibit 2.4 Organization Development Activities and
Scanlon Counterparts

OD	Scanlon
1. Diagnostic activities: attitude and opinion measurement, including formal measurement that comprises formal questionnaires or interviewing to ascertain the state of the organization	1. Trial year evaluation methods
2. Problem identification: process consulting to help perception and understanding of individual, group, and organizational-level issues	2. At all times in the involvement system
3. Goal setting and methods achievement: planning, utilizing information from problem solving, and to compare the real versus the ideal	3. Management's direction, especially through the screening committee and through the influence of the formula
4. Communication improvement: survey feedback activities, education and training activities, to improve coordination	4. All committees improve this, plus annual questionnaire will help
5. Conflict identification and resolution: third-party peacemaking, confrontation counseling to improve cooperation	5. Peer review of suggestions in production committees is a form of open problem solving
6. Task forces: team building intergroup activities to enhance cooperation	6. Group suggestion making is a very common outcome of the plan
7. Job design: technostructural activities to improve technical or structural aspects of work	7. One of the most common outcomes of Scanlon plans is acceptance of technical change
8. Measurement and evaluation: assessment activities to produce information on "where we are"	8. Annual survey, financial analysis, and annual Scanlon meeting

Adapted from B. E. Moore and T. L. Ross, *The Scanlon Way to Improved Productivity* (New York: Wiley-Interscience, 1978), 151.

worker offering the suggestion, the helping committee member, and management gain a new understanding and respect for one another. The suggestion may be enhanced and accepted. The committee member handles new tasks. Management acquires a new respect for the worker. The firm gains a productivity-related suggestion. None of these experiences happen in a training sessions which can be artificial. Rather, these are real experiences that become part of the human fabric of the firm.

The evidence for traditional gainsharing's role in organizational development is rapidly growing. Bullock and Tubbs[82] tested whether gainsharing plans with formal involvement structures had greater success than those without. Not surprisingly, they did. Innovation and labor-management cooperation were better in gainsharing plans with a formal involvement structure. Doherty, et al.[83] selected two long-term gainsharing plans out of a sample of 70 plans that had completed five or more years. The two selected were from manufacturing and service industries. They concluded that many organizational development objectives were achieved. These include, improved communication, reduced mistrust, increased cooperation, and increased awareness of employee performance. These outcomes are identical outcomes of OD hypothesized by Moore and Ross.[84]

Analogs to Involvement System

Exhibit 2.4 illustrates many subsequent steps or factors associated with OD and gainsharing involvement. An analog for each of these factors exists in the involvement system. For example, OD Activity 3 (Goal setting and methods achievement) often occurs as part of an OD training exercise, while gainsharing firms demonstrate a natural process of positive communication through the committee system. OD Activity 4 (Communication) here again is achieved in gainsharing firms through the committee system, the give and take of suggestion making and evaluation. Information is pushed down into the organization and suggestions percolate up via the committee system. Of course, there is also feedback from any annual surveys. Survey guided development is more easily conducted in the committee system. In sum, many identifiable OD activities are found in most traditional gainsharing firms.

According to Hatcher and Ross, gainsharing provides a visible structure that leads some organizations to higher levels of OD. In fact, as gainsharing becomes institutionalized, its functions become part of standard procedures. This structure helps the process of OD continue. Hatcher and Ross quote a president of one midwestern manufacturing firm:

> "I like the structure Gainsharing forces on a company. Without that structure, I don't know how to get participation, and I don't know how to support it. But if I've got someone telling me that we've got a gainsharing meeting at 3:00, I'll be there, and so will everyone else. The structure is the only thing that keeps the plan from dying a slow death."[85]

Hatcher, et al.[86] studied five manufacturing organizations to get a better understanding of which processes led to suggestion making. All five organizations revealed the usual pattern of successful gainsharing companies, i.e., a high level of suggestions made. Five thousand, four hundred, and thirty-five total suggestions were made by a total of 1,103 employees. Length of gainsharing plans ranged from 16 months to 72 months. While the totals are impressive, not all employees make suggestions, so their study design explored hypotheses on perceived job complexity and assisting behavior. In effect, support was found for higher rates of suggestion making when jobs were complex and enriched. This supports the claim of gainsharing and OD. Another interesting finding is that assisting behavior, while moderated by job complexity, is associated with higher rates of suggestion making. Assisting behavior consists of voluntary efforts or acts that are not part of one's official job description. Often termed organizational citizenship (Organ, 1988),[87] this behavior is associated with help given to peers, supervisors, and co-workers by assisting them perform job related tasks. Selecting employees for assisting behavior or developing organizational values for this pro-social behavior reflects concern for those factors which contribute to high levels of suggestion making.

Thus, there is growing empirical evidence that the OD model is stimulated by traditional gainsharing. Hanlon, et al.[88] and Gowen and Jennings[89] offer additional and positive findings on pro-social behavior and participation influencing gainsharing success. Personal growth and renewal by suggestion making are facilitated by gainsharing as new studies provide insights into the attitudes, values, job design characteristics, and social processes that moderate traditional gainsharing success.

SUMMARY AND CONCLUSION

The objective of this chapter has been to review the gainsharing literature. Other reviews[90] have focused selectively on the Scanlon plan, almost to the exclusion of other forms of gainsharing. Most reviews are purely descriptive. This chapter has attempted to provide some necessary context to the theoretical models of Chapter 1. Many of the calculations were presented, but with an eye toward their historical relevance. More extensive treatments are found in Chapters 4 and 5 as well as elsewhere in the book.[91]

Most of the early literature depicts "every man as a capitalist" and focuses on labor management cooperation and participation. Unfortunately, much of that literature is anecdotal. Fortunately, more contemporary research broadens the scope of evaluation to most forms of gainsharing, and methods used to assess gainsharing have become more quantitative. Certain key issues, such as size, involvement, presence of a union, and sources of failure, have been identified. We now know what gainsharing is, what it isn't, and we have a good grasp of what it can realistically accomplish. A growing amount of literature addresses how gainsharing works under specific circumstances. The factors associated with learning a new reward system are clearly the more interesting parts of the gainsharing literature since they offer so much promise.

The future of gainsharing as a reward system enhancing organizational development, is being explained by researchers. Understanding why gainsharing works is the goal of this research. Prediction of gainsharing success under specific circumstances will be the primary goal of this new research.

Notes

1. B. E. Moore and T. L. Ross, *The Scanlon Way to Improved Productivity* (New York: Wiley-Interscience, 1978).
2. A. W. Rucker, *Labor's Road to Plenty* (Boston: Page, 1937).
3. Moore and Ross, *The Scanlon Way.*
4. Ibid., p. 2.
5. B. Graham-Moore, "Gainsharing," *The Blackwell Dictionary of Organizational Behavior*, ed. Nigel Nicholson (Oxford: Blackwell, Ltd., 1995).
6. C. F. Frost, J.H. Wakely, and R.A. Ruh, *The Scanlon Plan for Organization Development: Identity, Participation, Equity* (East Lansing: Michigan State University Press, 1974).
7. F. G. Lesieur, ed., *The Scanlon Plan: A Frontier in Labor-Management Cooperation* (Cambridge: Technology Press of M.I.T. and N.Y.: John Wiley & Sons, 1958) 249–250.
8. B. E. Moore, *Sharing the Gains of Productivity* (Scarsdale, N.Y.: Work in America Institute Studies in Productivity, 1982); B. E. Moore, *A Plant-Wide Productivity Plan in Action: Three Years of Experience with the Scanlon Plan* (Washington, D.C.: National Commission Productivity and Work Quality, 1975).
9. J. P. Hoerr, *And the Wolf Finally Came* (Pittsburgh: University of Pittsburgh Press, 1988).
10. Moore and Ross, *The Scanlon Way.*
11. Moore, *A Plant-Wide Productivity Plan.*
12. Moore and Ross, *The Scanlon Way.*
13. Ibid.
14. J. F. Lincoln, *Incentive Management* (Cleveland: Lincoln Electric Company, 1951).
15. Moore and Ross, *The Scanlon Way* .
16. B.L. Metzger, *Profit Sharing in Perspective*, 2nd ed. (Evanston, Ill: Profit Sharing Research Foundation, 1966).
17. Moore and Ross, *The Scanlon Way.*
18. J.J. Jehring, "A Contrast Between Two Approaches to Total Systems Incentives," *California Management Review*, 1967, 7–14.
19. Frost, Wakely, and Ruh, *The Scanlon Plan For Organization Development*; F. G. Lesieur, ed., *The Scanlon Plan: A Frontier in Labor-Management Cooperation* (Cambridge: Technology Press of M.I.T. and N.Y.: John Wiley and Sons, 1958); Moore and Ross, *The Scanlon Way.*
20. C. Heyel, ed., *Encyclopedia of Management* (New York: Van Nostrand Reinhold, 1973).
21. P. J. Loftus, "Labor's Share in Manufacturing," *Lloyd's Bank Review*, (London), April 1969.
22. G. Copeman, "Wages and Added Value," *Management Today*, June 1977, 45–46; B. Cox, "Formulas for Value Added Incentives," *Accounting* (UK), February 1980, 113–116.
23. Moore and Ross, *The Scanlon Way.*
24. M. Fein, "An Alternative to Traditional Managing," in *Handbook of Industrial Engineering*, ed. Gavriel Salvendy (New York: Wiley, 1981).
25. R. S. Alanis and B. E. Moore, "Organizational Learning of New Incentive Systems: Improshare," (manuscript, The University of Texas at Austin, 1981).

26. Fein, "An Alternative to Traditional Managing."
27. Ibid., p. 481.
28. Ibid., p. 41.
29. Lincoln, *Incentive Management.*; Robert Zager, "Sharing the Wealth: HRD's Role in Making Incentive Plans Work," *Training*, January 1979, 30–31.
30. Fein, "An Alternative to Traditional Managing."
31. Michael Schuster, "The Scanlon Plan: A Longitudinal Analysis," *Journal of Applied Behavioral Science*, 1984, 20.
32. R.B. Gray, "The Scanlon Plan—A Case Study," *British Journal of Industrial Relations*, 9, 291–313.
33. Fein, "An Alternative to Traditional Managing."
34. J. Short and B. E. Moore, "Preliminary Findings of a Multivariate Analysis of Suggestion Systems Impact on Productivity" (Working Paper, Graduate School of Business, The University of Texas at Austin, 1975).
35. E. E. Lawler, *Pay and Organizational Development* (Reading, Mass.: Addison-Wesley, 1981); J.K. White, "The Scanlon Plan: Causes and Correlates of Success," *Academy of Management Journal*, 22 (June 1979), 292–312.
36. Ibid.
37. Lawler, *Pay and Organizational Development;* Moore and Ross, *The Scanlon Way.*
38. Lawler, *Pay and Organizational Development;* F. G. Lesieur and E.S. Puckett, "The Scanlon Plan—Past, Present, and Future" (Proceedings of the 21st Industrial Relations Annual Winter Meeting, 1968) 71–80; T. L. Ross and G.M. Jones, "An Approach to Increased Productivity: The Scanlon Plan," *Financial Executive*, February 1972, 23–29; R. Ruh, J.H. Wakely, and J.C. Morrison, "Education, Ego Need Gratification and Attitudes Toward the Job," (manuscript, East Lansing, Michigan State University, 1972); J. N. Scanlon, "Adamson and His Profit-Sharing Plan," Production Series no. 172 (New York: American Management Association, 1947) 10–12; G. P. Shultz, "Worker Participation on Production Problems: A Discussion of Experience with the Scanlon Plan," *Personnel*, November 1951, 209–211.
39. Frost, Wakely, and Ruh, *The Scanlon Plan for Organization Development*; Lesieur, *The Scanlon Plan: A Frontier*; William F. Whyte, *Money and Motivation* (New York: Harper and Brothers, 1955).
40. Jehring, "Contrast Between Two Approaches"; R. B. McKersie, "Wage Payment Methods of the Future," *British Journal of Industrial Relations*, June 1963, 191–212; T. L. Ross, et al., "Measurement Under the Scanlon Plan and Other Productivity Incentive Plans," (Manuscript, Bowling Green State University, 1975).
41. W. J. Howell, Jr., "A New Look at Profit Sharing, Pension and Productivity Plans," *Business Management*, December 1967, 26–42; G. Strauss and L. R. Sayles, "The Scanlon Plan: Some Organizational Problems," *Human Organization*, Fall 1957, 15–22.
42. Frost, Wakely, and Ruh, *The Scanlon Plan for Organization Development.*; Ruh, Wakely, and Morrison, "Education, Ego Need Gratification."
43. T.O. Gilson and J.J. Lefcowitz, "A Plant-wide Productivity Bonus in a Small Factory—Study of an Unsuccessful Case," *Industrial and Labor Relations Review*, 1957, 284–296; Gray, "The Scanlon Plan—A Case Study"; McKersie, "Wage Payment Methods."

44. Ibid.

45. P. S. Goodman, "The Scanlon Plan: A Need for Conceptual and Empirical Models" (Symposium, 81st Annual Convention, American Psychological Association. 1973); O'Dell, "Gainsharing"; White, "The Scanlon Plan: Causes and Correlates of Success."

46. Lesieur, *The Scanlon Plan: A Frontier*; McKersie, "Wage Payment Methods"; B. E. Moore and P. S. Goodman, "Factors Affecting the Impact of a Company-Wide Incentive Program on Productivity" (Final Report submitted to the National Commission on Productivity, 1973); Scanlon, "Adamson"; J. N. Scanlon, "Remarks on the Scanlon Plan" (Proceedings of the Conference on Productivity, June 4, 1949) 10–14; S. H. Slichter, J.J. Healy, and E.R. Livernash, *The Impact of Collective Bargaining on Management* (Washington, D.C.: The Brookings Foundation, 1960).

47. Frost, Wakely, and Ruh, *The Scanlon Plan for Organization Development*; R. Ruh, R.H. Johnson, and M.P. Scrontino, "The Scanlon Plan, Participation in Decision Making and Job Attitudes," *Journal of Industrial and Organizational Psychology* 1 (1973), 36–45; Whyte, *Money and Motivation.*

48. McKersie, "Wage Payment Methods"; Moore and Goodman, "Factors Affecting the Impact."

49. Lesieur, *The Scanlon Plan: A Frontier;* McKersie, "Wage Payment Methods."

50. Lesieur, *The Scanlon Plan: A Frontier.*

51. A. Anderson, "Devising Real Incentives for Productivity," *American Machinist*, June 1978, 115–130; Scanlon, "Adamson"; Scanlon, "Remarks."

52. Lesieur, *The Scanlon Plan: A Frontier*; Slichter, Healy, and Livernash, *Impact of Collective Bargaining;* Whyte, *Money and Motivation.*

53. R.B. Helfgott, "Group Wage Incentives: Experience with the Scanlon Plan" (New York: Industrial Relations Counselors, Industrial Relations Memo, 1962).

54. T. Hammer, "New Developments in Profit Sharing," *Productivity in Organizations*, J. Campbell, R. Campbell, and Associates (San Francisco: Jossey-Bass, 1988).

55. R. T. Kaufman, "Effects of Improshare on Productivity," *Industrial and Labor Relations Review*, January, 1992.

56. C. O'Dell and J. McAdams, People, Performance, and Pay (Houston: American Productivity Center, 1987).

57. S. E. Markham, K. D. Scott, B. L. Little, S. Berman, "National Gainsharing Study: The Importance of Industry Differences," Compensation and Benefits Review, January–February, 1992.

58. W. C. Hauck and T. L. Ross, "Is Gainsharing Applicable to Service Sector Firms?" *Productivity Gainsharing* (Englewood Cliffs, NJ: Prentice-Hall, 1983).

59. B. E. Graham-Moore, "Productivity Gainsharing in the Service Sector," *Personnel Management: Compensation Service* (Paramus, NJ: Prentice-Hall Information Services, 1987).

60. J. Jarrett, "Gainsharing in the Government Sector," *Gainsharing: Plans for Improving Performance* (Washington, D.C.: Bureau of National Affairs, 1990).

61. S. W. Bowie-McCoy, A. C. Wendt, and R. Chope, "Gainsharing in Public Accounting: Working Smarter and Harder," *Industrial Relations*, Fall 1993.

62. Markham, et al., "National Gainsharing Study."

63. Ibid.

64. M. Schuster, "The Impact of Union-Management Cooperation on Productivity and Employment," *Industrial and Labor Relations Review*, April, 1983.

65. B. Graham-Moore and R. Rodgers, "Productivity Gainsharing and Organizational Fit," unpublished manuscript, The University of Texas at Austin, 1986.

66. E. E. Lawler, III, "Gainsharing Theory and Research: Findings and Future Directions," Technical Report no. 85-1 (67) CEO, University of Southern California, 1985.

67. E. E. Lawler, III and S. A. Mohrman, "Involvement Management: Champions of Change," *Executive Excellence*, April, 1989.

68. Gilson and Lefcowitz, "Plant-Wide Productivity Bonus."

69. Gray, "The Scanlon Plan: A Case Study."

70. Helfgott, "Group Wage Incentives."

71. R.B. Johnson, "The Scanlon Plan: Criteria for Success in Non-Union Plants" (Master's thesis, School of Industrial Management, M.I.T., 1959).

72. Jehring, "Contrast Between Two Approaches."

73. R. Ruh, R.L. Wallace, and C.F. Frost, "Management Attitudes and the Scanlon Plan," *Industrial Relations*, 1973, 282–288; Ruh, Johnson, and Scrontino, "The Scanlon Plan, Participation, and Attitudes."

74. Ross, et al., "Measurement Under the Scanlon Plan."

75. Lesieur, *The Scanlon Plan: A Frontier.*

76. P. S. Goodman, personal correspondence, 1988.

77. J. G. Belcher, Jr., *Gain Sharing* (Houston: Gulf Publishing, 1991).

78. E. M. Doherty, W. R. Nord, and J. L. McAdams "Gainsharing and Organization Development: A Productive Synergy," *Journal of Applied Behavioral Science*, August 1989.

79. Scanlon, "Adamson"; Whyte, *Money and Motivation.*

80. *Hamilton* (Ontario) *Spectator,* November 18, 1980.

81. W. L. French and C.H. Bell, *Organization Development: Behavior Science Interventions for Organization Improvement* (Englewood Cliffs, N.J.: Prentice-Hall, 1973).

82. R. J. Bullock and M. E. Tubbs, "A Case Meta-Analysis of Gainsharing Plans as Organization Development Interventions," *Journal of Applied Behavioral Science*, August 1990.

83. Doherty, et al., "Gainsharing and Organization Development: A Productive Synergy."

84. Moore and Ross, *The Scanlon Way.*

85. L. L. Hatcher and T. L. Ross, "Organization Development Through Productivity Gainsharing," *Personnel*, October 1985, 49.

86. L. Hatcher, T. L. Ross, and D. Collins, "Prosocial Behavior, Job Complexity, and Suggestion Contribution Under Gainsharing Plans," *Journal of Applied Behavioral Science*, 1989.

87. D. W. Organ and M. Konovsky, "Cognitive versus Affective Determinants of Organizational Citizenship Behavior," *Journal of Applied Psychology*, 1989.

88. S. C. Hanlon, D. G. Meyer, and R. R. Taylor, "Consequences of Gainsharing: A Field Experiment Revisited," *Group and Organization Studies*, March 1985.

89. C. R. Gowen, III and S. A. Jennings, "The Effects of Changes in Participation and Group Size on Gainsharing Success: A Case Study," *Journal of Organizational Behavior Management*, 1990.
90. Moore, *A Plant-Wide Productivity Plan;* Moore, *Sharing the Gains of Productivity;* White, "The Scanlon Plan: Causes and Correlates of Success."
91. Moore, *Sharing the Gains of Productivity*; Moore and Ross, *The Scanlon Way.*

Chapter 3

Employee Involvement—The Key Link to Successful Long-Run Gainsharing

Timothy L. Ross and Ruth Ann Ross

What is the key to long-term gainsharing success? Although many "students" of gainsharing may argue over this issue, today most agree that the extent of employee involvement is important. Other issues key to success are covered in more detail in Chapters 2 and 6. The problem is not everyone agrees to what employee involvement really is. This chapter discusses the most common approaches of employee involvement and its evolutions used by gainsharing companies over the years. Our emphasis in this entire book is on employee involvement gainsharing, not just bonus plans as many studies research.

DISCUSSION OF EMPLOYEE INVOLVEMENT TECHNIQUES

In its most simple form, some people believe that employees writing up cost reduction or quality improvement suggestions or more communications up and down the organization or economic education on a quarterly basis to be employee involvement. Others believe that only self-directed teams are true involvement. It obviously can be formal or informal, long-term or short-term, and complex or simple.

Exhibit 3.1 gives a description of a common range from traditional (management directed) to self-directed (nonmanagement directed) involvement activities. Obviously, the whole area of employee involvement can become very complex in a hurry even with just a fast pass. Some people advocate total change in how organizations are managed whereas others promote a more

Exhibit 3.1   Range of Involvement Possibilities

limited change process. Some new organizational startups get employees involved in all of the above variables—something unheard of in the past.

TRADITIONAL GAINSHARING INVOLVEMENT—PLAN DESIGN

To help build identity, traditional gainsharing plans often used groups of employees to help design and perhaps renew the plan. Because of the complexities of the issues, these were heavily influenced by management or an outside consultant. In fact, many of the more packaged plans were and still are designed essentially by consultants with little input from employees. In unionized firms, the union officials often were heavily involved in determining the direction of the plan.

These design groups would search out consultants, read materials such as books and articles, and perhaps visit various locations to build their backgrounds in the gainsharing area. Some of the Scanlon oriented design groups were very sophisticated in their approach to the system with the intent being a true cultural change. They would spend many months and even years developing mandates for change, writing complex identity statements and developing detailed involvement systems in addition to developing the calculation and policy statements. The involvement system helps solve problems, gives employees the feeling that they can actually help earn the bonus, helps them more control their own destiny, and helps them develop a sense of ownership among other factors. This is why many traditional gainsharing plans had linked involvement systems.

The American Compensation Association's (ACA) Benchmark Study[1] gives a fairly good description of how plans have been designed and some other details on plan design.

__Designed By__	__Percent__
Initial plan champions	
Top management	60%
Human resources/compensation	24%
Plans covering some unit of larger corporation—approvals required	
Corporate management	78%
Corporate human resources	60%
Unit top management	80%
Plans designed by a task force (could be just management	80%
or both management and nonmanagement)	
Design teams having only management members	67%
Guidance on issues given by top management	
Plan objectives	57%
Payout measures	68%
Maximum payout	71%
Self-funding requirement	66%

Other issues found by the ACA study included: plans are better if not dictated by corporate; teamwork, business performance, and overall satisfaction are better if a design task force is used.

Financial-oriented plans take considerably less time to design according to the ACA study than operational plans, since the plan is often based on one broad measure of performance. Financial plans on the average take 30 employee days and operational 80 employee days because more detailed emphasis on measurement and multiple measures are often used. The financial plans were obviously mostly management developed and did not include formalized employee involvement systems.

To summarize, many traditional gainsharing plans were developed by some sort of design team, often controlled and often manned solely by management members. The more employees were involved, the more teamwork developed and the more the plans were viewed as successful. The ACA Benchmark Study reported primarily on bonus-oriented plans as contrasted to employee involvement gainsharing plans. Obviously, all employee-involvement-oriented plans should have employees involved at least in the design and implementation of such a system.

A key question should be raised here. Should nonmanagement employees be involved at a very early point? If a primary goal is to build identity with the system, the answer is yes. This puts severe "constraints" on the organization. Is top management likely to give up all of their ability to decide on the calculation or is a cultural change going to be required? What happens if you can't get corporate approval after the plan has been designed or corporate feels that they are being "blackmailed" into acceptance? These are complex questions, which is why we propose a two-staged design process as outlined in a later section of this chapter.

TRADITIONAL GAINSHARING INVOLVEMENT—PLAN OPERATION

Since gainsharing was started long before employee "empowerment" and self direction became common goals or techniques, the involvement systems were fairly limited in scope. Some of these are outlined below.

No Formal Involvement

The easiest way is to have no formal involvement and many plans were and still are installed in this way. It is doubtful whether this will survive difficult periods and in fact, most have not. Involvement has been limited to bonus communications and even that often has been done in a cursory manner.

One Level of Involvement

Many Rucker® plans had one level of involvement. Employees from each area of the facility were normally elected to serve on the Rucker Committee with top management. This group monthly reviews the bonus results, reviews economic conditions, and makes recommendations on suggestions submitted by employees to improve performance. Immediately after the Rucker Committee meeting, the employees held short meetings with people in their area to discuss the results and give other feedback. Employees were generally not actively involved in the design of the plan and involvement was limited to cost reduction and quality improvement areas. Although numerous Rucker Plans still exist today, the organization that promoted them has been disbanded.

Two Levels of Involvement

Many Scanlon oriented plans have employees much more actively involved. First, a relatively small group of employees helps design the plan and presents it to employees after various approvals are given. This group was often called a steering committee and now is frequently called a design team. They may work with a consultant. After implementation, most Scanlon Plans utilize an overlapping team concept as outlined in Exhibit 3.2.

Exhibit 3.2   Typical Scanlon Plan Involvement System

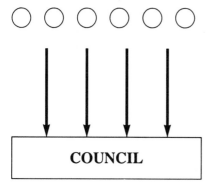

Area Teams or Groups of Employees

COUNCIL

Typical Involvement
- 3–5 people including a supervisor elected by employees
- Can implement ideas from people if:
  - Not over $X of cost
  - All agree
  - Only department affected or can get agreement
- Otherwise— referred to upper level (Council)
- Council: one nonmanagement rep from each team plus top management
- Council reviews bonus results, economic conditions, makes recommendations on larger ideas.

The area teams were originally called production committees and the council was called the screening committee. Terms have become more contemporary, but this involvement system has stood the test of time and still is used successfully today.

Some more traditional gainsharing plans have three or four levels of involvement. These were and still are very useful to increase employee involvement for larger and more complex operations. For example, if an organization has three or more shifts in an area, not much can be done on one shift that doesn't affect another shift. It's logical then to have a group working on interdependent improvement opportunities with perhaps greater decision-making authority. This pushes decision making down and reduces the number of ideas having to be referred to the top group such as the Council in Exhibit 3.2. Thus, it helps improve the effectiveness of the employee involvement system and the efficiency of getting things done.

OTHER SYSTEMS OF INVOLVEMENT

The Scanlon approach outlined above has been successful for over 50 years. It is a fairly easy way for a firm to start without requiring extensive training and culture change. It is a "parallel" system—it is not being integrated into day-to-day operations in a formal way because of the normal limited involvement to quality, cost reduction, and customer service areas. As such, this system must be carefully promoted and developed to be successful in the long term. Recognition and good feedback are very important.

The typical Scanlon involvement system is also more a vertical one, going up the organization from the bottom. Total Quality Management (TQM) and other more contemporary techniques concentrate on more horizontal or cross function groups or teams to be successful. In reality, *both* orientations are needed (i.e., vertical and horizontal groups) if major change is desired. Traditional Scanlon Plans formed cross-functional task forces to work on these larger issues.

But even self directed work teams need to have some formal involvement system or structure to help ensure that things get done. Formalized systems create bureaucracy but help ensure that things get done. Obviously, getting people involved in all of the items listed on Exhibit 3.1 makes the process much more complex and time consuming but also helps facilitate the change process. Each organization must decide how extensive a change process it desires, how formal the techniques must be, and what it can move to over time.

A STARTING PROPOSAL

What is a good way to get an employee involvement system started without taking years and requiring massive cultural change? Over the years, we have experimented with a wide range of systems because organizations have been so diverse. Remember that these are also organizations that want to change culturally at least somewhat. Self-directed organizations normally would do things a little differently. The approach outlined below does seem to work better than most others, although organizations need to adapt it somewhat based on their own needs and culture.

First, we would normally start with a fairly high level group to develop a draft of a plan including tentative purpose and goals, the involvement system to be used, the calculation, and various policies. This group is often called a steering committee or design task force. In a unionized firm, this group of 6–10 people typically would include some of the top union officials plus top management. In a nonunion firm, this typically would be just top management. The reason for this limited involvement is the trade-off between typical corporate approval processes and identity building. That is, if a larger cross section of the organization is involved and then can't get approval, there can be a major problem with very disappointed team members who have devoted time and emotional energy and with corporate managers who don't like to be pressured into decisions by employees. Obviously, if extensive proposal developments and approval processes are not required, perhaps this stage should be adjusted. Quite rightfully, however, top management will not delegate the entire responsibility of formula development to a group of lower level employees as the ACA Benchmark Study clearly found. In a unionized facility, this group can be permanent to review or renew the plan periodically. This group also tries to obtain tentative or final corporate approvals as necessary. All this would reinforce the findings of the ACA Benchmark Study.

Next, and extremely important, you must find a way to obtain commitment from the rest of the employees. This phase was apparently not even noted in the ACA Benchmark Study. We have found that this commitment can be achieved fairly well by having a broad, cross sectional group often called a "Development Task Force" or something similar. This group includes representatives, both management and nonmanagement, from all areas, normally selected by their department or area peers, shifts, and organizational levels to finalize the plan. This group may be from 25–50 or so people (or even larger), depending on the size of the organization. Obviously such a large group would have great difficulty in developing a plan from scratch. They work with the draft of the plan as composed by the design or steering committee to finalize it and present it to all employees. We actually had one group of over 100 people all meeting together although subgroups are often formed.

The goal of this group is to get 100 percent concurrence that all of its members can live with the plan as developed. This consensus building is extremely important and has been very successful in groups of even over 75 members. Members of this group would also make the presentations of the plan to the rest of the employees and be actively involved in forming the employee involvement system. Obviously, if it is just a bonus plan with no formal employee involvement, this group probably is unnecessary.

After the plan is finalized and presented to all employees we would encourage the formation of employee involvement teams similar to those outlined on Exhibit 3.2 at a minimum. This assumes that on-going involvement is desired after implementation. The overlapping team concept does work very well in most organizations and reinforces the concept of Changed Behavior = More Bonus Opportunities. This is lacking in many other change processes, such as TQM, and why they often probably fail. All of this is summarized on Exhibit 3.3.

Although appearing complex, the system outlined on Exhibit 3.3 has and does work better than most other systems that have been tried over the years and has existed for a long time. It is very useful even in self-directed workforce organizations. This system can be expanded to include more and more activities outlined on Exhibit 3.1 as elected by the organization. It can be put on hold for a while when the organization experiences major problems and reformed when the crisis stops without many difficulties although it ideally should be used to help the organization get through the difficult times. The system has to be reinforced with an active communication and recognition program to be effective in the long run since it is not part of the day-to-day activities of the average employee. This approach also should not cross the boundary into the area of practices found to violate the National Labor Relations Act in the widely publicized *Electromation* and *du Pont*[2] decisions by the National Labor Relations Board regarding management's domination of employee organizations.

Exhibit 3.3   A Proposed Employee Involvement System

Study and Implementation Stages

Design or Steering Task Force
Purpose: • Study plans
              • Develop plan draft: purpose/goals, involvement system if applicable, calculations, policies
              • Obtain tentative or final corporate approval
              • On-going evaluations
Members: • Top management of a facility; union officials if applicable (Note: some unionized firms get the union involved after management has discussed some of the key issues.)

Development Task Force
Purpose: • Finalize plan, develop identity/commitment, educate broader group, communicate plan to all employees
Members: • Cross section of entire organization (5–10 percent of workforce is typical); 2 or 3 ex-officio members from Design Task Force; can work successfully up to 60–70 members.

Operation of Plan

Area Teams
Purpose: • Implement ideas if not over established dollar limits, all agree, only area affected; concentrate on cost reductions and quality improvements
              • Meets monthly at least to discuss ideas, communications, teamwork, goals
Members: • One rep at least for each 5–10 employees or all employees in area plus supervisor

Council
Purpose: • Review economic conditions
              • Review bonus results
              • Decide or recommend on larger ideas referred by teams
              • Form cross functional teams as needed
              • Perform special studies
              • Set goals
              • Monitor area team activities
Members: • One nonmanagement rep from each team
              • Top managers
              • Others as needed

BENEFITS DERIVED BY EMPLOYEE INVOLVEMENT GAINSHARING

Like many other interdependent or behavioral variables, gainsharing can become quite complex in a hurry. But depending on the issues outlined in Chapter 1, we have found that a broad approach to an installation is desirable *if* the system is to survive long term. Listed in Exhibit 3.4 are some of the possi-

Exhibit 3.4 Possible Benefits of Gainsharing to Company and Employees

Possible Benefits to Company

Better cooperation
More goal orientation
More commitment to company
Better utilization of assets
Increased profits
Increased quality
Improved morale
Improved technology; improving or advancement
Decreased waste
Increased growth possibilities
Decreased turnover
Attract higher quality employees
Improved working environment
Streamlines decision process
Decreased grievances
Increased labor productivity
Increased quality of decision
Even out work loads
Decreased indirect costs (labor)
Increased customer service
Increased motivation of work force
Increased safety concerns
Improved customer relations and credibility
More money available for more improvement by improving performance
Increased development of supervisors
Increased job expertise
Increased quality of suggestions
Decreased downtime
Reduced absenteeism
Increased ability to change
Increased development of new products
Increased development and identification of leaders
Decrease/reduce medical costs
Decrease problem employees
Decrease payback time on investments
Increased link of pay and performance
Increase long-term security, plus allows more for long-term planning
Decreased management time on small items
Increased implementation of ideas
Increased shareholder satisfaction and value
Improved company public relations
Encourages employees to accept more responsibility and practice self-control
Increased/improved communication
Increased interest in company success
Job enrichment
Decreased fluctuations in many areas

Possible Benefits to Employees

Increased recognition
Increased job security
Increased job enrichment
Increased money
Improved relationships
Improved atmosphere
More problem solving
Increased communications
More involved employees
Have more fun
Increased control over jobs
Reduced frustrations
More fair share
Less friction
Increased hope—tomorrow will be better
Better understanding of business
Break monotony
More involved in decision making
More room for advancement and leadership skills development
Improved health
Understanding of other disciplines and areas
More pride
Make job easier
More and faster improvements
Develop communication skills
People listen more
Don't carry things home as much
Improved teamwork
Improved quality of work and personal life
More self-motivation
Fewer problems with management
Develop transferable skills

ble benefits often cited by participants of an employee involvement oriented gainsharing plan. Many of them will not occur without involvement. One should readily see that only in this way, does it become a Win/Win/Win situation for customers, company, and all employees. Each organization must decide which variables are most important; these and others are cited in the literature and in visits to existing employee involvement gainsharing organizations.

CONCLUSION

Our feeling is that some sort of formalized, structured employee involvement system should be an integrated part of a long-term gainsharing plan. This chapter reviewed some approaches that firms have used to help insure their plans are successful in the long term and the possible benefits to all parties. Studies have consistently shown that this is important to the long-term success of a plan since it helps the system survive good and bad times.

Notes

1. J. L. McAdams and E.J. Hawk, *Capitalizing on Human Assets: The Benchmark Study* (Scottsdale: American Compensation Association and Maritz, Inc., 1992).
2. *Electromation, Inc.*, 309 NLRB No. 163, 142 LRRM 1001 (1962), *enforced*, ____ F.2d ____, 147 LRRM 2257 (7th Cir., 1994), and *E.I. du Pont de Nemours & Co.*, 311 NLRB 893, 143 LRRM 1121 (1993). See also the Fourth Circuit's refusal to enforce an NLRB order requiring a Maryland hospital to disband an employee participation committee in *NLRB v. Peninsula General Hospital*, No. 94-1202, Oct. 18, 1994, 202 *Daily Labor Report* AA-1 (Oct. 21, 1994).

Chapter 4

Formulas for Developing a Reward Structure to Further Organizational Goals

Brian Graham-Moore

For too long, the means for developing a gainsharing reward structure has been "hidden" from view. Some gainsharing formulas are held to be proprietary; yet in their generic form none are. Possibly this area of our knowledge has been obscured because consultants have held this information close to the vest. Just as responsible, however, may be the general ignorance that prevails in any area of financial analysis. Put simply, the decision maker of the 1990s can no longer be held in the dark. Selecting an appropriate gainsharing formula should be an informed decision. Instead of selecting just one formula, perhaps several should be chosen and tested so that the tradeoffs can be fully understood.

Formula determination is the leading cause of disagreement among corporate officials, local management, human resource, and outside consultants. Proper formula determination consists of making a series of informed judgments in a rational way. This chapter presents a diagnostic tool for organizations to use in developing a gainsharing formula that will reinforce the positive properties of the organization specified in Chapter 1 (Exhibit 1.2). As a first step, organizations should address all of the issues in this chapter before implementing a gainsharing plan.

This chapter reviews the goals that should be specified when gainsharing is considered. Also, five generic formulas are presented along with some recent variants to illustrate how these organizational goals interact with the strengths and weaknesses of each formula. Then, assessment of selected formulas is delineated so that the decision maker can install a gainsharing formula with few surprises. This assessment portion of the chapter introduces the fact that hybrid gainsharing formulas can be developed once key decision makers specify the profile goals and understand the fit between goals and their organization.

Gainsharing formula selection is not easy; however, it is definitely a rewarding process. A clear understanding of how gainsharing fits within an organization creates a clearer understanding of the organization's culture and its policies.

THE DECISION-MAKING APPROACH

The sequential decision-making process recommended here reflects the concerns raised in the literature describing gainsharing failures, discussed in Chapters 2,5, and 6. Probably the estimated one-third of gainsharing installations that failed did so in the first year. Typically, the blame is placed on the formula. To avoid a poor selection of formula, a rational decision-making model should be followed. The sequential steps are these:

1. goal specification,
2. formula selection,
3. assessment of fit between the organization and the formula.

All organizations need to address the three steps listed above. Otherwise, failure to specify the objectives and carefully consider the formula and the organization's needs will result in intraorganizational conflict. Consider the following scenario: An individual in the organization hears of a way to improve productivity, possibly at a conference. A renowned consultant is brought in providing empirical evidence that her or his method has proved to increase performance. In fact, the consultants can even provide examples showing great success in improving performance. Who can argue with results? A gainsharing program is quickly adopted. What were the specific goals that the organization wanted to achieve? Was a serious search given to alternative gainsharing plans? Proper evaluation of gainsharing is unlikely since organizational goals weren't specified. The organization may have adopted a gainsharing plan that works but the reason for the selection was not well considered. The comparative approach specified above makes more sense.

In 1978, Moore and Ross presented the most comprehensive known discussion of (1) formula calculation, (2) alternative formulas, and (3) measurement problems in the context of traditional gainsharing.[1] This chapter goes beyond the issues they raised and attempts to examine a set of issues that build on this previous work. Specifically, this chapter outlines a framework for theoreticians, practitioners, and other decision makers that addresses the following issues:

1. What does the organization expect to gain from a gainsharing program formula?
2. Which criteria help an organization to select among alternative formulas?
3. What are the trade-offs between the various formulas?
4. How does an organization select a formula that will survive in a turbulent environment and permit institutionalization?

GOAL SPECIFICATION

Goal specification sounds like such an obvious step, yet gainsharing organizations often exhibit symptoms months after gainsharing implementation that suggest poor clarification of their goals. If a key manager says "I thought gainsharing would reduce scrap and waste and that hasn't happened," very likely the formula selected is a poor fit with organization goals.

Goals

Goal specification centers on honestly addressing all the goals listed here along with the theoretical issues discussed in Chapter 1. These goals and issues appear in many forms and in many combinations. Key decision makers need to understand this combination in order to make optimal use of their organization's particular profile. Clearly, one choice is to reject gainsharing as inappropriate for the company in question. In all cases, decision makers must attempt to select a program that fits best with the organization's technology and culture.

Process

The process of goal specification is also very important. That is, an obvious goal of gainsharing is to make organizational goals common across the entire organization. Often overlooked are ways to involve all the constituencies that make for successful gainsharing. Early task forces can include union representatives, staff members, and hourly wage earners. Key individuals who can and will influence gainsharing implementation, and later institutionalization, need to be part of the goal specification process.

Clarification

Clarifying what the organization means when it says it wants to improve performance is often a fascinating exercise. Most people agree that performance refers to the ratio of inputs to outputs. Taken to a deeper level, however, organizational performance can be viewed as the comparison of profits (outputs) to investments (inputs). If an organization wants to assume this financial definition of performance, a cash profit-sharing program may fit best. In contrast, performance can be viewed as the amount of output produced by a certain amount of labor. Using this definition of performance, a direct efficiency formula such as allowed labor can be implemented.[2] This type of formula, however, ignores overheads and offers no incentive for efficient management of resources. There are other gainsharing formulas that measure the ratio of goods produced to strictly labor inputs. One must remember that rewarding efficient management may weaken the relationship between pay and performance. Also, the broader the formula the more it will be affected by economic fluctuation, unless it is adjusted for these fluctuations.

Organizational Factors

The various gainsharing formulas express different behavioral and organizational objectives. It is a good idea for firms to establish that these gainsharing objectives "fit" with the organization's objectives. Once this has been accomplished, firms should adopt a rational approach for selecting a formula. All gainsharing formulas can be evaluated against most of the following seven behavioral and organizational factors:

1. strength of reinforcement,
2. scope of the formula,
3. motivation of harder work,
4. motivation of smarter work,
5. motivation of behavior to produce nonlabor savings,
6. ease of administration,
7. economic flexibility.

As indicated in Chapter 1, our purpose is not to support one kind of gainsharing plan, rather we suggest that formula can be constructed to best achieve the goals of a firm, whatever its current status. Goals should require a firm to stretch, but should not be so high that they contribute to frustration. Those firms embarking on a gainsharing program should specify their organizational goals. The firm should view these goals within the theoretical framework suggested in Chapter 1 so that it can select and evaluate a gainsharing formula against the factors discussed here.

Decision makers must first specify what they mean by performance. How extensive will the definition be? Who contributes? Each gainsharing formula has a different impact on the subgoals of performance, as the reader will see. Therefore, strategic planning in gainsharing should contemplate all relevant behavioral and organizational factors given the common understanding of the firm's view of performance.

Elaborated below is the list of seven behavioral and organizational factors that affect the attainment of the goals of gainsharing. This list should provide organizations with a starting point, but they may want to add additional factors or goals as they progress with the plan.

Strength of Reinforcement

The amount of the bonus can be small or potentially very large. Lincoln Electric has paid total bonuses equal to annual pay. Just how much the work force will be influenced by extrinsic rewards can vary as a function of compensation philosophy, cultural values, and individual differences. Annual average gainsharing bonuses range from 0 to 30 percent and higher.

Scope of the Formula

Does the organization want a formula to capture broad areas of performance or to focus narrowly on, say, output? The ability of the formula to assist decision makers and any participating employee groups in isolating evolving problems is often overlooked. For example, if quality of product or service is a desired goal, a narrow cost reduction gainsharing formula might work toward this objective. A more broadly based gainsharing formula that includes all controllable costs in the numerator and the market value of output in its denominator encourages all to share the final test of the marketplace.

Motivating Harder Work

Is the organization trying primarily to get its workers to work harder? While it seems organizations always want to encourage employees to work faster, it may not be possible to get a large increase in speed. In addition, other factors, such as safety, may prohibit attempting to achieve this apparently obvious goal. Organizations should seriously evaluate the desire and potential for harder work.

Motivating Smarter Work

Does the organization want to encourage workers to try to come with better ways to produce goods? While all organizations like to find better ways to produce goods, encouraging workers to make this type of contribution does not come without costs. Obtaining ideas from workers involves administration costs. In addition, supervisors may feel threatened when workers try to act smarter. Thus, organizations should assess the viability of this pursuit before undertaking such a program. The inability to implement employee-authored improvements will deter gainsharing success.

Motivating Nonlabor Savings

To what degree is it possible for workers to create savings on expenses (e.g., materials, equipment) other than labor? To the extent that such savings are possible, the organization may want to select a formula to reward expense savings that go beyond labor savings. Organizations should be aware that complex formulas can cause additional costs—problems with measurement, communication, and understanding.

Ease of Administration

While gainsharing plans offer the potential for dramatic increases in performance, they do require administrative work. Different formulas require different amounts of administrative work. Consequently, organizations need to specify how important it is to minimize administrative complexity. For example, bonuses can be reported and paid weekly or monthly. Information must be collected, processed and managed. Also, some gainsharing plans involve supervisors heavily. They must explain the formula and relate policy to employees and, thus, must receive special training in order to be effective.

Economic Flexibility

During economic downturns, a number of gainsharing firms have had to cut production dramatically. These cuts, unfortunately, may have an unexpected impact on the appropriateness of the standards used in a gainsharing formula. If organizations anticipate that economic fluctuations will affect the required level of production, a formula should be chosen that (partially) buffers the gainsharing plan from such changes. Seasonal variations can also affect the bonuses and deficits in ways which are independent of human endeavor. Simple gainsharing formulas do not offer the same opportunities to buffer these swings that a more complex formula can provide.

GENERIC FORMULAS

An organization typically begins the mechanics of traditional gainsharing formula determination by developing the expected (standard) amount of labor cost necessary to produce a given amount of goods based on historical data. Once the plan is completed, actual labor costs are compared to standard costs for each bonus period (e.g., a week, a month) and the bonus is based on labor cost savings. The five generic formulas outlined below vary in terms of what goes into the production costs. Each formula influences the behavioral and organizational factors in different ways. Sufficient information is presented to allow you the opportunity to understand and evaluate each of them. Before implementation, however, it is appropriate and necessary to examine a more detailed description of the mechanics of the desired formula via spreadsheet analysis.

To evaluate each formula with respect to a given organization, it is important to realize that the advantages and disadvantages of a given formula are only relevant to the extent that they affect that particular organization. Some of the considerations listed below would not have a serious effect on many organizations. Thus, an organization must attempt to select the formula with the most advantages and least disadvantages, since there is no perfect way to measure productivity.

Exhibit 4.1 displays the similar and dissimilar aspects of five generic gainsharing formulas. Each formula varies considerably in the construction of a balance sheet of items that go into making the formula operational. Focusing primarily on the behavioral and organizational factors, each generic gainsharing formula is reviewed below.

Impact of the Single Ratio Scanlon Formula

The mechanics of the single ratio formula dictate determining expected labor costs from historical data, preferably over a relatively long time frame.

Exhibit 4.1 Five Gainsharing Formulas—A Comparison

Traditional Scanlon	Expanded Scanlon Ratios		Improshare/ Allowed	Rucker/ Value-
Single Ratio	Split Ratio	Multicost Ratio	Labor	Added
HR Payroll Costs	HR Payroll Costs by Product	HR Payroll, Material, Overhead by Product & Department	Actual Labor Hours by Product & Department	Direct Labor
Net Sales or Production Value	Net Sales or Production Value	Net Sales or Production Value	Production Standard	Value Added

This is done by calculating the percentage of sales that has been used to pay labor expenses. This relationship of historical human resource cost to sales or output cost is termed the base ratio. Once this percentage is set, a bonus is earned in any period in which actual labor costs are less than the allowed (expected) rate.

Exhibit 4.2, Developing a Single Ratio, depicts the basic ingredients and typical steps followed in calculating a Scanlon single ratio. All human resource costs under the control of the worker for a year are totaled and then divided by either net sales or the prediction value for the year. Usually, three year's data are captured. Then, the stability of the base ratio is reviewed. In this case, the expected human resource cost ranges from 19 to 21 percent. Therefore, the historical base ratio of expected human resource cost is a value ranging from 19 to 21 percent.

Exhibit 4.2 Developing A Single Ratio

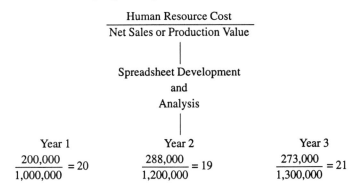

$$\frac{\text{Human Resource Cost}}{\text{Net Sales or Production Value}}$$

Spreadsheet Development
and
Analysis

Year 1	Year 2	Year 3
$\frac{200,000}{1,000,000} = 20$	$\frac{288,000}{1,200,000} = 19$	$\frac{273,000}{1,300,000} = 21$

Now consider a subsequent bonus period (e.g., a month) in which sales value of production is equal to $1,200,000 and labor costs are $210,000. The bonus pool would be equal to $30,000 (line 8) of Exhibit 4.3, Single Ratio Scanlon Monthly Report. This is merely the difference expected between payroll costs (line 6, $240,000) and actual payroll costs (line 7). The allowed or expected percentage on line 6 is 20 percent which was selected from Exhibit 4.3, wherein the choice ranged from 19 to 21 percent.

In actuality, a typical single ratio bonus calculation is very straightforward. Exhibit 4.3 illustrates how most Scanlon companies report their monthly bonus in the form of a balance sheet.

Even this simple (and original) Scanlon formula has its policy implications. In Exhibit 4.3, for example, line 9 reduces the bonus pool by 50 percent. If this deduction is taken by the firm, it serves as a hedge against future productivity improvements that are not a result of efforts by the labor force. Thus, by taking a share of each bonus pool the company is less likely to adjust the base ratio for each technological improvement.

Line 10 of Exhibit 4.3 shows a reserve for deficit months, a similar hedge for leveling out cyclical variations. In this way, a deduction for periods of very high productivity can be applied to the deficits incurred in periods of very low productivity. One of its purposes is to build long-term attitudes.

Line 11, reflecting employee share, is $11,250, which is divided by the participating payroll costs for the period. The result is a 6.7 percent bonus applied on top of the actual pay earned during the period. Thus, the bonus is differentially applied in terms of absolute dollars. That is, all employees—from

Exhibit 4.3   Single Ratio Scanlon Monthly Report

1. Sales	$1,100,000
2. Less sales returns, allowances, discounts	25,000
3. Net Sales	1,075,000
4. Add: increase in inventory	
(at cost or selling price)	125,000
5. Value of production	1,200,000
6. Allowed payroll costs (20% of value of production)	240,000
7. Actual payroll costs	210,000
8. Bonus pool	30,000
9. Company share (50%)	15,000
Subtotal	15,000
10. Reserve for deficit months (25%)	3,750
11. Employee share—immediate distribution	11,250
12. Participating payroll costs	168,750
13. Bonus percentage ($11,250/$168,750)	6.7%

Adapted from: B.E. Moore and T.L. Ross, *The Scanlon Way to Improved Productivity* (New York: Wiley-Interscience, 1978) 71.

the plant manager to the lowest paid worker—receive 6.7 percent of their respective monthly earnings. All gainsharing plans are not intended to change the regular reward structure, but rather to stimulate productivity. Therefore, the bonus is calculated on actual earnings in most gainsharing companies. Notice also that line 7, actual payroll costs, is greater than line 12, participating payroll. Normally, there are some exclusions to the participating payroll, i.e., the sales force, key management positions, and so forth. The participating payroll may be a lower value, yet total human resource cost is appropriately found on line 7.

Because of its simplicity, the single ratio calculation is easy to understand. However, its impact on the organization is not so simple. Exhibit 4.4, Effect of Single Ratio Formula on Behavioral and Organizational Factors, illustrates how this formula affects meaningful factors in gainsharing. For example, of the seven behavioral and organizational dimensions, the single ratio has a significant impact on strength of reinforcement, motivation of hard work, and ease of administration.

Note that the scope of the single ratio is relatively narrow for most organizations. That is, overhead, materials, and to some extent waste are not specifically

Exhibit 4.4   Effect of Scanlon Single Ratio Formula on Behavioral and Organizational Factors

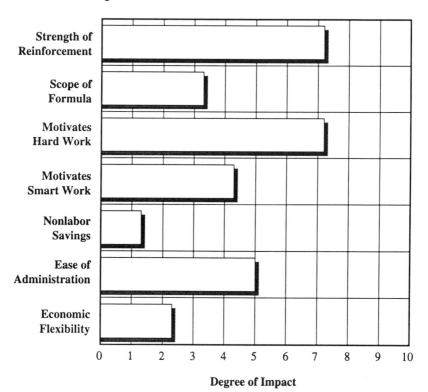

Degree of Impact

covered by this labor-only ratio. However, if an organization was very labor intensive and had low overhead, this ratio might have more appeal. Perhaps, in some service industries, such as cable television, the single ratio could be a reasonable choice (see Chapter 14 for service industry examples).

As Exhibit 4.4 shows, nonlabor savings are virtually nonexistent. Suggestions that improve methods to actually save raw materials in Scanlon companies affect the bonus in *labor* efficiency only. True, if gains in labor-saving methods were translated into increased sales or output, then an increase in the profit may be realized from the output. This increase would help to produce bonuses. Generally, it is fair to say that since single ratio plans do not calculate and transfer gains from nonlabor savings into bonus dollars, there is no direct relationship. If the scope of the calculations are broad, as in the multicost formula, then gains in nonlabor savings are shared more directly.

Sudden and significant changes in prices for raw materials can cause the denominator of the single ratio formula to reflect bonuses incorrectly if adjustments are not made for these changes. The single ratio may not account for inflation, changes in product mix, technological change, or capital investment. Rapidly peaking cycles of production cannot be easily smoothed by this formula either. None of these consequences of the single ratio are necessarily bad, if decision makers are aware of these facts.

Impact of the Split Ratio Formula

Exhibit 4.5, Effect of Split Ratio Formula on Behavioral and Organizational Factors, indicates the impact of the split ratio formula on the organization. This calculation develops the base ratio by product line or other functional cost category. Since this improvement overcomes the problem of changing product mix encountered with the single ratio formula, the split ratio formula can deal more accurately with economic flexibility and cyclical variations. Ease of administration does suffer somewhat, since more information must be processed and evaluated. And while this formula is inherently fairer, it is more complex. While this formula does reward all employees, it also demonstrates that some product lines contribute more to overall productivity than others. This identification of differing product performance may lead to conflict among areas of the firm. Some competition may be beneficial. However, if the conflict is not well managed, lack of cooperation and interdepartmental harassment can result. If the above is not a consideration, the motivational factors are about the same as the single ratio formula, yet performance measurement is improved.

Finally, it is important to understand exactly why the split ratio can be a choice for those firms with sufficient product mix to affect the bonus calculation. Exhibit 4.6, Assumed Bonus Calculation Under Single and Split Ratio Methods, illustrates why split ratio could be useful. In this example, the single ratio calculates a bonus pool of $60,000. Under the split ratio, the bonus is

Exhibit 4.5 Effect of Split Ratio Formula on Behavioral and Organizational Factors

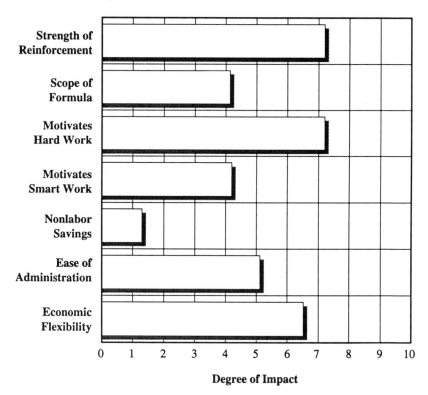

Degree of Impact

$20,000. Thus, the single ratio overpaid by $40,000. The true increase to productivity was reflected only in the Product B line.

Impact of the Multicost Split Ratio Formula

Exhibit 4.7, Effect of Multicost Split Ratio on Behavioral and Organizational Factors, depicts how the profile of behavioral and organizational factors changes under this formula, especially when compared to the Scanlon formulas previously described. Scope of the formula has a very high degree of impact since the formula is so comprehensive. Nonlabor savings can now be reinforced since the formula is almost a total performance calculation. Previously described formulas have little reinforcement of nonlabor savings. This formula also provides necessary adjustments for economic flexibility and cyclical variations. For example, utility prices that fluctuate wildly can be budgeted or normalized so that only their usage is reflected in the formula and not their great

Exhibit 4.6   Assumed Bonus Calculation Under Single and Split Ratio Method

	Typical Single Ratio	Split Ratios		
Period 1		Product A	Product B	Total
Sales value of production	$1,8000,000	$1,200,000	$600,000	$1,800,000
Allowed payroll costs:				
Single ratio: 20%				
Split ratio: 10% product A				
30% product B		120,000	$180,000	300,000
Actual payroll (assumed)	300,000	140,000	160,000	300,000
Bonus pool	$ 60,000	$ (20,000)	$ 20,000	$ 0

Assumptions:

Period 0

Two products (A and B) are produced with equal quantities and selling prices.
  Sales of product A = $600,000; sales of product B = $600,000
Labor costs allowed = 20% in total; A actually = 10%, B = 30%

Period 1

Sales of A increase by 100% ($600,000 + $600,000); B's remain the same ($600,000).
  Total sales now equal $1,800,000.

Split ratio calculation

When determining the original allowed amounts, indirect payroll costs were allocated to products based on sales and this continues for actual costs in subsequent periods.

Source: B.E. Moore and T.L. Ross, *The Scanlon Way to Improved Productivity* (New York: Wiley-Interscience, 1978), 75.

swings in actual price. Also, costs that tend to run above the standard are identified for problem solving. If these costs are under the control of the worker, the information system that supports the multicost calculation points to areas for productivity improvement. Obviously, the motivation of smarter work gets a boost—see Exhibit 4.7.

Overall, the impact of most of the behavioral and organizational factors increases favorably. However, this is a sophisticated formula requiring excellent accounting and information systems that some firms simply do not have. Firms may also encounter difficulties in administering this formula—especially if trust is not high. By way of contrast, the single ratio formula has often been called the simple ratio. Its ease of communication is heightened by its simplicity. When one looks at the multicost split ratio formula, it appears that its reinforcement value is less than that of the Scanlon ratios. This is because it more accurately reflects all the forces impacting on productivity. Therefore, this formula tends to

Exhibit 4.7 Effect of Multicost Ratio Formula on Behavioral and Organizational Factors

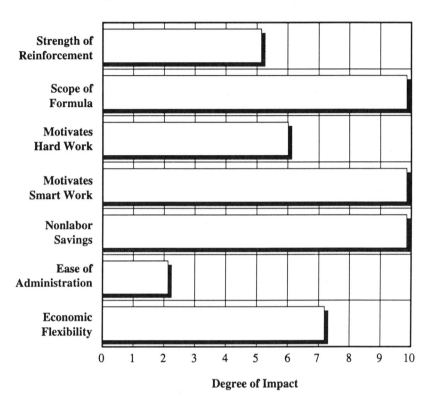

Degree of Impact

level payments while Scanlon ratios reflect labor productivity only and run the risk of over or underpaying. Since reinforcement is one of the primary reasons for choosing a gainsharing plan, this is no small consideration.

Looking more closely at the multicost ratio formula (see Exhibit 4.8), we see that it includes all production expenses (labor, materials and supplies, energy, and so forth) in the base ratio. This ratio is determined on historical data. In similar fashion as specified in the single ratio formula above, the base ratio is determined as follows:

$$\frac{\text{Production expenses by product or department}}{\text{Sales value of production}}$$

During any period in which actual expenses are less than the allowed rate, a bonus is earned. For example, assume that for every $1,000,000 of sales value of production, $800,000 of production expenses were historically

Exhibit 4.8   Multicost Split Ratio Monthly Report

1. Value of production (sales ± inventory, allowances, etc.)		<u>$1,000,000</u>
2. Allowable expenses (80% of #1)		800,000
3. Actual expenses:		
Labor (all employee costs)	$120,000	
Material and supplies	500,000	
Other costs (energy, etc.)	<u>160,000</u>	<u>780,000</u>
4. Bonus pool (#2–#3)		20,000
5. Company share (50% × #4)		<u>10,000</u>
6. Gross bonus (#4–#5)		10,000
7. Reserve for deficit months (40% × #6)		<u>4,000</u>
8. Bonus pool (#6–#7)		<u>6,000</u>
9. Participating payroll		<u>80,000</u>
10. Bonus percentage (#8/#9)		<u>7.5%</u>

Adapted from: B.E. Moore and T.L. Ross, *The Scanlon Way to Improved Productivity* (New York: Wiley-Interscience, 1978), 79.

incurred. If during a particular period sales value were equal to $1,000,000, while actual production expenses equaled $780,000, then

$$\text{Bonus pool} = (\$1,000,000 \times .80) - \$780,000 = \$20,000.$$

In contrast to the single ratio formula, this formulation extends the scope of expenses to cover virtually any costs under the employee's control. That is, this formulation increases the likelihood that employees will find ways to save nonlabor expenses. This calculation also places the potential for more bonuses in the hands of the workers. For example, working smarter includes trying to conserve virtually every controllable cost. The multicost ratio, however, requires greater administrative expense, is harder to understand, and may frustrate and demotivate workers if they lack much control over materials, energy, and so forth.

Exhibit 4.7, Effect of Multicost Split Ratio Behavioral and Organizational Factors, correctly shows that the multicost split ratio formula has maximum impact on scope of the formula, motivating smart work, and nonlabor savings. The factor that suffers, of course, is ease of administration. Also, as discussed in Chapter 1, there is greater tendency by management to overcontrol with this calculation. In effect, there is a risk it will become a control system rather than a reward system.

Again, referring to Exhibit 4.7, the strength of reinforcement is an interesting trade-off between magnitude and frequency of the gainsharing bonus. Single ratio calculations tend to pay higher bonuses in good months, but the multicost plan appears to pay bonuses more frequently. For example, a company with a single ratio Scanlon plan may report six deficit months while the same company using a multicost formula is more likely to report nine bonuses plus a year-end bonus, although all of these bonuses will be smaller. In terms of learning, more frequent, but smaller bonuses have higher reinforcement value.[3]

The multicost formula can also obtain the benefits of the split ratio formula by calculating a sub-bonus pool for each product based on multicosts and adding the sub-bonus pools to obtain the total bonus pool. These advantages, however, give rise to the problems of sensitive information systems and their understanding by all employees.

Moore and Ross strongly recommend that a company new to productivity gainsharing should not start out with a multicost formula.[4] They argue that the formulation is too confusing for employees to relate to and understand. They suggest that organizations desiring a multicost formula should use a two-stage implementation plan, whereby a single ratio is implemented, accepted by the work force, and then modified to a multicost format some years later. See Chapter 5 for other alternatives.

Impact of the Allowed Labor or Improshare Formula

Exhibit 4.9, Allowed Labor/Improshare Calculation, shows how Improshare computes the Base Productivity Factor or BPF. In many ways it looks different from other gainsharing calculations. Invented by Mitchell Fein in 1976, it is an organizationwide bonus based on the individual-level Halsey Premium Plan. By aggregating this measure and folding in nonmeasured work, such as staff, Fein has created a very useful variant of gainsharing which has numerous advantages and disadvantages.

Let's deal with Exhibit 4.9, Allowed Labor/Improshare Calculation, first, then evaluate this calculation against the behavioral and organizational factors. Step 1 in Exhibit 4.9 indicates that our example is a small firm with a total of 100 employees. Of that 100, let's say that 75 are hourly wage earners and the remainder are staff and managers. Their hours worked in the previous year totaled 200,000. Step 2 merely divides total hours worked by the output, which is 50,000 units. Thus, the average time required to produce one unit is four hours. Step 3 shows that "standard hours" to produce 50,000 units were 105,000. Standard hours simply refers to the engineered standards or work measurement done by industrial engineers, e.g., Motion-Time Analysis (MTA), Methods-Time Measurement (MTM), Master Standard Data (MSD). Conceivably, these standards could come from less direct methods of industrial engineering such as an empirical analysis of time records. Nevertheless, Allowed Labor and Improshare require specification of a standard. Step 4 reminds us that total hours are not the same as standard hours. Indeed, fixed and variable payrolls can present problems in gainsharing calculations because the fixed payroll is unmeasured and is assumed to co-vary with the variable payroll. If staff, as overhead, are headed at a value greater than the assumed (via organizational

Exhibit 4.9 Allowed Labor/Improshare® Calculation Steps

1) 100 Employees produced 50,000 units in 50 weeks for a total hours worked of 200,000 or (100 employees × 50 wks × 40 hrs = 200,000)

2) Average time per unit produced:

$$\frac{200,000 \text{ hours}}{50,000 \text{ units}} = 4.0$$

3) Standard hours to produce 50,000 units is 105,000.

   In the past 50 weeks the engineered standards account for 105,000. Total hours are higher because not all produced hours are in the standards, e.g., shipping, mainte-nance, set up, overhead, staff, etc.

4) Total hours   200,000

5) Convert engineered standards to reflect 50 weeks of productivity and to factor in all nonproductive time

$$BPF = \frac{\text{Total hours worked}}{\text{Total standard hours produced}}$$

or,

$$BPF = \frac{200,000}{105,000} = 1.905$$

6) Multiply all standard output by 1.905 to create the *base ratio.*

   For Example:

   If standard hours = 105,000 × 1.905 (BPF) = 200,000 = earned hours

   If actual hours = 100,00 × 1.90 (BPF) = 190,500

   Then, there is no change for bonus. Bonus hours = 9,500 (200,000 – 190,500)

7) Divide 9,500 by 2 since company share is one-half.

8) Bonus Distribution = $\frac{4750}{200,000}$ = 2.38%

Note: The BPF measures total hours required in an acceptable base period to produce 1.0 standard hour of product. Obviously, this BPF can be multiplied by each standard for a product line and then be aggregated to give the total BPF, i.e., the expected hours.

change, growth, etc.), then this variable payroll "eats up" real productive gains made by the variable payroll group, i.e., the hourly wage earners.

Step 5 shows how the BPF of Improshare is calculated. Its purpose is to gather production and nonproduction related costs (both variable and fixed) into one statistic. BPF is analogous to the Base Ratio in other gainsharing plans. In our example shown in Exhibit 4.9, this BPF equals 1.905. Step 6 shows that if we multiply 1.905 times our "standard hours" we can convert that product to a bonus/nonbonus statistic for *any given interval of work.* This fea-ture is important because many Improshare companies can pay the bonus weekly because of the ease of this conversion factor. Step 7 demonstrates the policy, very common among Improshare companies, of dividing the bonus in half. Obviously, the company favors this policy since it gets one-half of all labor productivity gains. Valuing the hours according to average wage rates leaves dollars available for distribution. This distribution policy is similar to other gainsharing plans in that the bonus is contingent on the value of hours worked, i.e., dollars earned. Where the Improshare system differs greatly is in frequency of payout. It can, and, in contemporary practice, does pay a weekly bonus. Typically, however, a four-week rolling average is used to smooth out the highs of a bonus and the lows of the deficits. There is no reserve account as seen in Scanlon and multicost calculations. All of the bonus and all of the deficit are included in the four-week rolling average.

Improshare calculation is associated with many policy recommendations of its inventor. For example, Fein has suggested that Improshare programs include these essential stipulations:

- Work-hour standards should be frozen at the average of the base period.
- Standards should not be changed except when new capital equipment is acquired and changes are made in technology.
- An agreed-upon ceiling should be established on productivity sharing. The excess over the ceiling is to be carried forward to future time periods, i.e., banked. If appropriate, standards may be "bought back" with a single cash payment.[5]

Whereas these descriptions of Improshare's calculation and policies are correct, this gainsharing plan, more so than any other, takes many shapes. For example, it can be tailored to serve a group, such as hourly wage earners, or subdivisions of the organization, such as departments. This plan is often installed as a financial incentive program only; however, it is also found as an organization-wide bonus system and combined with an involvement system, such as Quality Control Circles or labor-management committees. It is clear that Fein favors an organizational culture that fosters clear communications and productivity suggestions similar to the philosophy espoused in Scanlon companies.

Exhibit 4.10, Effect of Allowed Labor/Improshare on Behavioral and Organizational Factors, displays the impact of this calculation. This profile is remarkably different from the three previous profiles. The reason for this great difference is *that there is no comparable denominator in the Allowed Labor calculation.* Sales bring about productivity, but their volatility can influence the Scanlon-like calculation in inequitable ways. This calculation reduces this source of instability. It's fair to say reduced since the Allowed Labor and Improshare formulas pay a bonus on acceptable finished goods—in the case of manufacturing. Without controls in the form of good sales forecasting and good inventory control, the reality of the marketplace is absent in the calculation. The positive side of this, of course, is the ability to pay the bonus weekly. For that reason, the Allowed Labor/Improshare formulas get high marks when it comes to strength of reinforcement. Bonuses can be more frequent than in other gainsharing plans and can be as high as 30 percent. If they exceed 30

Exhibit 4.10   Effect of Allowed Labor/Improshare® Formula on Behavioral and Organizational Factors

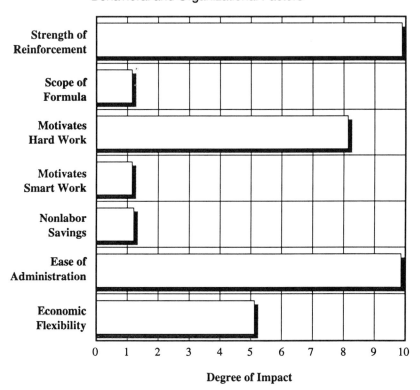

Degree of Impact

percent (which is 160 percent of base productivity), certain controls are employed to bring them in to the 160 percent range.

Equally affected by this type of gainsharing calculation is the motivation for harder work. There is no question that this calculation places its emphasis on quantity of output. This is the most direct way to influence the bonus since the volume of the output is not factored into the calculation. Conversely, the scope of the formula is very narrow, i.e., it encompasses labor only. Therefore, the factors of working smarter and making suggestions, which can affect other gainsharing plans, are usually omitted in these plans. Since these are forms of nonlabor savings, why make suggestions in that direction when the labor-only calculation excludes their potential bonus value? Quality controls must be good before acceptance of finished goods.

This type of calculation was created to avoid some of the problems associated with the economics of the marketplace, and that is why ease of administration is evaluated so highly. Those organizations with good industrial engineering and excellent information systems, which, in turn, drive good budgeting practices, can put this calculation into place in days. Ironically, however, the estimate of economic flexibility depicted in Exhibit 4.10 is only average when compared to Scanlon-type calculations because the same information systems have to be excellent in the areas of forecasting and inventory control. It would appear, for example, that the Allowed Labor/Improshare calculation would benefit continuous process manufacturing companies with low labor content and machine-processed and paced jobs since the information systems and controls are of necessity well planned.

When one looks at the obvious advantages of the Allowed Labor/Improshare calculation, it is clear that a full understanding of the behavioral and organizational factors is very important. This is why the theoretical positions reviewed in Chapter 1 take on so much significance. Without defining the culture of the organization, its technology, and what is meant by productivity, the choice of an appropriate gainsharing calculation can be risky, and this calculation is very narrow in focus.

Impact of the Value-Added/Rucker Formula

Volatility of outside prices for raw materials and energy can be a factor that results from unstable environments or transfer pricing practices. These sources of uncertainty are actually out of the control of the worker, so why burden his or her learning of gainsharing with this kind of information? When indicated, the Value-Added or Rucker plan makes sense as a refinement to the Scanlon-type calculations. Remember that the simplest definition of value added is the difference between the selling (or manufacturing cost) of the product and the price for raw materials. By subtracting the price of outside purchases, some of the volatility in that price is removed. The outside purchase price does, however, go into the selling price or manufactured cost—our denominator. Therefore, the employee has influence of usage and gets rewarded for it if it is less than the standard. See Exhibit 4.11, Value-Added/Rucker Monthly Report.

Step 1 of Exhibit 4.11 reflects the difference between the selling price and price adjustments for seasonality. Step 2 reflects subtractions for outside purchases, such as materials, supplies, and energy. Value added of $340,000, or 34 percent of the selling price is reflected at Step 3. At Step 4, the historical average of labor value added is applied. This is often called the Rucker Standard. In this example, 41.17 percent ($140,000) is the allowed (or expected) labor cost. Step 5 shows that the actual labor cost was $130,000. Thus, Step 6 exhibits a bonus pool of $10,000. A 50/50 split is a common policy and Steps 7 and 8 reflect this. Steps 9 and 10 show a policy of a reserve for deficit months (as in the case of many Scanlon companies). Since the participating payroll is $80,000 (Step 11), then the bonus percentage becomes 3.75 percent in Step 12. The exclusion of outside purchases permits adjustments for inflationary pressures. Also, cyclical variation in other outside purchases and nonlabor costs are

Exhibit 4.11   Value-Added/Rucker Monthly Report

Value-Added Calculation Method — Month X

1. Value of production (sales ± various adjustments)		$1,000,000
2. Less outside purchases (material, supplies, energy)		
Material and supplies	$500,000	
Other outside purchases, nonlabor costs	160,000	660,000
3. Value added (#1–#2)		340,000
4. Allowed employees costs (from diagnostic historical analysis) #3		
× 41.17%)		140,000
5. Actual labor (employee costs)		130,000
6. Bonus pool (#4–#5)		10,000
7. Company share (50% × #6)		5,000
8. Employee share (#6–#7)		5,000
9. Reserve for deficit months (20% × #8)		2,000
10. Bonus pool (#8–#9)		3,000
11. Participating payroll		80,000
12. Bonus percentage (#10/#11)		3.75%

Adapted from: B.E. Moore and T.L. Ross, *The Scanlon Way to Improved Productivity* (New York: Wiley-Interscience, 1978) 81.

kept out of the formula. Thus, Exhibit 4.11 accurately reflects how these two factors are well handled by the value-added formula.

Exhibit 4.12, Effect of Value-Added/Rucker on Behavioral and Organizational Factors, illustrates how the Value-Added, or Rucker formula interacts with these factors. The relative strength of its reinforcement value is equal to the single and split ratio formulas. In fact, most of the behavioral and organizational factors have similar profiles to those in the single and split ratio formulas. The key differences are in the area of economic flexibility. Most traditional Scanlon formulas do not deal well with the inflationary effects on the sales value of production and have to be adjusted. Double-digit inflation can undermine the appropriateness of the base ratio used in most Scanlon calculations.

Value-added formulas subtract outside purchases (material and supplies, energy, etc.) from the sales value of production to determine the value added by the production prices. Based on historical data, allowed labor costs are computed as a percentage of the value added. This makes the Value-Added/Rucker calculation very similar to the Scanlon single and split ratio calculations, yet certainly not as simple nor as understandable. The scope of the formula is slightly more comprehensive than the simpler formulas (it deals with usage of materials), but not as comprehensive as the multicost. Its ability to motivate hard work is similar to the Scanlon ratios.

The Value-Added/Rucker rates slightly higher on its impact on working smarter than Scanlon or Allowed Labor/Improshare since its involvement sys-

Exhibit 4.12 Effect of Value-Added/Rucker Formula on Behavioral and Organizational Factors

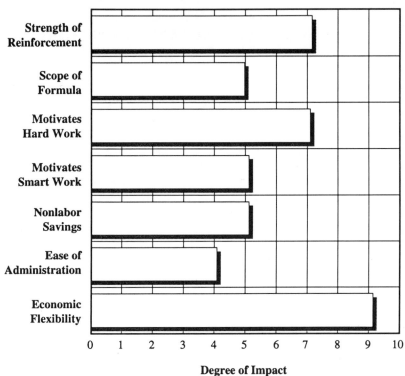

Degree of Impact

tem rewards the efficient usage of outside purchases. For the same reason, non-labor savings are improved by this calculation, but not as greatly as by the multi-cost formula. Ease of administration is rated below the levels shown in the Scanlon and Allowed Labor formulas, but higher than in the multicost. For example, Value-Added/Rucker plans don't pay weekly bonuses as the Impro-share plan does. Assembling price and cost data require time, and there are necessary pulses and flows to this process. All of these factors, make the Value-Added/Rucker plan more similar to the multicost where ease of administration is concerned; however, less manipulation of price and cost data is required than there is in the multicost formula.

Lastly, but most importantly, economic flexibility is rated highly because of the one significant difference of this calculation—separating out volatility of outside purchase prices. Since gainsharing asks employees to take more control of their work and become more responsible, the gainsharing calculation that buffers those factors outside the control of most employees has greater motivational force. Unfortunately, value added is a different concept for U.S. employees to comprehend.

ASSESSING THE FIT BETWEEN GAINSHARING AND ORGANIZATIONAL FAIRNESS

No assessment of the appropriate gainsharing calculation can be addressed without a discussion on fairness. As mentioned in Chapter 1, fairness is the cement that holds a gainsharing program together. If both the employee and the company believe that the gainsharing calculation is fair, then both have an equal stake in making it work. In fact, a gainsharing calculation that is fair will build trust within the organization. If both sides are committed to fairness, how can the calculation and its policies make a difference? One issue is understandability of the calculation itself, perhaps even its availability for audit. The Scanlon single ratio is simple. It simply says beat yesterday's performance. The multicost is complete and requires some aptitude, if not knowledge, in the area of cost accounting. Thus, the simplicity of a gainsharing formula can influence perception of fairness.

Gainsharing policies can also influence perceptions of fairness. For example, most gainsharing companies distribute the bonus as a constant percentage of pay, but that means it is variable in actual dollars—depending on pay classifications and hours worked. When a task force undertakes the challenge of assessing which gainsharing plan meets the organization's needs, an honest discussion of fairness will be revealing. For example, gainsharing will not work if the standard or base ratio is set at such a level that neither side believes in it. Both management and all other employees have to believe that the base ratio is fair and not likely to be changed without fair reasons.

Is one gainsharing calculation inherently more fair than another? To some extent, the answer is yes. Rightly or wrongly, the Scanlon single ratio is probably perceived as more fair than other calculations. This is a logical result of its visible and favorable history. It tends to pay slightly higher bonuses than other calculations. Its measurement properties are not as precise; thus, it doesn't run the risk of becoming a control system. So, initially these factors reinforce the perception of fairness to the majority of the employees. However, if management loses its confidence in the Scanlon ratio because of its poor measurement properties, then they feel that fairness to the stockholders is being jeopardized. As always, fairness is a two-way exchange. If a balance is not struck gainsharing will fail.

Scenario Generation

Five generic traditional gainsharing formulas have been presented with their respective behavioral and organizational profiles. Critical issues surrounding choice of each gainsharing formula have been examined. The key decision makers should accept the responsibility to consider the differences between the gainsharing formulas as they fit into their own organizational culture and technology. As Chapter 1 indicated, this process requires a thorough understanding of the organization's status and climate, what beliefs its people espouse, and how the organization expects to achieve its objectives.

Comparisons of Formulas

The best way to make a rational choice is, after thorough discussion, to select at least two formulas, build a database of relevant historical data, and create spreadsheets to generate "what if" scenarios. This exercise will accomplish many things—

1. It will structure a discussion concerning how gainsharing policies fit into the organization's goals.
2. It will clarify and make operational the working knowledge of the key decision makers.
3. It will permit empirical testing of different gainsharing formulas under normal and "stressed" business constraints.
4. It will build confidence in any appropriate gainsharing calculation—particularly if it has to be sold or defended to higher level decision makers.
5. It will lead to a judgment on selecting a fair standard.

If a rational plan of gainsharing formula assessment is pursued, then management may choose to tailor a calculation to the organization. For example, Exhibit 4.13 reflects gainsharing calculations that evolved within an integrated steel company. After much study and review of the five generic formulas discussed in this chapter, this company developed two different "hybrid" gainsharing formulas for two substantially different parts of its organization, rather than imposing one uniform gainsharing calculation throughout. Exhibit 4.13 displays one year of a base period spreadsheet for the blast furnace operation of this large company. As discussed earlier, the formula used is a multicost ratio, in that labor, operating cost, and yield are the three parts of this comprehensive calculation. As such, it is designed to achieve the behavioral and organizational objectives found in Exhibit 4.7. That is, have medium reinforcement, comprehensive scope, motivate hard, but especially smart work, share non-labor savings, and have good economic flexibility.

Obviously, the plan will be complex and difficult to administer. For that reason, key decision makers chose to use the best known measure of labor productivity in steel, work-hours per net ton. This measure is more similar to the Allowed Labor/Improshare calculation since it is based on engineered standards for most hourly jobs. There is great continuity to this measure since it is found in government reports, industry reports, annual reports, and the union

Exhibit 4.13 Hybrid Multicost Formula of Blast Furnace Cost Data by Quarters, 1987

	Jan.	Apr.	Jul.	Oct.	Year-End/ Average(x)
1. Net tons produced	181,669	171,185	148,494	159,144	1,971,784
2. Equivalent employees	309.4	306.5	321.2	318.7	3760.2
3. Total all hours	0.295	0.310	0.374	0.347	0.330(X)
4. Distribution standard = 0.330					
5. Workhours @ standard	59,951	56,491	49,003	52,518	650,690
6. Actual workhours	53,523	53,027	55,560	55,142	650,516
7. Workhour savings (loss)	6,428	3,464	(6,557)	(2,624)	174
8. Save (loss @ $12.50)	$80,350	$43,300	($81,963)	($32,800)	$2,175
9. Operating cost per net ton produced	($2.91)	($4.73)	($3.36)	($1.08)	($2.85)(X)
10. Standard per ton	($2.85)	($2.85)	($2.85)	($2.85)	
11. Savings (loss)/ton	$.06	$1.88	$0.78	($1.77)	
12. Total savings (loss)	$11,213	$312,614	$116,139	($282,137)	$8,081
13. Average 1987 yield	61.47	61.47	61.47	61.47	61.47
14. Actual yield	61.52	60.61	62.33	61.96	
15. Gain (loss)	0.05	–0.86	0.86	0.49	
16. 1% effect per ton	$0.536	$0.536	$0.536	$0.536	$0.536
17. Total savings (loss)	$4,869	($78,909)	$68,450	$41,798	$5,970
18. Total savings (loss) all combined	$96,432	$286,005	$102,626	($273,139)	$16,226

contract. Comparisons of work-hours per net ton can be made over very long periods of time and can be made with foreign competition. Therefore, combining this statistic with operating costs and yield makes sense.

Thus, this hybrid gainsharing formula measures the blast furnace productivity by measuring the mean of 1987 for work-hours per net ton at 0.33 (see line 3, Year-End Totals or Average). This weighted average for the entire facility of around 325 employees reflects total work-hour per ton at this location. The year 1987 was considered to be representative of a good year of productivity; 1985 and 1986 were not thought to be as good.

Line 4 of Exhibit 4.13 reflects the distribution standard or mean of all work-hours divided by net tons produced. It is .33 and is the distribution standard being tested in this spreadsheet. Here again, the message of gainsharing is to beat yesterday's productivity. Applying the mean against actual 1987 data, we can see that line 8 reports seven bonus months and five deficit months with a total annual payout of $2,175 but only four months are shown on the exhibit. Since deficits are shared equally in this example, a total labor-only payout of $2,175 divided by some 325 employees wouldn't have much impact.

Now, there are two other components to this calculation—operating cost and yield. Line 9 of Exhibit 4.13 shows actual operating cost while line 10 applies the standard which is based on the mean of twelve good months. Line 11 reflects increases or decreases when this standard is applied. Line 12 shows that efficiencies in operating cost contributed to seven bonuses and five deficits in the full spreadsheet with year-end savings of $8,081. Fifty cents of each dollar saved below the expected operating cost would be shared under this plan.

Finally, the third component of this calculation is yield. This reflects the efficiency of the blast furnaces throughout. That is, low work-hours per ton and low operating cost could still lead to a poor finished product. Therefore, this company wishes to share the gains of high quality output. Again, 1986 was a year wherein all decision makers agreed that product quality was never higher. The average yield of this year is 61.47 (line 13). When applied to 1987 actual yield, only six months produce a bonus in the full spreadsheet. Notice that the statistics from these months do not co-vary perfectly with the labor and operating parts of the calculation. In April, for example, line 8 shows labor produced a modest bonus (3,464 hours below the expected hours). Operating costs in April were excellent (see line 12). Therefore, if people work smarter with materials and energy, they can conserve costs. Unfortunately, the yield was below the expected level by $78,909 (see line 17 for April). Thus, the combined effect of two bonuses and one deficit nets out at $286,005 for April. One-half is distributed to the entire work force, leaving $143,002.50. The percentage of an individual's bonus is calculated by dividing total earnings for the month of those on the participating payroll into 143,002.50, which was 325 times average wage of $12.50 per hour. In this test the bonus was approximately 3 percent of earned wage and salary. In summary, if the reader scans the lines of the spreadsheet, then add lines 8, 12, and 17, the total savings or loss reflects the three components of this multicost calculation.

In keeping with the objectives of the decision makers, this hybrid, multicost formula focuses attention on all aspects of this plant's technology. While it is a capital intensive process using costly materials, human performance is of great impact. Constant attentions to the conservation of raw materials and utilities, along with good quality control, help to keep yields high. A three-part formula of labor, materials, and yield emphasizes the contribution each makes to total productivity. This spreadsheet analysis permits "what if" scenario testing of this formula against the contingencies this steel company may face. It also permits a better understanding of what this calculation can do.

Goal Sharing

The movement of gainsharing from manufacturing to service industries (which include nonprofit and public sector organizations) has caused a shift from cost-based calculations to goal-based calculations. Sometimes termed goalsharing or win sharing,[6] these calculations constitute new attempts to bring the traditional gainsharing philosophy to new strategies of manufacturing and of service organizations alike. Chapters 9 and 14 delve into some of the special issues and problems found in goal sharing calculations.

Traditional gainsharing has tried to pay bonuses out of cost savings. In goal sharing calculations, cost savings becomes redefined as cost avoidance since sales or revenue is either zero or negligible. Remember, if the price for a manufactured product remains relatively stable, then reducing the product's cost affects of ratio of cost to sales in a meaningful way. Conversely, if a non-profit or public sector organization reduces its cost in department A, then an expected operation cost was avoided and budgeted monies are shifted to other departments. The mission or goal of the organization is to serve.

For example, if a police department avoided expected gasoline usage when peace officers drive carefully, then the expected cost was avoided. Very likely, it will be reallocated to defray another cost that is higher than expected. One might argue that this leaves little incentive to drive carefully to save gasoline.

Evolving gainsharing calculations in service-only applications reflect a commitment by management and boards of directors to value service goals monetarily, then share increases in performance via gainsharing type formulas. Involvement systems are definitely needed to stimulate and create those behaviors associated with improved performance. Some of the following factors have been used exclusively in service organizations, and some are combined with traditional cost saving calculations and found in manufacturing:

- retention of customers
- on-time performance
- safety via reduction of accidents or hours lost
- customer complaints via reductions in a rolling average
- customer service, e.g., a utility report using a reduction in outage minutes per customer

These goal sharing calculations, for the most part, make sense, but continuity of the calculation over time is subject to unique pressures, at least in the public sector. This is because of the commonly held view that "true" cost savings are not being factored into the bonus. Thus, if working smarter and harder contributes to cost avoidance, is it possible that public sector bonuses can be supported? Obviously, this is less true of not-for-profit service industries where the service is valued in the marketplace. Then, costs savings tend to work the same way they do for manufacturing.[7]

The bottom line is that new and rapidly evolving form of goal sharing calculation is being added to the track record of traditional gainsharing. Service organizations, private or public, that meet market conditions, and charge for their services will probably find goal sharing useful. Purely public sector organizations will find it difficult to continue goal sharing calculations because of cost avoidance arguments. The organizational cultures that support traditional gainsharing in the private sector survive managerial succession. For example,

Scanlon plans in a particular Dana Corp. plant may have experienced three or four managerial changes in leadership. Conversely, public sector managers have great difficulty creating conditions that favor long-term continuity. Chapter 9 will develop some of these issues. Therefore, when nonprofit and public sector service organizations find goal sharing appealing, the risks are considerable. The first risk, of course, is achieving a fair measure of the goal. Goals, by their very definition, are normative and very likely reflect management's view of what is important. For example, most people would agree that a good product at a fair price is a reasonable goal. Since this type of goal is measured by most traditional gainsharing calculations, its measurement isn't particularly problematical.

Now, if reduction of workman's compensation claims is a goal of management, while many employees may resent the deviant actions of a few, they may resent even more that it becomes a goal affecting their bonus. Thus, goal sharing can actually become de-motivational unless there is a buy-in by employees on the selection and measurement of goals.

Goal sharing represents a natural evolution of the hybrid gainsharing calculation. As such, it faces some challenges. That is, the concept and application is sophisticated. Understanding of the calculation will require a larger educational effort. Acceptance of goal sharing is instrumental for this calculation's success, but it is difficult to achieve. However, there is no reason why such an approach cannot be used in the private sector as will be shown in Chapter 5.

SUMMARY

The decision-making approach to formula development has been detailed throughout this chapter. Indeed, when one reviews Chapters 2 and 6, gainsharing failure literature often cites imprecise or poorly designed formulas as a prime contributor to the lack of success. If decision makers rely on the steps of goal specification, formula selection, and then proper assessment of the fit between the organizational characteristics and the formula, they will avoid one common pitfall of gainsharing failures.

Developing a gainsharing reward structure looks like a financial task. To some extent it is, but this chapter delineated the behavioral and organizational factors that have been shown to be important for formula development. Gainsharing is really a behavioral mechanism to change the culture of a given organization. This fact is easily seen in Chapter 5, "Solving Some of the Measurement Issues." Gainsharing formula development is less a financial task than it is a behavioral design.

Strength of reinforcement, while often only an expectation, was reviewed in order to allow decision makers to honestly discuss *their beliefs about what potential rewards could or should be.*

Scope of formula is actually an underlying theme through most of this book since many different kinds of gainsharing are possible. Plans vary most on this dimension, that is, how broad does the organization wish participation and involvement to be.

Motivating harder work is distinguished from motivating smarter work in this chapter because these are two distinct ideas. They can be achieved together, but in many gainsharing applications, working smarter is the message most typically sent. Rather than send an incorrect message that may lead to demotivation, these behavioral factors require honest discussion.

Motivating nonlabor savings, as a specific issue, was discussed in order to require decision makers to explore whether nonlabor savings can be shared. Also, if they are to be shared, what mechanisms need to be in place to help those behaviors that permit nonlabor savings.

Ease of administration, so often overlooked, was reviewed so that decision makers could estimate the amount of resources required to deal with gainsharing. Here again, ease of administration may have a significant impact on the organization's ability to feed back productivity information and achieve its gainsharing fulfillment goals.

Economic flexibility is useful for a task force to discuss since it will lead to a better understanding of when and how bonuses are possible. This kind of understanding will shape more accurate expectations. In turn, accurate expectations will have greater motivational force.

Goal specification, as discussed, becomes a crucial step. When there is full understanding and agreement on the organization's goals, gainsharing formula development becomes a simpler task. This chapter reviewed those behavioral and organizational factors that must consciously fit into the organization's specified goals.

Generic formulas of gainsharing were reviewed to emphasize that there is no one gainsharing plan or one gainsharing formula. Comprehension of all the trade-offs of each formula type will build confidence in the appropriate formula. This chapter has made clear that hybrid formulas are frequently developed to mesh the organization's goals more securely with the gainsharing reward structure.

Goal sharing represents a potentially exciting development of traditional gainsharing. While service-type goals can be a part of a hybrid gainsharing plan in manufacturing, it is probably the only way to create gainsharing for nonprofit /public sector organizations. Most of these organizations are mission driven and deliver a service. Great care must be used in the design of goal sharing for these organizations to avoid gimmickry. Apparently, St. Luke's Hospital in Kansas City, Missouri, a not-for-profit institution, has overcome some of these problems. Since 1985, its goal sharing plan is based on comparing costs to a rolling average of the preceding two years then linking this measure to overall hospital financial performance.[8] This is a sophisticated goal sharing calculation requiring strong educational effort to insure employees understand it.

The assessment of fairness is dealt with separately in this chapter to stress its importance. It is a primary requirement that the human resource and management believe that the gainsharing calculation is fair. This chapter discussed the most common ways to build that concept. It bears repeating that understandability and simplicity of the formula not only reinforce the concept of fairness but stimulate trust as well.

This chapter encouraged the thorough testing of competing gainsharing formulas to improve understanding. Scenario generation through spreadsheet analyses can be a task force exercise that puts "numbers" to the design decisions. The rational choice mode, which is the theme of the chapter, is best elaborated when various scenarios, and various gainsharing formulas are tested side by side.

Lastly, the assiduous use of the ideas reflected in the measurement chapters of this book will, in itself, be a rewarding process. No task force can pursue gainsharing formula development without developing an appreciation of the dynamics of goal specification, organizational culture, and productivity enhancement. Since formula determination has been shown to be a significant cause of failure, the diagnostic tools available and the information base about gainsharing must be acquired and used.

Notes

1. B.E. Moore and T.L. Ross, *The Scanlon Way to Improved Productivity* (New York: Wiley-Interscience, 1978).
2. Ibid.
3. B.E. Graham-Moore and R. Rodgers, "Productivity Gainsharing and Organizational Fit," unpublished manuscript, The University of Texas at Austin, 1986.
4. B.E. Moore and T.L. Ross, *The Scanlon Way to Improved Productvity,* note 1, above.
5. M. Fein, "An Alternative to Traditional Managing," in *Handbook of Industrial Engineering,* ed. Gavriel Salvendy (New York: Wiley, 1981).
6. J. G. Belcher, Jr., *Gain Sharing,* (Houston: Gulf Publishing, 1991).
7. B. E. Graham-Moore, "Productivity Gainsharing in the Service Sector," *Personnel Management: Compensation Service,* (Paramus, NJ: Prentice-Hall Information Services, 1987).
8. Belcher, *Gain Sharing.*

Chapter 5

Solving Some of
the Measurement Issues

Timothy L. Ross and Ruth Ann Ross

Although gainsharing has been around for many years, probably more has been written about the employee involvement, communications, and other behavioral aspects of gainsharing than the measurement aspects. In addition, misconceptions have developed over the years for a variety of reasons. For example, many writers refer to the Scanlon Plan ratio as labor cost related to sales value of production, whereas in reality Scanlon-oriented plans have used calculations ranging from standard versus actual labor time, to return on investment, to multiple pools, and many types in between.

Although many methods can be used to evaluate calculation alternatives, essentially the issue becomes one of value system orientation along with a few practical issues. Key among these issues are:

1. Whether to aim for a narrow or a broad profit orientation,
2. Ease of attaining the financial goal or goals established,
3. Whether to reinforce long-run or short-run thinking,
4. How much financial information will be disclosed,
5. Whether the plan will have a moving or static base,
6. How much approval or support will the plan get from the corporate structure.

These and other issues are reviewed in this chapter. Traditional gainsharing is reviewed in concert with current and expected future trends. Much is happening in gainsharing measurement.

CONCEPTUAL CRITERIA
FOR SELECTING AN APPROACH

Before delving into some key measurement issues, some conceptual framework for measurement must be established. Such a framework is necessary even where the more packaged gainsharing approaches such as the Improshare and Rucker plans are applied.

Physical Versus Financial Performance

There are two polar types of performance—physical (or operational) and financial—and all gainsharing calculations can be evaluated against these extremes. Some firms do however like both and end up with a little of each.

Physical performance can be equated to a coal miner producing forty tons of coal in forty hours, or one ton per hour. This is how most employees think of productivity: widgets per hour, reports per week, people processed per day, and the like. This is an important performance or productivity concept, and some calculations are based on it.

If in the next week, the miner produces forty-four tons in forty hours, physical performance increases to 1.1 tons per hour, or a 10 percent increase. It may have been caused by mix changes, better equipment, shorter walks to the coal, and so on, over which the miner may have little control, or by working smarter or harder, less waste, or more cooperation and teamwork, over which the miners as a group may have control. Some firms may want to adjust for the different causes, whereas others may not. Yet almost everyone would agree that the miner's performance has increased, whether the increase is attributable to the miner or not.

But if between week one and week two, the selling price of coal dropped by 25 percent, has the miner's performance increased? Obviously, both yes and no. The miner's physical performance has, but his financial performance has not. Since most employees think in physical performance terms while top managers think in terms of financial performance (e.g., profits), some compromise is probably appropriate. For example, one might consider starting the calculation somewhere between the two extremes and then moving toward one extreme or the other. From our experience, it seems that many more firms move toward financial rather than toward physical performance over time. Some firms like physical or operational measures but base the amount going to employees on profitability; it's like having your cake and eating it too.

Control Versus Reward Orientation

However, the real issue regarding physical or financial performance is: Which side is suitable for a particular company? Since we promote a "systems" approach to gainsharing, we believe that a full range of calculations should be considered, but we still believe that it is essential to narrow the options to reduce costs, time commitment, and confusion. After exploring many alternatives, we now generally use a simple contrasting approach that we call the control/reward evaluation.

We find that in a majority of firms, most managers have a shared group of attitudes that can be described as being primarily either control-oriented or reward-oriented. These orientations require different sets of gainsharing characteristics, which are contrasted in Exhibit 5.1.

To illustrate further, a control-oriented manager would have no difficulty saying to employees: "You did a great job this month even though we did not make much profit." The reward-oriented manager would have difficulty with this. On the other hand, the reward-oriented manager could tell employees that they earned a bonus because the firm was able to raise selling prices; the control-oriented manager would have difficulty accepting this.

This control/reward comparison is extremely useful in narrowing calculation alternatives in perhaps 75 percent of all cases. The remainder need to evaluate the full range of alternatives. In some of the latter cases, an easy compromise is developed between control and reward. Many multiple pool calculations have characteristics of both.

Other Conceptual Criteria

In addition, once a preliminary calculation is developed, we often evaluate each calculation against a set of criteria that includes the following questions:

Exhibit 5.1   Gainsharing Characteristics Associated with Control and Reward Orientations

Control Orientation	Reward Orientation
Performance productivity-based	Financial productivity-based
Prices of outputs do not influence	Prices of outputs may influence
Prices of inputs do not influence	Prices of inputs may influence
Isolation of group contributions (e.g., direct and indirect labor) is desired	Isolation of group contributions not as important
Some adjustment for volume influence	Less or no volume adjustment
Frequent adjustment for capital and other items	Infrequent adjustment of outputs and inputs
Smaller number of items affect the bonus (more variable items)	More items affect bonus (could include all costs)
Disclosure often limited	Full disclosure, including perhaps profits
More physical-based	More dollar-based
Not necessarily related to profits	More directly related to profits

1. Will it be perceived as fair by participants (probably the most important criterion)?
2. Does it meet management's objectives as indicated by its orientation to control or reward? (If not, management at all levels will be less than enthusiastic about it.)
3. Can it be understood by those who make the effort?
4. Does it incorporate flexibility to changing conditions, or do constant adjustments need to be made?
5. Can it be easily administered?
6. Will it direct attention properly, e.g., not waste excluded resources?
7. Will it violate disclosure limitations?
8. Will it be useful in isolating problem areas?

These and other criteria are extremely useful in evaluating a calculation after installation.

Basic Traditional Gainsharing Calculations and Issues

The basic calculations can be grouped around three fundamental types:

1. physical or operational performance (control oriented),
2. financial performance (reward oriented),
3. prospective target (future oriented).

The first two are normally established by developing a historical relationship or ratio between inputs and outputs. The third approach is discussed later in this chapter. Note that the lists below move from broader to narrower bases of calculation.

Some common inputs used in formulating the calculations include the following:

1. all costs,
2. all costs minus some noncontrollable items,
3. only controllable costs,
4. only variable costs,
5. only payroll costs including fringes,
6. only wages and salaries,
7. direct and indirect labor time,
8. only direct labor time.

Some common outputs used in formulating the calculations are:

1. sales (usually net),
2. sales plus or minus work in process and finished goods inventory change,
3. value added (sales minus outside purchases),
4. total standard costs,

5. total standard direct labor cost,
6. total standard direct labor hours earned,
7. physical outputs (thousand board feet, gallons, students taught, and so on).

Physical-oriented performance calculations would include ratios such as Input 6/Output 5 or Input 7/Output 6, above. The latter ratio basically represents how Improshare is calculated.

Financial-oriented performance calculations would include Input 1/Output 1 or Input 2/Output 2, above. The first one is essentially a form of profit sharing, with a hurdle rate, whereas the second stops somewhat short of profit. A whole series of these ratios could be and have been used. The ACA Benchmark Study found that 17 percent of the plans were combination plans having both physical or operational and financial measures.[1]

Using the financial-based calculations, we normally analyze the past five years (three years is a minimum unless the business has totally changed or the data are not available) and the most recent year on a monthly basis to evaluate both cycles and seasonality. This helps to determine the base period percentage—that is, the base period input/output ratio—to be allowed and whether a reserve is needed to adjust for the normal ups and downs of production, such as seasonability and various spikes in activities. Simple simulations can be done by hand or computer to evaluate the effect on the bonus for, say, 10 percent increases in volume with no increases in costs. Forecasted performance is also carefully considered to assess its effect on the bonus.

A Traditional Calculation Example

An example at this point might help clarify the issues. Suppose that a management cannot decide whether it is control- or reward-oriented and therefore wants a middle-of-the-road calculation. This includes, say, wages, salaries, supplies, and scrap (for a manufacturing firm) as its inputs (Input 6 and part of Input 4, above), and sales plus or minus work in process and finished goods inventory change as the output (Output 2, above). Going beyond mere sales is advantageous because most firms find that employees relate more to production than to sales. Another benefit to the use of sales ± inventory change is that actual costs rather than some combination of actual and standard cost can be used. But for manufacturing firms, inventories cause problems if they fluctuate significantly, as will be discussed below.

Historically based on, for example, the most recent three years, we determine that actual wages, salaries, supplies, and scrap were 25 percent of value of production (i.e., sales ± inventories). The calculation is illustrated in Exhibit 5.2. You could use a very recent period, forecasts if more applicable, or even a combination of the two.

A brief discussion of the calculation should help explain the various issues. In Exhibit 5.2, lines 1 and 2 were taken from the actual records for the

Exhibit 5.2   A Sample Calculation (Month x)

1. Sales	$ 900,000
2. Inventory change (at cost)	+100,000
3. Value of production	$1,000,000
4. Allowed costs (25% based on history)	$ 250,000
5. Actual costs for Month x	230,000
6. Bonus pool	$ 20,000
7. Employee share (assume 50%)	10,000
8. Less: year-end reserve (assume 25%)	(2,500)
9. Net bonus	$ 7,500
10. Participating payroll	$ 150,000
11. Net bonus % (9 divided by 10)	5%
12. Balance in the reserve	$ 2,500

month, as was line 5 (actual costs of wages, salaries, supplies, and scrap).
These would be separately monitored and disclosed. If we were to value the
change in inventory (line 2) at estimated sales prices, a practice some firms find
desirable for employee comprehension, then the output would be the sales
value of output or production rather than the value of production (with sales at
sales value and inventory at cost, as in Exhibit 5.2). This difference will vary
from firm to firm. Obviously, if mix is a major problem, one can do the same
procedure by each product line, adjusting the base input/output ratio (line 4) as
appropriate. We call this procedure the split single ratio.

The employee share of the bonus pool in Exhibit 5.2 is 50 percent (line 7),
a percentage that seems to represent the trend today. The two packaged
approaches, Improshare and Rucker®, often pay 50 percent and 100 percent
respectively of the savings. But there are numerous exceptions to these sharing
formulas. The sharing decision will depend in part on past/target performance
and the ease of improving upon it. Also, the broader, more financial-oriented
calculations seem to share less with employees, with the exception of the
Rucker Plan. The ACA Study found a wide range of employee sharing and also
found that some firms don't pay bonuses as a percent of wages.[2]

Many firms establish a reserve (line 8) to reduce the spikes or to avoid
having to pay large bonuses during the easy-to-earn periods and share losses
during negative periods. If the reserve is negative at the end of the year, it is
normally absorbed by the firm at that time; if positive, it is distributed to
employees. The reserve also helps to reinforce a long-range employee outlook.
Improshare plans seldom establish a reserve because of their control orientation, but they do use a four-week moving average. The percent of the reserve
depends on corporate philosophy and extent of seasonability. More conservative firms reserve more and 50 percent is common. Other options are possible,

such as having to make up any negative amount in the reserve before any bonus can be paid out.

The net bonus percentage in Exhibit 5.2 (line 11) represents the normal method of distribution because of legal and other issues. Regardless, overtime must be considered unless there is true profit sharing. The balance in the reserve is just a running total and obviously not really a liability until the end of the year, even if some firms do accrue it for financial purposes. These issues will be discussed in more detail later in this chapter.

SUMMARY OF BASIC TRADITIONAL CALCULATIONS

Exhibit 5.3 is a broad summary of the various basic calculations, high-lighting the changes that mark the evolution from performance to financial calculations.

Obviously, variations of these exist in practice. We have also had considerable success with an expansion of an allowed labor or Improshare type of calculation. Essentially, this calculation develops one pool for labor and another for such items as supplies, material quantity variance, and scrap. The pools are then aggregated to form one bonus.

While we do not cover all common traditional calculations in detail, a careful reading and reviewing of the list of outputs and inputs and the sample calculation should give the reader a feeling for the different calculation approaches. By reviewing the inputs and outputs presented above, one should be able to evaluate and choose from many alternatives. A historical analysis would give significant insight into which costs are more variable and which are more fixed.

NONTRADITIONAL CALCULATIONS

In recent years, firms have found that gainsharing in general and pay for performance can become anything you want it to be. It can be long term or short term (one group espouses an annual sunset policy); organization-wide or small group oriented; paid annually or monthly with little difference expected in behavior (the ACA Benchmark Study found that 69 percent of "financial" plans paid only annually and 24 percent of operational plans paid primarily weekly and use of every other payment period under the sun[3]); based on goals (one group calls it goal sharing and another "gain management") or past performance; complex (one organization had 28 pools including one based on the number of people smoking) or simple; and so on. Three or four pooled plans are very common.

These nontraditional approaches increase gainsharing's flexibility in responding to the rapidly changing business conditions and increases its applic-

Exhibit 5.3　Characteristics of the Basic Traditional Calculations

Calculation Type	Performance Type	Common Outputs	Common Inputs	Advantages	Possible Problems
Standard labor	Physical (control)	Standard direct labor cost Standard direct labor hours Physical output	Labor costs (direct/indirect) Labor hours (direct/indirect)	Considers some mix problems Prices do not affect or can be easily adjusted Easier to install Employees relate to Limited financial disclosures	Only limited inputs included Could result in bickering over standards Standards may have to be frozen Cost of maintaining New product difficulties Difficulty of adding other inputs, such as overtime
Single ratio	Physical/financial (control if prices adjusted for)	Sales or Sales ± inventory or Total standard costs	Labor costs Limited other costs	Easy to understand Simple way to start Limited disclosure required Related to employees costs	Mix may influence (different base ratio for each product line) Inflation influences Neither reward nor control Inventory may influence more
Value added	Financial (reward)	Sales minus outside purchases	Labor Some other costs	Broader More financially oriented Increases flexibility Handles some mix problems	Some items still excluded Defining an outside purchase (e.g., material, supplies) Determining what to do with capital (Is it an outside purchase?) More difficult to understand
Multicost	Financial (reward)	Sales Sales ± inventory Total standard cost	All variable costs Most costs	Shares overall success Most costs included Congruent with management's broad goals Adaptable to mix changes Increases possibilities for commitment	Not performance productivity based More difficult to educate employees More information dissemination Changing pricing strategies may influence Requires more involvement
Profit sharing/Return on investment	Financial (reward)	Sales	All costs	Similar to multicost	Similar to multicost, plus not a gainsharing concept unless a hurdle is established Lack of controllability of some items

ability to many more situations but also increases the chances of manipulations by management. In a way, this trend has made its installation simpler and faster in some situations, but it has also made gainsharing more complex and confusing for some people.

Reasons for the Recent Trends

Frankly, the traditional calculations could not easily handle the rapidly changing conditions that confronted many organizations. Additionally, it was difficult to find one single measure of performance that adequately reflected the performance of an organization. Also, the traditional calculations were difficult to use in new plant start-ups or other major change processes, and finally, among other reasons, some of the traditional calculations really didn't tie into the businesses' objectives in many cases. As new people were attracted to gainsharing from a research or consulting basis, they were not wed to the more traditional calculations and started to experiment with other approaches, with some success.

Early Changes

First came some "tampering" with the traditional calculations, such as weighting returns more heavily or deducting for customer complaints. Next, firms started to develop separate pools with each having its own inputs and outputs. Examples would be as follows:

Pool 1: Labor productivity (standard versus actual time or single ratio)
Pool 2: Quality and customer service (rework, scrap, overtime, returns related to some measure of output such as pieces, standard time, standard cost or sales)

A third pool was commonly added for other controllable costs or perhaps safety. Each could have its own base ratios, percents to employees, reserve, and frequency of payments to name a few of the issues. The multiple pool has been very good if nonmanagement employees are involved in the design since it breaks the system down into more dissectable portions. Some calculations stayed very narrow, physical or operational oriented; and some were fairly broad, including most costs depending on whether management was control (more physical, operational) oriented or reward (more financially) oriented.

More Recent Approaches

In more recent years, firms have used a whole range of other approaches to include more and more items in the calculation in a variety of ways. Some of these are listed below:

Quality and customer service activities (see Chapter 11 for some
   examples)
Safety
Rejects
Customer complaints
Sales growth
Fill rates for warehouses
Inventory control
Reducing hazardous waste
Machine utilization
Waste reduction
Impurities in final product
Attendance/turnover

Probably the most common additions are in the areas of quality and customer service activities, safety, and inventory control. Quality and customer service has always been heavily emphasized in gainsharing, but new calculation modifiers place even more emphasis on it. Some of these are self-funding by reducing costs, but others may not be. These issues are discussed later in this chapter.

Because the approaches used have been very innovative and often very simple, gainsharing can now be applied in many new situations including new company start-ups. Some of the common approaches are as follows:

1. Indexing approach. Create an index by calculating the ratio, of, for example current on-time shipments to past or targeted on-time shipments. If the index is greater than 1, the normal calculation is indexed up (see Chapter 11 for an actual example).
2. "If" or goal approach. If you reach a set goal, you get a specified bonus amount. This can be scaled up or down as appropriate. For example, if labor productivity is at X percent, everyone gets $10 for the month. Some can be negative so one can offset another. Normally there is a scaling effect up and down and three to six or seven factors are included (e.g., labor productivity, safety, customer complaints, on-time shipments, cost performance). This is really more of a goal approach.
3. Scale or modifier approach. In this case, you would create a scale. For example, if there are 100 customer complaints –5 percent is applied, 80–100 = –2 percent, 60–80 = 0, 40–60 = +5 percent, 20–40 = +15 percent, less than 20 = +25 percent. Other factors could be added to develop a net weighting which then would be used to adjust a more financial, self-funding pool.
4. Point approach. In this approach, if employees do something positive or attain a certain level of performance, they get so many points. All the points are added together and then weighted by some dollar value.

By using such approaches and other special focus bonus pools, a firm can add activity measures to the calculation and adjust the weighting, depending on how important they are. Some of the goal-oriented approaches have two goal levels above zero: minimum level equates X bonus and maximum equals Y bonus. Obviously such an approach allows an organization to control the maximum amount of bonus that will be paid. Even with all these approaches, a firm often must still use a traditional calculation if the plan is required to be self-funding.

We feel that such approaches give gainsharing a much more flexible posture and increases its applicability to many more situations. In addition, we expect these trends to continue and accelerate in the future. In fact, gainsharing plans based on goals are even used in departmental reward systems and new company start-ups.

REFINING THE CALCULATIONS

Some of the information that we have presented on choice of calculation is found in most gainsharing books and in Chapter 4. What follows are a number of other issues related to refining the calculations for particular situations that are not discussed adequately in the literature. Most of the decisions associated with these issues are made essentially independently of the type of calculation employed, except in obvious cases—for example, the issue of standards pertains primarily to standard-based plans such as Improshare. These are issues of traditional and nontraditional calculations.

Limited or Poor Past Performance (Base Ratio Movement Considerations); Continuous Improvement Included

If the firm is new, a moving rather than a static ratio base is often used with no period allowed to be higher than an average of the past periods. That is, performance cannot become worse. For example, the base ratio (line 4) in Exhibit 5.2 could go from 25 to 24 percent but not to 26 percent. More recent periods are sometimes given extra weight. We normally have a comprehensive quarterly review to maintain equity until a stable base is determined. Forecasted figures are often used in conjunction with past performance.

If the firm is not new but has had poor past performance for whatever reason, should a bonus be paid for improvement upon an unacceptable level of performance? Some managers say no, or at least not 50 percent of any improvement. One obvious approach is to reduce the percentage going to employees to, say, a 20 to 30 percent range. Another approach is to weight good performance periods more heavily. Another is to use a moving average by:

1. adding each new period to the old,
2. adding each new period while dropping an old,
3. weighting recent periods more heavily, or
4. always adding forecasted performance as one of the periods.

Another approach is a little more complex: It consists of increasing the percentage going to employees as improvement occurs. For example, employees may get 20 percent if improvement occurs to a certain point, 30 percent if improvement reaches the next hurdle, and so on. If industry statistics are available, they are generally acceptable for setting hurdles in firms with good trust levels. Many firms force the concept of continuous improvement in their calculation. New variables can be added later.

In any case, an attempt must be maintained to develop perceived equitability between the shareholders, employees, and customers. Management does itself no justice by allowing the earning of bonuses too easily, and if such a practice decreases the firm's ability to compete, no one gains in the long run. Similarly, if management tries to limit the bonus artificially, the system will also deteriorate, to the detriment of everyone for many of the behavioral reasons covered in Chapter 4. We normally suggest an annual comprehensive review to evaluate equitability. But a final question should perhaps be asked: "In today's competitive environment, can an organization afford to pay forever for a one-time improvement in performance?"

How to Consider Volume

Many managers do not desire to pay large bonuses just because volume increases, even if the increase really is a productivity improvement. That is, if the amount of output is doubled with the same level of input, productivity has increased. But the improvement may be due to fixed or semivariable factors. Detailed monthly simulations will help determine whether this could occur, and how great a problem it is likely to be. We often use simple regression analysis (i.e., plotting inputs against outputs) to evaluate a cost's fixed and variable portions. Several options are available to help solve this problem:

1. reduce the fixed portions of inputs in the calculation,
2. reduce the semivariable inputs included,
3. put a cap on a period's bonus,
4. pay over a longer period (e.g., bimonthly or quarterly).
5. reduce the share to employees
6. separate more fixed portions and pay separately, for example, annually.

In actual practice, various combinations are used.

Some novel approaches are being used, especially for semivariable costs. One is a flexing approach. If, for example, standard labor earned should increase over a norm of some level, increased quantity or costs of semivariable inputs would be allowed but not a proportional increase. That is, if standard direct labor earned should increase by 10 percent over a period's norm, 2 percent more semivariable labor would be allowed; if a 20 percent increase should occur, then 4 percent more semivariable labor would be added and so on at each level. Although complex, this does help solve the objection to paying large bonuses just because volume increases.

If you want to include, say, all wages for philosophical reasons, fixed labor costs can be included based on a head count allowed at the beginning of the year or adjusted for approved reasons, and at an average wage. Still more complex options are used, but we do not believe they are desirable. Perhaps the more fixed costs should be excluded if management feels strongly enough about reducing the volume impact.

Two points should be made, however. First, costs or hours to be included is a separate decision from that of who participates in the bonus plan. (Everyone participates in its operation but does not necessarily share in the bonus.) These are two completely separate decisions, which many confuse. Second, reducing the volume impact on the plan is really a form of smoothing or reducing the bonus highs and lows. Frankly, we see no reason why bonuses should not be high when volume is high and vice versa but would feel uncomfortable with a 30 percent to 40 percent bonus or higher in one period and a zero bonus the next solely because of volume. Corporate staffs also seem bothered by such fluctuation possibilities, although we personally have never seen this degree of short-run volatility in plans that are installed, even if we have seen it in calculations under consideration. We have heard of such situations, however, so they can occur.

Caps and Leverage Effects of Labor Costs

To correct for major spikes in performance, some managers like the idea of caps on bonus size. Improshare normally imposes an automatic weekly payment cap of *60 percent with one half returned to the company*. Others set a lower cap of 10 percent to 20 percent, with any gain in excess frequently credited to the reserve. Others dislike caps and let bonuses go up. We have heard of bonuses exceeding 100 percent for a period. Large, easy-to-earn bonuses, especially if the calculation has a large fixed component, can be a problem because of heightened expectations, so we are not against caps in such situations. Also, corporate staffs of large companies whose units are installing gainsharing systems are more receptive to such plans when there are caps.

A final caution in the area of caps and volume applies to firms where labor is a small component of all costs. If wages and salaries are less than about 10 percent of total costs, a firm is practically precluded from using one of the broader calculations, such as value added, multicost, or even more profit sharing based on a hurdle rate, unless large bonuses are acceptable. Such bonuses result from the high leverage relationship between output and labor costs. If wages are 5 percent of sales and one saves 1 percent on other costs either because of volume or cost reduction, the contribution to the bonus is 20 percent (1 divided by 5). In fact, in almost all cases of large bonuses—that is, bonuses over about 30 percent—the calculation normally is fairly broad and labor is a small percent of costs. Watch for this possible problem by completing numerous simulations on specific periods. A goal-oriented approach often helps preclude these types of events.

Bonus Size and Bad Times

Most studies indicate that long-term bonuses average in the range of 5–7 percent, with smaller bonuses distributed in earlier years and often larger ones in later years. Obviously, many exceptions can be found. Not all organizations pay bonuses as a percent; some just pay a specific amount to employees.[4]

With respect to bonus size and bad times, some firms' policy is that if the profits are negative, no bonuses are paid, regardless of how they are computed. This smacks to us of management trying to have its cake and eat it too. Management should live with the results of its choice of a reward- or control-oriented calculation, although some limitations may have to be imposed at the outset to get corporate approval. A scaling effect up and down to adjust the percent of sharing probably makes more sense in some situations. Many organizations that install gainsharing really are not profit centers, however.

Building long-term identity with the system is extremely important to the plan's survival during difficult times. During the most recent recessions, many firms' plans survived with little difficulty, but only because identity was developed.

Inventories and Accounting of the Bonus

As mentioned earlier, inventories pose a calculation problem because of their relationship to the standard cost system and accounting systems in general. After a certain point of production, the actual cost of inventory items is not separately determined—just the standard cost in manufacturing organizations. Because of this, most firms base their calculations on production rather than sales. But to maintain a close ratio between costs and output for more financial-based productivity calculations, one should compute inventory change at sales prices rather than costs. For those firms that do not, a standard markup for changes can be developed, if appropriate. Computerization makes the whole area of inventory adjustments somewhat easier. Obviously, inventories are not a problem for many service sector firms. Likewise, most manufacturing firms are exercising closer controls so inventory fluctuations are much less of a problem as was traditionally the case.

One reason why firms are attracted to such standards-based plans as Improshare is their somewhat easier handling of the inventory problem. But if the inventory cycle is long, "what goes in the box" at the end of the period is not entirely acceptable as the sole measurement point. The key is to do simulations of various "what ifs," carefully monitoring changes, and attempting to be fair and open about the problem.

Some managers also do not want to give any credit toward the bonus until the product is sold, since only at that time are resources available to pay the bonus. Employees normally seem to understand and accept this thinking, even though it is not related to physical performance, or at least to production.

A final note is necessary on how to account for the bonus. From a purely accounting standpoint, the bonus is a cost, and is normally accounted for as an overhead item but not charged against the plan; otherwise the plan has to pay for the bonus twice—once when earned and then when paid.

Mix Changes and Capital

Narrow, standards-based calculations and broad ones such as multi-cost/profit seem to handle mix problems the best. Mix problems can be of several types, and each must be analyzed separately to determine their impact and the calculation change required.

1. *Substitution of capital for labor.* If capital is not included in the calculation, some adjustment is probably necessary if significant capital investments are made. Standards-based calculations are probably easier to adapt. For example, standards-based types of calculations such as Improshare often have a policy of adjusting the standard for 80 percent of the change so that everyone benefits somewhat from the equipment. Many other approaches are used, ranging from no adjustment to an immediate adjustment for 100 percent of the change, or in some cases, allowing the standard to remain as is until the end of a period. Combinations are also sometimes used. These approaches may be used for various lengths of time with a decrease in the percent of change as time goes by and as the impact of the change decreases.
2. *Outputs and inputs increasing or decreasing in price levels at different rates.* Standards-based calculations need not be adjusted at all if prices are excluded. Broad calculations adjust almost automatically. Also, reward-oriented managers, who tend to use broad calculations, are not as concerned about this issue as control managers because of their philosophy. But major pricing strategy changes can seriously affect some broad calculations, and these will have to be evaluated before a plan is established. Calculations of intermediate breadth must be monitored and adjustments made as required. As part of the normal study and evaluation, consider such fluctuations for this and other mix issues.
3. *Changes among the physical components of a product, such as changing from one quality of material to another.* Some calculations handle these changes easily, but others do not. Each such possible change in this area should be considered and planned for. Major adjustments can be made without difficulty if sufficient details were incorporated into the base period ratios and were maintained after installation.

Issues involving mix and different margins have resulted in some novel approaches over the years, such as split multicost. This entails separate calculations for each facility, for example, or each product line, which are then aggregated. Careful monitoring is necessary, and equity must be maintained.

New Products

Some plans have a stated philosophy of allowing the same bonus potential for new as for old products. These are normally standards-based plans, such as Improshare, since broader calculations are fairly well insulated from these problems unless profit margins fluctuate considerably for new versus old products. This approach is difficult for some managers to accept because they feel their ability to produce new products may be reduced if they have to pay a large portion of past productivity increases to employees for new products.

We tend to accept this logic and feel some tightening is acceptable, provided a process review is maintained. For standards-based plans, running a comparison with a sample of old and new products can help evaluate how great a problem, if any, there will be after installation. Sometimes one or two trial runs are made before developing standards, which are then reviewed at a later date. Again, intermediate types of calculations seem to present more difficulty than very narrow- or very broad-based types when adjusting to fundamentally new products and must be more carefully monitored for equitability. If a company can capture the performance improvement by recalculating the standard of new products, this helps to keep them competitive. Since there is generally a mix of new and old products, opportunities for bonus represent a tradeoff between incentive equity and market competitiveness. Goal-oriented systems can include such factors in the goals.

Individual Incentives and Gainsharing

Most experts claim that individual incentives are incompatible with gainsharing. This is certainly an overstatement, and successful applications of both have been made in some firms, including Lincoln Electric, Steel Case, and Textron. But the individual orientation prevalent in some individual incentive systems is certainly incompatible with the group or teamwork concept underlying gainsharing.

At any rate, the combination of individual incentives and gainsharing would probably not work in most cases because most individual incentives are not as effective as firms anticipate. In fact, we have isolated 21 reasons why firms get rid of individual incentives, the most common reasons being the impact on quality and the cost of maintenance. There are also numerous ways to eliminate individual incentives, the most common of which are some form of buyout and the red circling or guaranteeing wage levels of higher-paid employees for some period. A reduction of job classifications is often instituted along with elimination of incentives to increase the flexibility of the work force.

Management likes the idea of introducing gainsharing when individual incentives are eliminated, since in this way the inducement to increase productivity is maintained. Unions generally find individual incentives a problem and will often cooperate somewhat in their elimination unless union leaders are among those earning high bonuses. When gainsharing replaces individual incentives, the former, unlike the latter, is usually outside the union contract by mutual agreement. The union does not want management to use the argument in bargaining that large gainsharing bonuses are being earned so wage increases are not needed. Gainsharing normally includes all employees, not just union members, which is not true of individual incentives. Obviously, some education is also needed on how to manage in a nonincentive environment.

Loose or Tight Standards

Managers often say they cannot install a standards-based system because their standard cost system is poor. Although this is partially true in all cases, it is not very relevant. To start gainsharing, one merely has to determine the relationship between standard time (or costs) earned and actual time (or costs), if the labor calculation portion is productivity based. All that tight or loose standards do is change the relationship. Exhibit 5.4 should help explain this (some readers may disagree on our definition of loose and tight standards).

In the two situations, if standard hours earned increases by 10 percent to 66,000 hours and 49,500 hours respectively while actual hours stay the same and 66,000 is multiplied by 1.5 and 49,500 by 2.0, the result is allowed hours of 99,000 in both cases. Thus, each yields the same bonus earning opportunities (i.e., 99,000 allowed minus 90,000 actual hours).

Exhibit 5.4   Loose and Tight Standards

Situation 1: Loose standards (one-year period)

1. Actual direct labor hours	= 50,000 hours
2. Actual indirect labor hours	= 40,000 hours
3. Standard hours earned	= 60,000 hours

$$\text{Base productivity:} \quad \frac{50,000 + 40,000}{60,000} = 1.5$$

Situation 2: Tight standards (one-year period)

1. Actual direct labor hours	= 50,000 hours
2. Actual indirect labor hours	= 40,000 hours
3. Standard hours earned	= 45,000 hours

$$\text{Base productivity:} \quad \frac{50,000 + 40,000}{45,000} = 2.0$$

But the process of changing the standards does weigh heavily in the decision to apply a standards-based system. In such a case, two sets of standards must be maintained—one for gainsharing and another for scheduling, pricing, and so on (which is not entirely bad). Obviously, if the system is not standards based, the problems are reduced considerably, and standards are not as sensitive an issue. Firms that have major problems with trust in standards are likely not to select a standards-based system and, if one has already been installed, are likely to move away from it. Accounting rather than engineered standards are also frequently used.

Percent to Employees and Percent Versus Flat Amount

The percentage of measured savings returned to employees range from around 15 percent to 100 percent depending on management, the broadness of the calculation, and base period, and corporate philosophy. Many multiple pool calculations have different percentages for different pools; goal-oriented systems often eliminate this problem entirely. This issue is perhaps more philosophical than technical. As stated earlier, 50/50 has a good ring if adjustment procedures are adequate to maintain equitability and the base period performance is adequate. The more the pools, typically the smaller the percentage returned to employees.

Whether to pay the bonus as a percentage of gross wages or as a flat amount per hour of work is one of the most sensitive issues of gainsharing. A percentage is probably more uniform in its motivational impact and is probably more fair because it is congruent with normal pay systems. But many employees, including most managers, feel that a flat amount per hour of work is more fair because the bonus results from a team effort.

From the point of view of federal regulations, a percentage of pay including overtime is probably the only consistently acceptable payment method. The Fair Labor Standards Act states that the computation of overtime must be based on a calculation of regular wage (that includes production *and* other bonuses plus numerous other items such as shift premium). Excepted from recomputation are profit sharing *and* bonuses based on a percentage of all wages including overtime. Profit-sharing plans apparently can pay the bonus on a flat basis to everyone. A few firms distribute the bonus on hours with overtime weighted at 1.5 or more times but no formal ruling has been made on this approach that we know of, so check with your attorney in your state. This is less of a problem in countries outside of the United States. Technically you can pay the bonus any way you like; but if paid as a flat amount, you have to include bonuses when calculating overtime, which increases overtime costs. Many options are possible including two pools, one for exempt employees paid as a flat amount and one for hourly employees paid as a percent.

Quality Considerations

Most gainsharing firms place great emphasis on quality. There are often double and triple or more penalties for employee-generated quality problems, such as returns. We believe that this approach is desirable. It can take the form of a direct charge as a cost against the plan, an addition to returns and allowances, or some other procedure. This approach must be especially emphasized in certain service-sector firms such as hospitals (see Chapter 14). For examples of quality and customer service considerations, see Chapter 11.

Targeted Performance Instead of Past Performance

In some instances, because of philosophy, nature of the situation, unique measurement problems, or short history, past performances may not be an acceptable base. For example, using past performance has limitations if one wants to add numerous performance and financial productivity measures; to tie the system into one's business plan; or to apply it to contracted performance, government, some other nonprofit organizations, some job shop situations, or some very important performance measures. Goal-oriented systems by definition are based on expectations.

In such cases, a targeted performance approach is sometimes preferable. Calculations can be formulated through indices, contract costs, or ratios allowed, and, in some situations, targeted return on investment. Such approaches are readily accepted if identification, involvement, and communications have been effectively developed before installation and are maintained thereafter. Obviously, a good level of trust in management is also necessary.

Trade-off of Resources

People obviously focus on what is important to the bonus. Narrow calculations based, for example, on standards, may encourage a waste of resources to save on labor. Care must be exercised to help prevent this from happening by establishing a frequent review and a plan of action for dealing with a trade-off if it should occur. The most commonly wasted resources are materials, supplies, tooling, and, in some situations, energy. Care should be taken, both before installation and during operation, to evaluate possible impacts in these areas and who or what group should be involved in evaluating the consequences and developing some plan of action.

Reserves and Frequency of Payment

As stated earlier, many firms like the idea of maintaining reserves to help protect against spikes in performance and reinforce a long-run view. Reserves range from 10 percent to 70 percent of the employee share of the bonus pool, depending often on seasonality, past history, and corporate input (which normally means higher reserves). If positive at the end of the year, it is normally paid on the same basis as the normal periodic bonus. If negative, it is normally absorbed by the company.

Although most firms calculate and pay each period separately, some make the plan pay back any deficit in the reserve before paying any bonus in subsequent periods. If the reserve is 25 percent of positive periods and 100 percent of negative ones, it could become negative rapidly. Consequently, some firms increase the reserve to something like 50 percent of positive periods while always paying out something for positive periods, even if a deficit for the previous period has not yet been fully paid back. Other options are used, but these are the most common. Obviously, some employees would prefer no reserve so as to maximize their possible return, but they are not sharing equally in the deficits, which would be unfair to the shareholders. Also, it would mean that long-run attitudes were not being reinforced.

Frequency of payment ranges from weekly for some standards-based calculations to yearly for a few firms. Monthly payments may be the most common. We find little perceived difference in success between firms that pay monthly or quarterly; it really reflects whether the orientation is short run or long run. Although we do not have problems with large reserves, other consultants seem to, so some have developed other options. These include a rolling payout to smooth results and recover any losses before a bonus is paid, and, year-to-date payments (total bonus minus amount already paid).

Additive or Separate

The multiple pool and goal-oriented systems can be additive (i.e., the minuses, if any, are subtracted from the positives) or each pool (or some of them) can be calculated and paid separately. Frankly, some firms make them additive and others make them mutually exclusive with each standing on its own. Many firms have special focus pools that stand separately from the normal calculation.

Self-Funding or Activity Based

Many firms require the plans to be self-funding, which means that you can't pay just for such activities as improving on-time shipments. These are conceptual issues that must be considered by each organization. We think both are important and at least some payment should be possible for improving important activities.

Profit Sharing Versus Gainsharing and a Profit Link or Not

Perhaps the most frequently asked question is: "What's the difference between profit sharing and gainsharing?" Frankly, much disagreement exists here. Some think that profit sharing is a whole separate system and that gainsharing is narrower, more control oriented, and paid more frequently. This may suffice in some situations, but, unfortunately, such a definition eliminates perhaps one third of the excellent firms that call themselves gainsharing but use profit improvement as their measurement system. We feel that if a plan has a hurdle rate ("gaining" aspect), pays bonuses more often than once a year if earned, and a formal link to an employee involvement system, then it is a form of gainsharing independent of the measurement system used. We realize that some people may disagree with the definition.

Most gainsharing plans are also installed in cost centers rather than in true profit centers. In most of these organizations, the goal should be primarily to reduce costs and perhaps improve other variables. But if the unit is a profit center, many organizations like to have some tie to profits even if physical or operational based. The easiest way is to tie the year-end reserve payout to profitability. That is, if profits are at X amount, everyone gets 50 percent or 100 percent or 150 percent of the year-end reserve as an example. Alternatively, you could base the percent of sharing based on profitability levels. Finally, some firms have a profitability hurdle rate before any bonus is paid.

Unique Industries

Although the techniques discussed in this chapter probably apply to many, if not all situations, some unique perceived or actual measurement problems can be found in some industries. These must be solved by using the conceptual approach discussed earlier or developing simpler sharing techniques such as lotteries, departmental prize awards, or unique measurement techniques. In just about all cases, however, some sharing formula can be developed if the firm really wants one regardless of whether management is control or reward oriented or how major a change process it desires. The key is to be convinced that something will work rather than to try to discover the "perfect" measurement system. A workable formula is generally possible, but a perfect one does not exist.

SUMMARY

This chapter, along with Chapter 4, should provide significant assistance in investigating, implementing, and monitoring a gainsharing calculation. Perceived fairness and meeting organizational objectives are probably the most important factors to long-term success. Some more complex/broader calculations require much more education than do others. The key is to conceptually decide on the calculation orientation and then reinforce it after implementation. In most situations however a calculation can be developed and maintained without major difficulties. New calculations allow gainsharing to be applied in practically all situations, including new company start-ups.

Notes

1. J.L. McAdams and E.J. Hawk, *Capitalizing on Human Assets* (Scottsdale: American Compensation Association and Maritz, Inc., 1992), 20.
2. Ibid, p. 52.
3. Ibid, p. 48.
4. ACA, 1992; many statistics are offered depending on the type of plan. Also see J.L. McAdams and E.J. Hawk, *Organizational Performance & Rewards* (Scottsdale: American Compensation Association, 1994).

Chapter 6

Why Employment Involvement Gainsharing Works and Sometimes Doesn't

Timothy L. Ross

Most experts in the field of gainsharing would probably say that the success rate is not over 65 percent. (This percentage includes firms with marginal plans, which is a common practice). No one really knows the success rate, since most of the plans have been installed by consultants who are frequently unwilling to share their client's experience with others. In the ACA Benchmark Study, only 13 percent of respondents were dissatisfied with their plans.[1]

Overall, failure of gainsharing is most often linked with the managerial expectation of increased performance with little effort directed toward making it happen. This increased performance rarely occurs, and when it doesn't, disenchantment may set in. Similarly, if employees expect significant bonuses without major behavioral changes to increase performance, they are likely to become discouraged if bonuses do not materialize. Expectations and changed behavior are the key elements of success or failure. They always have been and probably always will be the most important variables.

OVERALL REVIEW

We could state very simply that firms that do not develop the variables outlined in Chapter 1 to a significant degree would probably see their plans fail. Firms install gainsharing for many good as well as poor reasons. Those whose plans fail exhibit in high probability the following characteristics to an extensive degree:

A. *Organization and Labor Force Variables*
  1. low trust or confidence in management, low accountability, low levels of participation, and lack of direction,
  2. poor communications among and within departments, and communications patterns that are primarily from the top down (i.e., "don't listen" managers),
  3. inability of people to relate to the system,
  4. low control over revenue and unstable employment,
  5. low levels of identity with organization, its past, present, and future opportunities and problems,
  6. inequitable wages when compared with other employees and area firms.

B. *Social, Cultural, and Institutional Variables*
  1. poor industrial relations and confidence; poor union relations,
  2. low level needs for involvement and commitment.

C. *Financial Information and Competition Variables*
  1. poor internal financial information system,
  2. lack of accuracy of the financial system,
  3. low levels of financial understanding or ability to relate to the system,
  4. lack of knowledge of, or dedication to beat, the competition,
  5. unstable conditions in output or input markets; declining markets,
  6. severe competitive conditions and limited commitment to change,
  7. severe governmental constraints,
  8. management manipulation of the bonus
  9. bonus calculation poorly designed—doesn't accurately reflect business conditions; too easy or impossible to earn a bonus.

The more these variables are present in a firm, the greater the risk of failure. But if one analyzes them carefully, one should not be surprised to note that they are the variables commonly cited as important to the success of any organization. That is, if the company is unsuccessful or lacks improvements, in all likelihood its gainsharing plan is doomed to failure unless drastic actions are taken. Thus, to be successful as a gainsharing company, an organizational need to change or to be better than others must exist. Without these attitudes, neither the employees nor management are likely to make the changes necessary on a continuing basis and the system will likely fail. The more a firm experiences the above problems, the greater the rush to failure. Unfortunately in these trying and rapidly changing times, probably no organization has the ideal environment in which to install such a system, nor is it likely to get any easier. Frankly, most firms that have installed such systems have significant problems of some sort before installation. Employee involvement gainsharing has been very successful in changing organizations. That is, they have been used to lead organizational change rather than lag or support it.

SOME EVIDENCE FROM THE LITERATURE

Several studies have attempted to explore correlates of gainsharing success. For example, in order to assess the differences in managerial attitudes, Ruh, Wallace, and Frost contrasted managerial attitudes in 10 firms with active gainsharing systems with those in 8 firms that had implemented and abandoned their plans. Their general findings were as follows:

1. Managers in firms that abandoned their plans perceived the rank-and-file employees to demonstrate significantly less judgment, creativity, responsibility, dependability, pride in performance, initiative, self-confidence, and willingness to change compared with managers in firms with continuing gainsharing plans.
2. Managers in firms that abandoned plans had less favorable attitudes toward participative decision making than continuing firms' managers. The same results were found regarding the perceived impact of participation on morale and performance.[2]

Of the abandoned plan firms, the expectations of managers regarding success were negative either before or after installation. Nevertheless, the firms obviously did not sink into bankruptcy or experience other dire consequences as a result of gainsharing failure.

Although generally congruent with our predictions, the study did not validate any cause/effect variables in that the failure of the plans may have been caused by the poor attitudes or may have been the result of the plans. Obviously, such pregainsharing attitudes as these could spell failure. But variables outlined above could also have actually caused the abandonment of the plans and, as is often the case, differentiating and isolating the cause/effect variables is difficult.

White found a number of corroborative pieces of evidence in his study of 23 gainsharing firms, 12 of which had abandoned their plan at the time of the study.[3] All were manufacturing firms. Some of his major findings follow.

1. High levels of failure are associated with low levels of employee participation. That is, if participation is perceived by employees to be low, the plan is likely to be marginally effective and perhaps doomed to failure.
2. Larger size does not seem to be a major factor for failure. Obviously, larger firms must be committed to significant communications and participation.
3. Low levels of managerial confidence in participative management are strongly associated with failure or marginal success. This variable should be useful in predicting gainsharing success if the system is participation-oriented.
4. The longer the plan is in existence, the less likely that the firm will abandon it. High expectations of immediate change tend to lead to dis-

appointments. (Some longstanding firms do of course eventually abandon the plan because of economic downturns, managerial changes at the top, and so on.)

5. When installing a plan, realistic favorable expectations are important. Consequently, organizations with poor employee attitudes should not be selected for gainsharing plans. Getting the proper people involved at the beginning is also important.

6. If a high-level executive does not take a leading role, the plan's failure probability increases.

7. Technology does not seem to be positively or negatively related to failure.

Numerous other researchers have hypothesized problem areas and possible failure from a series of cases or conjectures over the years. Although these are not definitive, they provide valuable insights into the forces that may play in an actual situation and indicate where possible problems may arise. Problem areas are not listed in order of importance but generally expand on the studies discussed above.

1. poor calculation,[4]
2. lack of bonuses or opportunities to earn them,[5]
3. poor union/management cooperation and leadership,[6]
4. lack of supervisors' commitment,[7]
5. management defensiveness,[8]
6. lack of management's commitment of time, money, or enthusiasm,[9]
7. little perceived need to change or be different,[10]
8. poor communications or information sharing,[11]
9. lack of support for continuance from the top of the organization.[12]

The evidence seems to substantiate many of our propositions. If future researchers and businesses use the model shown in Chapter 1, we feel that most of the variables included there will provide extremely useful information in predicting both success and failure. A successful gainsharing system does not occur by chance but is carefully developed and nurtured over the years. It can survive managerial succession if support from the top is high.

TWO OTHER STUDIES

In the following sections two analyses made by Ross are examined based on studies completed. The first is a general study of accountants and supervisors, and the second is a record of an actual failure, where the employees voted for abandoning the plan after a year's trial period. The data and identity are disguised for purposes of anonymity.

Study 1. Accountants and Supervisors Contrasted

In an attempt to partially validate primarily the financial aspects of our model, a group of 22 accountants (mostly controllers) and supervisors at existing gainsharing firms were requested to rank a set of 22 variables of gainsharing success from very important (1) to very unimportant (5). These variables ranged from bonus earning opportunities (number 1) to departmental goal setting (number 22). A day was then spent discussing the implications of the findings. The overall findings are outlined in Exhibit 6.1.

Regarding areas of significant differences between the two groups, six areas in particular stand out. These are:

Q3.   accuracy of standards (ranked 2.6 by accountants versus 1.4 by supervisors),

Q4.   knowledge of competition (2.8 versus 1.8),

Q8.   simplicity of calculation (2.7 versus 1.8),

Q10. government constraints (3.2 versus 2.3),

Q18. control over sales growth (2.5 versus 1.6),

Q19. current pay levels (2.5 versus 1.4).

In all cases, supervisors perceived these six areas to be of more importance than did accountants. Each was discussed in detail to find the reasons for the differences and how to close the gap. The results follow.

In most cases, standards do not affect the bonus directly. If they do, then their accuracy is very important, even as perceived by accountants. If they are just tools of performance expectations, then they are less important directly to gainsharing as perceived by the participants. Supervisors perceived accuracy of standards to be more important to success than did accountants. But everyone agreed that accurate standards are important to a successful firm for a variety of reasons. Most agreed on the undesirability of standards that are too loose. Supervisors also seemed to want to become more involved in the whole standards area, which would be a good opportunity for more involvement. No significant ideas were offered to help people to overcome the fear of changing standards.

Regarding control over sales growth, supervisors again believed that this was more important, due mainly to inefficiencies that result when production is pushed too hard to increase sales. This probably affects a supervisor's tasks more than the accountant's. Supervisors desire more stability. One participant compared uncontrolled growth to a form of cancer.

Supervisors also believed pay levels to be more important because low pay makes it difficult to retain employees. They have a strong need to maintain a stable and skilled work force.

Knowledge of competition was extensively discussed. Some points made included: (1) accountants more than supervisors realize how complex this issue is, (2) this may be more important to sales than to production, and (3) the area needs to be more heavily emphasized for all gainsharing firms of the future. This area must be kept simple and built on over time.

Exhibit 6.1   Variables Important to Gainsharing Success/Failure

	Means	
	Accountants	**Supervisors**
1. Bonus earning opportunities	1.6	1.4
2. Understanding of the calculation	1.9	2.2
3. Accuracy of standards	2.6	1.4
4. Knowledge of competition	2.8	1.8
5. Stability of selling market	2.3	1.6
6. Trust in accounting staff	1.7	1.4
7. Market growth potential	2.4	1.6
8. Simplicity of calculation	2.7	1.8
9. Type of work force	2.4	2.0
10. Government constraints	3.2	2.3
11. Knowledge of company's (plant's) performance	1.3	1.2
12. Accuracy of production/inventory control system	2.0	1.4
13. Trust in accounting system	1.3	1.2
14. Stability of materials market	2.6	1.8
15. Success of company (profit)	1.3	1.4
16. Product pricing practices	1.9	1.6
17. Frequency of new products	2.0	1.8
18. Control over sales growth	2.5	1.6
19. Current pay levels	2.5	1.4
20. Stability of employment	1.9	1.4
21. Departmental performance feedback	1.4	1.2
22. Departmental goal setting	1.6	1.2

Scale: 1 = Very Important   3 = Undecided   5 = Very Unimportant
           2 = Important   4 = Unimportant

Highly ranked by both groups included:
1. Bonus earning opportunities,
2. Trust in accounting staff,
3. Knowledge of company's (plant's) performance,
4. Trust in accounting system,
5. Success of company (profit),
6. Departmental performance feedback,
7. Departmental goal setting.

(Obviously, any actions or programs directed in these areas should contribute significantly to success or failure if the results are validated for all groups of managers.)

Although differences between accountants and supervisors regarding trust of accounting staff and understanding of the calculation were not great, the participants believed that both are of about equal importance.

People can relate to broader calculations but they are frustrated by their inability to do much about them. An effort must be made to get to the lowest common denominator to increase understanding, and accountants probably do a poor job in this area.

Most participants agreed that one need not have a bonus in the short run but that expectations for a future bonus are important. (Some newer gainsharing participants disagreed, since the bonus is a common goal.) Some perceived the bonus as an add-on but some did not; goal clarity is at issue here. Others viewed the participative management aspect as the most important aspect. But how far can one go without a bonus? There was much disagreement on this point. Recently we had one plan survive there years without a bonus by placing heavy emphasis on other aspects of the plan.

The question was asked, Do people really want to be involved? Movement is toward more participation even if some workers resist. Many employees want more from their job than just money. But it takes much effort to get them to participate in a gainsharing system. If they do become involved, problems can result if management discontinues it for any reason because of the build up of employee commitment.

Another inquiry area focused on whether a plan could be successful if everyone knew that a bonus would not be earned without a large layoff or other drastic measures. Much disagreement existed on this point. Most believed that it would be a mistake to sell it on this basis.

The key question brought up by most was, What turns an employee or group on? This is the key to measuring success. To some it is money or bonus, but to others, it might be involvement, recognition, or job security. If employees relate strongly to bonuses, then they should understand why one is or is not being earned.

An extensive discussion took place regarding whether people should know who is and who is not earning or contributing to the bonus, a possibility to document with some calculations. This can be divisive but also can be quite constructive, depending on how used. Who really earned and contributed to a bonus is frequently difficult to establish because of the complexities of cause and effect.

Likewise, considerable differences were expressed regarding how much individual recognition should occur. Most agreed that the best recognition is the type in which the entire organization is recognized. Effort should also concentrate on both low and high performers.

All of these areas need considerable research before definitive answers can be developed.

Study 2. A Case of Failure

This is a fairly brief case of a gainsharing failure. The background is as follows:

The firm in question was a small, 60-employee manufacturing firm, involved primarily in assembly operation, located in a depressed area of a large city. The highest profit in the five years prior to the installation of the plan was less than 1 percent of sales before corporate charges and interest. The firm had made no profits during four of the five years. The work force consisted of minority workers with low skill levels; wages were approximately 50 cents above minimum wage requirements. Although the work force was unionized, the firm received no interference from the local. In fact, it succeeded in obtaining wage concessions. It was further hampered by weak financial information systems. Training and other activities were severely limited by financial conditions. Its market was declining and sales were decreasing in absolute dollars. The firm was part of a major conglomerate and was given a "last chance" to improve its performance.

A behavioral evaluation was conducted, including an employee survey. A management team effectiveness profile indicated low evaluation of fellow managers, especially of the president. A survey of employee attitudes indicated the following key summarized results. The survey was on a five-point Likert-type of scale with 5 being the most positive mean and 1 the most negative.

		Mean
1.	How satisfied would you say you are with your earnings?	2.36
2.	How would you rate cooperation between departments?	2.40
3.	How would you rate communications between departments?	2.20
4.	To what extent do you have confidence and trust in your supervisor?	2.90
5.	Is management willing to accept suggestions you make?	2.74
6.	Is the take-home pay here as good as similar companies in the area?	2.20
7.	Do you feel that the pay for your job is fair compared with the pay for other jobs in this plant?	2.10
8.	The feeling of satisfactory relationships with management?	2.20
9.	How much confidence and trust is there in management?	2.00
10.	How much concern is there for controlling costs?	2.60

Obviously, conditions were poor for the installation of a plan on several key variables:

1. Because of very low earnings, employees would probably view the plan as a substitute for equitable wages.
2. Poor communications were apparent.
3. There was little trust in management and little reason to trust them.
4. Supervisors were poorly trained.
5. There was low concern for controlling costs.
6. Written comments indicated severe feelings of discrimination, pressure for performance, and poor equipment.

Additional problems centered on inadequate available time or money. Finally, neither employees nor managers perceived a real need to change in spite of the financial conditions. Also, they had low levels of expectations in general on eight key questions regarding such activities as costs, quality, productivity, job security, and need for involvement. They were obviously discouraged and frustrated.

When the plan was finally presented to the employees following completion of the work of a steering committee, a confidential vote was taken for a trial period of one year. The vote was exactly 75 percent, too low a commitment for good initial success. (Note: it was requested that the president not be present or many employees would definitely vote against the plan.)

This was, of course, a high-risk situation at best as outlined earlier. However, the plant and divisional management believed that little could be lost by trying the plan even though they were cautioned against thinking it could work. Quite simply, they were told to do something—and plans had saved other firms from going under.

The results of the first and only year of operation are outlined below:

1. A major layoff in the first month of operation resulted in a one-third reduction of the work force. Three layoffs occurred the first year.
2. Bonuses were not paid until the fourth month of operation (5.1 percent). This was the largest of four bonuses, the rest consisted of 3.5 percent, 5.0 percent, and 2.2 percent of wages, or about 1.5 percent total for the year.
3. Volume continued to erode over the previous year; backlogs continued to erode.
4. Wide fluctuations in sales and inventory made it difficult to evaluate whether direct labor productivity increased, but management believed that it had somewhat.
5. No one served as coordinator, and communications dropped substantially after the first few months, including feedback on suggestions.
6. No training programs were established for supervisors or team representatives. Some existing teams did not meet on a regular basis.
7. Supervisors were on the screening (plantwide) committee and dominated the discussions.
8. Indirect employees were not laid off anywhere near proportionally to direct labor employees.
9. Employees had much difficulty relating to gainsharing with the fluctuations in volume and employment.
10. Because of volume fluctuations and pressures to improve performance, production control apparently deteriorated.
11. Because of erratic volume, trust in management had probably deteriorated.
12. Little emphasis was placed on communications, including calculation education, feedback of performance, follow-up of suggestions.
13. Inconsistent supervision was a constant throughout.

14. Misunderstandings occurred between the office and factory.
15. Bickering among management continued to expand.
16. Less than 50 percent of employees submitted suggestions, and follow-up procedures were frequently not completed.
17. Wages increases were nominal.

Considering the above problems, there is little wonder that the employees voted the plan out in December, at the conclusion of the trial period. Management made no attempt to salvage either their own or their employees' commitment to the system.

Obviously, this is a perfect example of where not to install a plan. Most of the variables in our discussion above were obviously violated. A perceived need to change does not bring change about. In this particular case there was need for change in many areas. Although the firm went through the motions of instituting a plan, management obviously missed the opportunity to make a major change.

A final note to this summary is appropriate. In spite of the problems outlined above, operating profit for the first 11 months went from a negative $57,000 to a plus $114,000. Was the plan a total failure? Perhaps it did help to save the firm from extinction although no one would certainly consider it a success.

OTHER COMMON FACTORS OF SUCCESS

In addition to the factors mentioned above and in Chapter 2, many factors important to success have never really been studied. However, experience would indicate that they are important in most situations. Each is discussed in some degree.

- New or old firms. Most applications have been in existing facilities that have some track record for developing good base performance results and this makes sense. But we have seen six plants install gainsharing almost from day one all based on goals until some historical information is developed.[14]
- Small or large size. The statistics on this issue are probably biased by combining some large organizations' profit sharing or other systems. Employee involvement gainsharing seems somewhat difficult though for very small firms (less than 20 people) for some reason and would be very difficult for large firms (over 2,500). But both could obviously have just a bonus plan with no difficulty. People in small organizations perhaps have to wear too many hats. Large facilities are fairly bureaucratic although you could have several separate gainsharing plans within a plant as Motorola had for years. Obviously, exceptions to these conclusions are found in practice.

- Management beliefs. Management need not be totally participative, but they must believe in people's ability and desire to contribute and grow. Douglas McGregor's Theory Y assumptions are perhaps good assumptions. Unfortunately, many managers do not share these beliefs.
- Bonus tied to organizational objectives. Whatever bonus calculation is used, it must not be contrary to the values of the organization in the long run. Instances of contrary calculations might be to increase labor productivity while reducing quality and customer service, or paying a significant bonus while profits are dropping when management is financially oriented. It pays an organization to assess the plan against its overall values or those of management.
- Seasonality. This can cause a major problem for some firms but can be solved with various leveling approaches, such as larger year end reserves; moving averages; making up any deficits; or increasing the bonus period (from monthly to quarterly) to mention a few of the more common approaches including personnel subject to frequent layoffs and call backs can also be a problem, which is why many firms are using temporary or part-time personnel much more extensively. Generally, but not always, these more temporary personnel are excluded from the plan.
- Interdependency. Employee involvement gainsharing seems to work best if there is a lot of interdependence between areas and departments. Rotating shifts with four shifts makes this difficult even if important. Large organizations also make this more difficult but some of these organizations have the dedication and resources to work on this important issue.
- Management and nonmanagement employee commitment. As the ACA Benchmark Study showed, gainsharing is probably never installed unless top managers support the concept of employee involvement and sharing. In a way, it is like the classic question of which is more committed to a bacon and eggs breakfast, the pig or the chicken. Even "chicken" commitment can run to a very, very small egg. Hence, you must make it very specific if long-term commitment is desired, including replacing managers who do not support it. Management must support the ideas, help them get implemented, and encourage employees. Employee commitment can also be a major problem if employees have been abused in the past or if bad union leadership exists. Both of these issues must be tackled in a very specific way so everyone knows what to expect. The development task force approach discussed in Chapter 3 helps considerably, and the next section offers some more specific suggestions.
- Key accounting personnel. It really helps to have top people in this area who believe in employee involvement gainsharing, believe in educating people, are good communicators, and are trusted.

- Union support. Although the ACA's Benchmark Study found that only 24 percent of the firms they studied were unionized, in reality the actual statistics are probably higher than this. Union support is important to the success of a good long-term employee involvement gainsharing plan. This happens by getting them involved on the design task force and including some site visits. Chapter 10 discusses this in more detail.
- Importance of an evangelist. Like any other interpersonal situation, it really helps to have one or more key upper people who really support the system against all of the negatives. A good coordinator is extremely important if the system includes a formal, structured involvement system.
- Stability. Although mentioned earlier in Chapters 1 and 2, rapid changes because of technology, expansion, or other factors interfere with a good plan. Traditionally, rapid changes caused more problems than today because the calculations were more static. With the more fluid, multiple pool and goal oriented calculations today, this is less of a problem but can still cause some companies significant difficulties. Planning for them and getting employees involved in the change processes are the keys to handling change.
- Openness. Management must be willing to share a significant increase in information compared with what traditionally has been disseminated. Some data must be kept confidential because of competitive reasons; accountants must be imaginative in disclosing important factors that influence the bonus.
- Corporate support. This certainly helps. Without it, the system will *not* spread to other units. This is always surprising to people. Corporate management is often "fearful" (what a shame) that if it is a big success, all other units will want to do it. This typically only happens if corporate management is sincerely dedicated to spreading the word and even then, very few units will want to install it. The ACA Benchmark Study found plans "dictated" by corporate were less successful than those developed by a local design team.
- Workforce characteristics. Employee involvement gainsharing works best with a fairly well educated, committed, and technically competent workforce. The workers should be interested in involvement, continuous improvement, financial and other operational information, and be dedicated to change.
- Technical support. This system emphasizes working smarter rather than harder. Consequently, the involvement and ideas submitted places most pressure on "technical" support areas, such as engineering, maintenance, purchasing, scheduling, and customer service and quality. These groups must be supportive of the system.
- Recognition and communication efforts. People underestimate the importance of these factors to long-term successful employee involvement

systems. Each organization contemplating installation of any such system should be prepared to expend considerable effort in these areas if success is really desired. This is especially true in difficult periods.

- At risk plans. Most gainsharing plans are not "at risk" plans and probably will not be in the foreseeable future. The ACA study found that 16 percent of the plans studied were at risk. The at risk plans based on operational measures also were more successful overall.[13] Unfortunately, Americans do not trust management sufficiently to put some of their pay at risk as do the Japanese. Hopefully that will change some day, and in fact is already happening in "pay for performance" plans.

MANAGEMENT COMMITMENT—
THE KEY VARIABLE

When everything is said and done, perhaps with all systems in general and certainly with most employee involvement systems, obtaining and maintaining management commitment is the key. But in reality, management is often under a great deal of stress with many countervailing forces exerting pressures from all different directions and is often not long-range oriented. Frankly managers need help in deciding what they can and cannot do to help make the system succeed in the long run.

Obviously, each organization will have to decide what it can do to help in this area, but we have found the following list simple enough to obtain commitment from most managers. More specific guidelines are preferred to more general ones.

- Full-time coordinator with specific responsibilities if over 200 employees. At least half-time coordinator for smaller firms.
- Monthly meetings between coordinator and top manager to assess performance of all departmental involvement systems, education, management commitment, and so on.
- Top managers attend organization-wide monthly meetings and other meetings regularly (e.g., quarterly with rotation).
- Meetings with all employees at least once a quarter to discuss broad issues of business, gainsharing performance, and problems.
- Long-term commitment to education occurs (e.g., at least 25 hours per year of education for all levels of managers).
- Include documented commitment to gainsharing in formal managerial evaluation systems.
- Insure that ideas are investigated and the results are fed back; make sure that low idea areas and high rejection rate areas are investigated and action taken. Review whether ideas are implemented in a timely fashion.
- Make sure that meetings are held as scheduled and that they are action oriented.

- Openly support managers/supervisors in their gainsharing efforts—reward commitment, ideas, group meetings.
- Top manager visits implementation organization frequently to talk up gainsharing and give recognition.
- Top managers offer ideas themselves and encourage others to do the same.
- Provide good meeting facilities.
- Encourage involvement by recognizing it and making it important.
- Allow time to complete gainsharing activities.
- Have a good library and circulate good articles.
- Monthly meetings (15–20 minutes) with all employees in small departmental groups to discuss the bonus results and communication areas.
- Hold short meetings with all supervisors once a month to discuss gainsharing.
- Insist on periodic evaluations of gainsharing system—at least annually.
- Get managers involved as advisors to all department/area teams.
- Get at least one top manager to be an evangelist.

An organization can go way beyond this listing if appropriate. Another list could be prepared for nonmanagerial employees and union officials if applicable.

SUMMARY

Obviously, the perceptions of success and failure of a plan become very complex as the reasons for installing it. If gainsharing is installed solely as a form of contingent compensation with little effort directed toward building commitment, communications, employee involvement, or even need to improve in an already successful firm, one should not be surprised when little improvement occurs. The key is to develop management and nonmanagement commitment to the system while still maintaining reasonable expectations.

To summarize, it is important to agree on philosophy of installation, commitment required from everyone and a structure of involvement/communications which reinforce the entire system. Continuous reviews of these and other variables are extremely important to long-term plan success.

Notes

1. J. L. McAdams and E. J. Hawk, *Capitalizing on Human Assets* (Scottsdale: ACA and Maritz, Inc., 1992).
2. R. A. Ruh, R. L. Wallace, and C. F. Frost, "Management Attitudes and the Scanlon Plan," *Industrial Relations*, 1973, 282–288.
3. J. K. White, "The Scanlon Plan: Causes and Correlates of Success," *Academy of Management Journal,* June 1979, 292–312.
4. J. J. Jehring, "A Contrast Between Two Approaches to Total Systems Incentives," *California Management Review,* 1967, 7–14; B. E. Moore, *A Plant-Wide*

Productivity Plan in Action: Three Years of Experience with the Scanlon Plan (Washington, D.C.: National Commission on Productivity and Work Quality, 1975); T. L. Ross and G. M. Jones, "An Approach to Increased Productivity: The Scanlon Plan," *Financial Executives,* February 1972, 23–29; A. Ashburn, "Devising Real Incentives for Productivity," *American Machinist,* June 1978, 115–130.

5.　R. Helfgott, *Group Wage Incentives: Experience with the Scanlon Plan,* (New York: Industrial Relations Counselors, Industrial Relations Memo, 1962); Ashburn, "Devising Real Incentives," note 4, above.

6.　R. W. Davenport, "Enterprise for Everyman," *Fortune,* January 1950, 50–58; R. B. Gray, "The Scanlon Plan—A Case Study," *British Journal of Industrial Relations* 9, 191–213; E. Puckett, "Productivity Achievements—A Measure of Success," in *The Scanlon Plan: A Frontier in Labor Management Cooperation,* ed. F. G. Lesieur (Cambridge, Mass.: Technology Press of M.I.T. and New York: Wiley, 1958); Helfgott, *Group-Wage Incentives,* note 5, above; H. Thierry, "The Scanlon Plan: A Field Experimental Approach" (Symposium, 81st Annual Convention, American Psychological Association, 1973).

7.　Moore, *A Plant-Wide Productivity Plan in Action: Three Years of Experience with the Scanlon Plan,* note 4, above; Helfgott, *Group Wage Incentives,* note 5, above; Thierry, "The Scanlon Plan," note 6, above; Ashburn, "Devising Real Incentives," note 4, above.

8.　H. R. Northrup and H. A. Young, "The Causes of Industrial Peace Revisited," *Industrial and Labor Relations Review,* October 1968, 31–47; R. J. Doyle, "A New Look at the Scanlon Plan," *Management Accounting,* September 1970, 48; F. Whyte, *Money and Motivation* (New York: Harper and Brothers, 1955).

9.　Moore, *A Plant-Wide Productivity Plan in Action: Three Years of Experience with the Scanlon Plan,* note 4, above; C. F. Frost, J. H. Wakely, and R. A. Ruh, *The Scanlon Plan for Organization Development: Identity, Participation, and Equity* (East Lansing: Michigan State University Press, 1974); G. P. Shultz, "Variation in Environment and the Scanlon Plan," in *The Scanlon Plan: A Frontier in Labor Management Cooperation,* ed. F. G. Lesieur (Cambridge, Mass.: Technology Press of M.I.T. and New York: Wiley, 1958): A. J. Geare, "Productivity From Scanlon-Type Plans," *The Academy of Management Review,* July 1976, 99–108; Helfgott, *Group Wage Incentives,* note 5, above.

10.　Helfgott, *Group Wage Incentives,* note 5, above; C. F. Frost, "The Scanlon Plan: Anyone for Free Enterprise?," *MSU Business Topics,* Winter 1978, 25–33.

11.　G. S. Burtnett, "A Study of Causal Relationships Between Organizational Variables and Personal Influence Variables During the Implementation of Scanlon Plans, (Ph.D. dissertation, Michigan State University, 1973): Helfgott, *Group Wage Incentives,* note 5, above; Ashburn, "Devising Real Incentives," note 4, above.

12.　G. P. Schultz, "Worker Participation on Production Problems: A Discussion of Experience with the Scanlon Plan," *Personnel,* November 1951, 209–211.

13.　J. L. McAdams and E. J. Hawk, *Capitalizing on Human Assets,* note 1 above.

14.　Timothy L. Rose, "Self Management and Gainsharing: A Winning Duo," *Journal for Quality and Participation,* June 1994, 10–15.

Chapter 7

Making Productivity Programs Last

Paul S. Goodman and James W. Dean, Jr.

In the 1970s and 1980s we saw a proliferation of new forms of work organization projects designed to improve on productivity and quality of working life. In many ways the new forms were revolutionary because they represented fundamental changes in how work should be organized, in how organizations might be designed, and in the nature of labor-management relationships. Some examples of these new forms are discussed below.

Autonomous work groups represent one new form of work organization. Basically, these are self-governing groups organized by process, place, or product. There is a substantial shift in authority and decision making as the group takes over such responsibilities as hiring, discipline, and allocation of production tasks. Most autonomous groups encourage job switching. Pay is based on knowledge of jobs rather than actual job performance.[1]

Labor-management problem-solving groups represent another common form of change. In this type of program, a hierarchy of linked problem-solving groups is superimposed on the existing organizational structure. The groups are generally arranged following the current organizational structure, with lower-level groups dealing with problems specific to their areas, and higher-level groups dealing with problems that cut across multiple organizational units. These groups meet regularly. Products from these groups include, for example, work simplification, flex-time projects, and new performance appraisal systems.

This chapter is adapted from B.E. Graham-Moore and T.L. Ross, *Productivity Gainsharing,* Chapter 8, "Making Productivity Programs Last," by P. S. Goodman and J. W. Dean, Jr. (Englewood Cliffs, N.J.: Prentice-Hall, 1983).

121

Companywide gainsharing programs represent another organizational change strategy that has proliferated over the past 20 years. These programs, which typically include organizational changes and new monetary reward systems, are designed to improve productivity.

Many other organizational changes have been introduced during this period. They all represent fundamental changes in an organization's communication, decision-making, authority, and reward systems. They also create fundamental changes in the relationships among people within the organization.

Beyond merely enumerating work organization projects, we now turn our attention to the focus of this chapter—whether these programs last. That is, after some period of initial success, do these productivity programs persist or remain institutionalized? Are they just temporary phenomena? Why do some projects decline while others do not? What factors shape whether new forms of work organization have some long-term viability?

SIGNIFICANCE

The importance of understanding more about the concept of persistence of new programs or institutionalization of change should be apparent. If one is interested in bringing about long-term change in productivity, in quality of working life, and in labor-management relationships, then we must know more about why some change programs remain viable while others decline.

Unfortunately, there are few well-developed frameworks for understanding this problem area.[2] So it is difficult to go to the organizational literature to gain insights, in some systematic way, of why change programs do or do not decline over time. Yet there is some evidence that some of these new forms of work organization projects do not last.[3] Goodman and Dean examined the persistence of change in a heterogeneous sample of new forms of work organization projects. They selected organizations in which the change program had been successfully introduced and where some positive benefits had been identified. They interviewed participants four to five years after the project had been implemented. They wanted to know whether the change activities had persisted. Only one-third of the change programs designed to increase productivity and quality of working life exhibited some reasonable level of persistence. Two-thirds were either nonexistent or in decline. The program that exhibited the strongest persistence was a Scanlon Plan.

Of course, it is difficult to ascertain any national percentages about the number of these change programs that exhibit persistence. We will never know exactly how many of these new projects will decline and fail. However, common sense and growing empirical findings suggest that maintaining change is a significant problem for labor leaders, managers, and practitioners of organizational change.

INSTITUTIONALIZATION

A Definition

Institutionalization in this chapter is examined in terms of specific behaviors. We are assuming here that the persistence of employee involvement-type change programs can be studied by analyzing the persistence of specific behaviors associated with each program. For example, job switching is a set of behaviors often associated with autonomous work groups. To say that these and other behaviors associated with a program are practiced over time is to say that program is institutionalized. An institutionalized act, then, is defined as a behavior that is performed by two or more individuals, persists over time, and exists as part of the social reality or culture of the organization.

When we say that a behavior, such as making productivity suggestions by a high percentage of the work force for many years, is "part of the organization," we mean that members of the organization know how to make productivity suggestions, like to do it, and consider it appropriate for all its members to make suggestions. Remember, institutionalized behavior does not depend on any one individual; it is an organizational phenomenon.

In summary, the defining characteristics of institutionalization of an organizational change program are performance of the change program behaviors, persistence of these behaviors, and the incorporation of these behaviors in the daily functioning of the organization.

Degrees of Institutionalization

It should be clear from our definition of institutionalization that an act is all or nothing. Yet, an act may vary in terms of its persistence, the number of people in the organization performing the act, and the degree to which it exists as part of the organization. The problem in some of the current literature on change is the use of the words success and failure. This language clouds the crucial issue of representing and explaining degrees or levels of institutionalization. Most of the organizational cases we have reviewed cannot be described by simple labels of success or failure. Rather, we find various degrees of institutionalization.

The basic questions are: What do we mean by degrees of institutionalization? How do we measure these degrees?

We have identified five factors that constitute the degree of institutionalization.

1. *Knowledge of the behaviors.* Here we are interested merely in how many people know about these behaviors, and how much they know. Do they know how to perform these behaviors? Do they know the

purposes of the behaviors? For example, making productivity suggestions is a part of many gainsharing programs. However, if only some people know that they are supposed to make suggestions, the change program is not very institutionalized. This is why knowledge of the behaviors is important.

2. *Performance.* Here we are interested in how many people perform the behaviors, and how often they perform them. This is not as simple as it sounds. First, some behaviors are supposed to occur more often than others. A labor-management committee, for example, may be expected to meet occasionally, say, once a month, while team meetings are held weekly. This does not mean that team meetings are more institutionalized than the labor-management committee because they are more frequent. Second, some behaviors are supposed to be performed by more people than others. Most employees would be involved in team meetings, but only a few would take part in a labor-management committee. The idea is not merely to count the number of persons or the frequency of the behaviors, but rather to compare numbers and frequency to the levels required by the change program. Only then can reasonable comparisons be made.

3. *Preferences for the behaviors.* Here we are interested in how much people either like or dislike performing the behavior. In well-institutionalized change programs, most organizational members will like the critical program behaviors. In change programs on the decline, negative feelings are generally expressed toward the critical program behaviors.

4. *Normative consensus.* This aspect of institutionalization measures two levels of awareness among individuals in an organization: (1) that other people are performing the behaviors, and (2) that other people feel they should perform the behaviors. Normative consensus means the work group expects all members to support the expected program behaviors (e.g., suggestion making).

5. *Values.* The final measure of institutionalization is the extent to which people have developed values about the behaviors in the change program. Values are general ideas about how people ought to behave. For example, many change programs include behaviors consistent with the values of freedom and responsibility, as in autonomous work groups. In gainsharing, we expect to see the emergence and strengthening of values of cooperation, communication, and participation. The more people have developed these values, and the more aware they are that others have developed these values, the greater degree of institutionalization for the change program.

The five aspects above represent measures of the degree of institutionalization. But how do we combine them to get an overall measure? The answer is relatively simple, because the five aspects of institutionalization generally occur in the order we have presented above. People develop (1) knowledge about the behaviors, (2) they begin to perform them, (3) they start to develop feelings about the behaviors, (4) others come to be aware of these feelings, and (5) finally, values start to evolve concerning the behaviors. The further this sequence has progressed, the more the program has become institutionalized. Thus, in one program, people may know about the behaviors and perform them, but the other aspects of institutionalization may not be present. In another program, the behaviors may be known, performed, liked, and supported by norms and values. The latter program is obviously more institutionalized.

Summary

A change program designed to increase productivity and quality of working life is institutionalized when the behaviors required by it are performed by two or more persons over a period of time, and persist over time. We have argued that institutionalization is not an all-or-nothing question, but a matter of degree, and we have identified five aspects of institutionalization that measure the degree to which it has occurred. A program is institutionalized to the extent that it has progressed from levels of knowledge to performance, and finally to preferences, norms, and values that support the new institution.

FACTORS THAT AFFECT INSTITUTIONALIZATION

Now that we have a way to represent the degree of institutionalization, we can try to explain how and why it happens. Why are some gainsharing programs more institutionalized than others? Five processes affect the degree of institutionalization. These processes are important in explaining why some programs decline, while others grow and persist over time. The processes are:

1. *Training.* This is a broad category, which includes any source that helps an employee learn about a program such as gainsharing.
2. *Commitment.* High-commitment individuals invest a lot of themselves into a gainsharing program, and they will resist attempts to change behaviors that facilitate such a program. Commitment toward a new form of work behavior is enhanced when people voluntarily select that behavior in some public context.
3. *Reward allocation.* This refers to what rewards are distributed in the program, who gives and who gets them, and why they are distributed.
4. *Diffusion.* This refers to the extension of productivity programs into new work areas. If a productivity program is introduced into Department A, and it is transferred to Department B, diffusion has occurred.
5. *Feedback and correction.* These refer to the processes by which the organization can assess the degree of institutionalization, feed back

information, and take corrective action. Many organizations have no way of measuring how well their programs are doing. Therefore, they have no way of taking corrective actions. One advantage many gainsharing programs have are monthly bonus meetings where progress of the program is reviewed and changes are initiated.

We believe that these five processes are the major factors in predicting the degree of institutionalization a program will attain. There are, however, other important factors that affect these five processes. They are the structure of the change program and its organizational characteristics. Structure of the change program means such things as the goals of the change, how general it is, the critical roles associated with the change (consultant, facilitator, and so on). Organizational characteristics are the existing arrangements in the organization prior to the change program. It is the canvas on which the program will be painted. Organizational characteristics include such things as work force skill level, labor-management relations, and existing values and norms. It should be emphasized that these factors are important only to the extent that they affect the five processes listed above. For a clear example, see Chapter 4, which assesses how organizational characteristics affect whether gainsharing would "fit" into a particular organizational context.

EMPIRICAL FINDINGS

This section will discuss the findings of the authors, as well as others, about the processes and other organizational factors related to institutionalization. We will consider findings about the processes, structure of the change, and organizational characteristics, to see if studies bear out what we have argued in the section above. The main results are from a study by Goodman and Dean,[4] but the findings of other authors have been included where appropriate.

FIVE PROCESSES

Training

Training is providing information to organization members about new work behaviors. Training is important in three major situations: training as the program is started, retraining after the program has been in place for a while, and training of new incoming members of the organization. Most organizations do an extensive amount of initial training but are less consistent in retraining and in the training of new members.

Golembiewski and Carrigan report that retraining can lead to persistence.[5] In a program designed to change the practices of high-level managers in the sales division of a manufacturing firm, they found that a retraining exercise several months after the program was instituted strengthened the persistence of the program. Similarly, Ivancevich compared Management by Objectives programs in two large manufacturing firms.[6] One firm had a retraining exercise, while the other did not. After three years, the program in the former plant was more institutionalized. Goodman, in a study of a change project in an underground coal mine, reports that a decrease in frequency of training after the first year of the project contributed to its decline.[7] Organizations vary in their attention to training new members once a program is in place. Goodman and Dean[8] found that programs which trained new members were likely to be more institutionalized.

Commitment

Commitment refers to how much of themselves people are willing to invest in a new program. For example, a high degree of commitment toward a gainsharing program should increase the chances that behaviors would continue or be institutionalized. Commitment to a behavior is increased when people voluntarily select that behavior in some public context.[9] For example, an autonomous work-group program seemed to grow and develop when personal choices were carried out freely. Later in this program, when the organization required others to participate in the program, it began to decline. Also, it is found that programs offering more frequent commitment opportunities were more institutionalized than those with limited commitment opportunities. Ivancevich attributes the failure of a Management by Objectives program to lack of commitment by top management.[10] Walton, on the other hand, notes high levels of commitment in several successful programs of work innovation.[11] Other studies report that consistent levels of commitment throughout the organization are necessary for persistence of a change program designed to increase productivity and quality of working life.[12] Chapter 8 reviews nineteen years of experience with a Scanlon plan, wherein commitment by top management has contributed significantly to gainsharing viability.

Reward Allocation

This is the process by which rewards are distributed to employees in connection with the change program. Three aspects of the reward allocation process are important in understanding institutionalization: (1) the types of rewards that are available, (2) the links between behaviors and rewards, and (3) problems of inequity in the distribution of the rewards. The types of rewards related to work are generally categorized by psychologists as extrinsic or intrinsic. Extrinsic rewards, such as pay and promotion, are given by someone else. Intrinsic rewards, such as feelings of responsibility and accomplishment, come from within the individual. Many organizational change programs have been based on the assumption that intrinsic rewards are sufficient for institutionalization. However, Goodman and Walton have questioned this assumption.[13]

Programs that combine both extrinsic and intrinsic rewards have attained the highest degree of institutionalization,[14] while programs with intrinsic rewards alone have been less institutionalized. Of the programs evaluated, gainsharing made available both types of rewards.

The second aspect of reward allocation concerns the link between the behaviors required by the change program and the rewards. It is important that rewards be linked to the actual performance of the behaviors, as opposed to mere participation in the program. We have found that there is a higher degree of institutionalization in programs where the link between performance and rewards is strong. This is consistent with statements by Vroom and Lawler concerning reward allocation.[15] Reward allocation links are found to be psychologically strong in gainsharing studies.

A final aspect of reward allocation is the potential for problems of inequity. Inequity problems occur when employees feel they are not being fairly compensated for the work they are doing. Results of studies have shown that new programs often become complicated by these problems. For example, Locke, Sirota, and Wolfson report on a job-enrichment program in a government agency that did not become institutionalized.[16] The major reason was that workers were not compensated financially for the new skills they had learned. It is important to note that they had never been promised more money, but the fact that they were accomplishing more for the same pay was perceived as inequitable. Goodman reports similar problems developed among autonomous work groups in a coal mine.[17] Part of the program involved job switching, whereby each new member would eventually learn all the jobs in the crew. The problem evolved because the entire crew was to be paid eventually at the same (higher) rate of pay originally earned only by certain crew members. Since it had taken years for some of the workers to attain this rate, they felt it inequitable that the other crew members should come up so easily. This contributed to the decline in the change program. There are no reported problems with inequity and gainsharing. Its reward allocation structure complements the overall organization reward system. Obviously, if the overall system is unfair, gainsharing will reinforce those areas of inequity.

Diffusion

Diffusion refers to the spread of the change from one part of an organization to another. Diffusion is significant because the more the change program becomes diffused, the stronger the level of institutionalization. As long as the program is restricted to one part of the organization, people may not feel compelled to take it seriously, or they may object to it. But as diffusion occurs, people in other parts of the organization will begin to consider whether they should participate. As the program spreads, there also are chances for counterattacks on its validity.

The importance of diffusion for institutionalization has been noted by Goodman in the coal mine study mentioned above.[18] In this case, when the intervention failed to diffuse beyond the original target group, it was perceived as inappropriate and failed to become institutionalized. Similar findings have been reported in a study of work teams in several plants of a large manufacturing company.[19] When the innovations continued to be limited to a few parts of the organization, they were seen as inappropriate to the company as a whole and failed to become institutionalized. However, the researchers in this study caution against diffusion that is too rapid, without the supports of widespread understanding, acceptance, and resources that are needed for such an effort. Without these requisites, the program will collapse under its own weight. In general, then, a moderate course must be found between no diffusion and diffusion that is too ambitious for the resources supporting it. When applied to gainsharing however, diffusion is slightly different, since gainsharing is organizationwide by definition, and the entire organization is affected at the same time. Nevertheless, in multiplant organizations, diffusion of gainsharing across similar plants is important to ensure long-run viability of these programs.

Feedback and Correction

Feedback and correction are the processes by which an organization finds out how well the program is doing and takes steps to correct problems that have emerged. One of the common findings was that what actually occurred in change programs was often different from what was intended.[20] The organizations had seldom established any formal way of detecting whether the intended change was in place. Only in the most institutionalized programs in our study did mechanisms exist for feedback and correction. Walton says that lack of feedback and correction mechanisms is a major cause of the failure to institutionalize.[21] In another study, feedback mechanisms were in place, so that information about the program was available.[22] However, no one did anything about the problems that were detected. Perhaps the information was not available to those who had the power to do something. Or perhaps the information was available to them, but they had other reasons for their inaction. In any case, both sensing and correction mechanisms are important in attaining a high degree of institutionalization.

STRUCTURE OF THE CHANGE

Now that we have discussed the findings about the processes, we can discuss some of the factors that affect the processes. First, we will discuss the structure of the change, which refers to the unique aspects of the change program. Specifically, we will talk about the goals of the programs, the formal mechanisms associated with the programs, the level of intervention in the programs, how consultants were used, and sponsorship for the programs.

Goals

One way to characterize goals is by whether they are specific and limited or general and diffuse. In our study,[23] we found that programs designed to improve productivity or quality of working life with specific goals became more institutionalized than those with diffuse goals.

Another way to characterize goals is by whether they are common or complementary. Common goals are those desired by both parties to the change (for example, improving safety). Complementary goals aim to give each party something it wants, but the parties want different things (for example, productivity for management and bonuses for employees). In *Assessing Organizational Change,* Goodman indicates that common goals can contribute better to institutionalization.[24]

Formal Mechanisms

Most change programs have some new organizational form and procedures associated with them. These include, for example, the self-governing decisions made by autonomous work groups and by gainsharing production and screening committees. Here we are interested in how formal these arrangements are. For example, are meetings scheduled in advance? Are procedures written down? In general, we have found that programs with more formal mechanisms and procedures attain higher levels of institutionalization. For example, well-institutionalized gainsharing organizations operate with a "Memo of Understanding," which describes the goals, policies, procedures, and structure of gainsharing.

Level of Intervention

Here we are interested in whether the productivity program was introduced in a part of the organization, or in the whole organization. In our study, programs that were introduced throughout the organizational unit became more institutionalized than programs limited to a part of the organization. One of the problems with smaller-scale intervention is that people from other parts of the organization sometimes attempt to sabotage the program. This was true in four of the organizations that we studied, none of whose programs were very institutionalized.[25]

Consultants

Many organizations that undertake a change program employ a consultant to help them. Some organizations use consultants for considerably longer periods than others. We found that firms that rely on consultants for a long time are less able to develop their own capacity for managing the program. Consequently, after the consultant leaves, they are less able to institutionalize the program. The greater the dependence on the consultant, the less successful the program.

Sponsorship

Another factor that appears to affect the degree of institutionalization is the presence of a sponsor. The sponsor is an organizational member in a position of power who initiates the program, makes sure that resources are devoted to it, and defends it against attacks from others in the organization. If the sponsor leaves the organization, often no one steps in to perform these necessary functions, thus making it harder for institutionalization to occur.

The withdrawal of sponsorship can arise from common organizational practices. For example, Crockett reports a major organizational intervention in the State Department, in which substantial changes were observed to persist for years.[26] However, when the initiator of the project, a political appointee, left office, the organization reverted to its traditional form. The new administrator was not sympathetic to the values and the structure of the change program. As support and legitimacy of the program decreased, the degree of institutionalization declined. Similar effects are reported by Wanton[27] and Levine.[28] In some cases, the sponsor left temporarily;[29] in other cases, the sponsors focused attention on other organizational matters.[30] In all cases, however, the persistence of the new structures declined.

The key factor is not so much the success of sponsors, but whether the replacement provides the same level of sponsorship. In some gainsharing programs we have observed, the programs exhibit institutionalization although there was natural turnover at high plant levels. In these cases, sponsorship from the new manager was still in place.

ORGANIZATIONAL CHARACTERISTICS

Organizational characteristics are those aspects of the organization that exist prior to the change program and have an effect on the degree of institutionalization a program can attain. These characteristics are important to the extent that they affect the five processes we have discussed—training, commitment, reward allocation, diffusion, and feedback/correction. Chapters 3 through 6 focus on those organizational characteristics known to affect gainsharing success and failure.

Congruence with Organizational Values and Structure

Whatever the nature of the change program, one important factor for institutionalization is the degree of congruence or incongruence between the change program and existing organizational characteristics. In general, the more congruence exists, the greater the likelihood of institutionalization. Various organizational characteristics may be important in understanding congruence. In all cases studied by the authors, congruence between the change program and management philosophy led to higher degrees of institutionalization.

Several other authors have come to similar conclusions about congruence and institutionalization. Fadem suggests that when there is a great degree of incongruence between the change program and corporate policies, the project is less likely to be institutionalized.[31] Seashore and Bowers explain the level of institutionalization in terms of the congruence between the organizational change and the values and motives of the individual participant.[32] They found that a higher level of institutionalization resulted when the changes were more congruent with the values and motives of the employees. Mohrman, et al., studied organizational change in a school system.[33] They found that change programs were more likely to become institutionalized when the intervention structure was congruent with the existing authority system. Walton has shown that in some change programs, there is a gap between the behaviors required by the change and the skills possessed by the employees.[34] The greater the gap (or the more incongruence), the lower the expected degree of institutionalization.

Levine describes a set of innovations attempted at a state university.[35] Some of the innovations were more congruent with organizational norms and values than others. Over time, those innovations that were congruent were more likely to persist than those that were incongruent. Similar conclusions were drawn by Warwick and Crockett about a major organizational change undertaken in the State Department.[36] The new structure favored the taking of initiative by lower level officials, although this was incongruent with the reward system. Not surprisingly, the change did not last. Finally, Miller shows that a change program must be congruent with cultural norms and values, as well as with those peculiar to the organization.[37] An organizational innovation in several weaving mills in India was hampered because it did not provide for the workers' need for recognition by superiors, which is strong in the Indian culture. Chapter 8 shows how a gainsharing change program, which was congruent with an organization's culture, achieved long lasting changes in cooperation and participation as measured by suggestion making.

In summary, we have shown that programs can decline as a result of incongruence with existing organizational or cultural norms and values, the organizational authority system, or individual skills and motives. Of course, if those are already in conflict with one another, it will be difficult for programs to be congruent.

Stability of the Environment

From the evidence reported so far, it should be clear that institutionalizing a change program in an organization is a difficult task, even in the best situations. In some situations the added instability of the environment only makes things worse. In our study, there were only two cases of instability in the environment.[38] In these cases there was a major decline in demand for the organization's products, which led to curtailments in the work force. This, in turn, changed the composition of many of the groups that were an integral part of the change program. These groups became less effective, lowering the degree of institutionalization. Similar results were observed in another study as an economic recession led to layoffs and bumping.[39] Environment instabilities such as these represent a major obstacle to institutionalization.

Union

The union can play a major role in determining the degree of institutionalization. If there are high levels of labor-management conflict in the collective-bargaining area, we expect this to spill over to the productivity programs and negatively affect their viability. If the relationships at the plant or site level are cooperative, the productivity plans will exhibit longer-term viability. In other studies there is evidence that the quality of the relationship between the local district and the international has a critical impact on the viability of any productivity program.[40]

HOW DO YOU MAKE
PRODUCTIVITY PROGRAMS LAST?

The above discussion identifies a set of factors that can contribute to the persistence of productivity and similar types of labor-management programs. It is important for the reader to remember that these factors to promote institutionalization, which are reintroduced below, are based on empirical findings, not on just the opinions of the authors.

What should we do to make productivity programs last?

1. *Selecting Organizations.* Some organizations simply should not get involved in productivity-type change programs. A careful diagnosis is needed to be sure an organization is ready or not. The more that labor and management can acknowledge that some of their organizational units should not get involved, the more realistic their working relationship will be, and the more likely that a change program, when initiated, will last. Some of the reasons for not getting involved include:
   a. Unstable economic environment. Organizations experiencing economic instability and high fluctuations in their labor force will be hard put to mount a successful long-run productivity program.
   b. Instability in leadership environment. If there is likely to be turnover in key labor or management sponsors of the change program, it is best to delay the start of a program or abandon it.

    c. Mistrust between employees and management or union and management. If there are some basic problems in the relationships between employees and employers or union and management, a productivity program change effort should not be introduced. These problems need to be solved before a program such as gainsharing is considered.

2. *Plan for Institutionalization in the Beginning.* In most of the labor-management change programs we have reviewed, attention has been devoted largely to starting up a program. Little attention has been given to maintaining the program. A program has greater chances of success if mechanisms for maintaining it are considered in the early planning stages. That is, maintenance needs to be designed into the front end of a program.

3. *The Fit Problems.* There needs to be a good fit (or congruence) between the organization's values, philosophy, and structure and the nature of the change program. When the proposed change program (e.g., autonomous work groups or gainsharing) is in conflict with the organization's value system (e.g., high authoritarian), it simply will not last. How does a low-trust, high-authoritarian hierarchical system move toward a more participative system? The answer has to be in a carefully designed evolutionary change program that will occur over an extended time period.[41]

4. *Characteristics of Changes.* While no one program is suited to all organizations, the following characteristics should ensure a long-run effort.
    a. Specific statement of goals, written out and approved by labor and management.
    b. Specific procedures to implement labor and management program activities. These activities are complex processes. Failure to clarify them can lead to trouble. Where feasible, there should be some formalization of issues, such as who should be in the labor-management committee, when it should meet, how members should rotate, what are the boundaries of the committee's work. Formalization increases long-run viability of the change program.
    c. Total system intervention. Change programs that can be introduced into the total organizational unit, rather than in part, will last longer, but only if sufficient organizational resources are allocated to them.

5. *Training Over Time.* Most productivity programs advocate training to start up a program. We advocate periodic retraining over time to reaffirm program change principles. Special training programs for new organizational members are necessary to ensure long-run viability.

6. *Commitment.* High commitment will facilitate the persistence of most labor-management change programs. High commitment comes from (1) voluntary participation in program activities, and (2) opportunities

for recommitment over time. Productivity programs that offer continuous opportunities for recommitment exhibit higher levels of persistence.
7. *Effective Reward Systems.* The design of organizational rewards systems can substantially determine the longevity of a productivity program. An effective reward system should:
   a. Include both extrinsic (e.g., pay) and intrinsic (e.g., more autonomy) rewards.
   b. Link rewards to specific behaviors required by the productivity program (e.g., assuming greater decision-making responsibilities).
   c. Introduce a mechanism for revising the reward system. It is unlikely rewards will maintain their attractiveness over time. A successful program will need some procedure, approved by labor and management, to revise rewards over time.
   d. Minimize problems of inequity over compensation issues.
8. *Diffusion.* As the productivity program is introduced in one unit (e.g., a department), it must be quickly spread to include all organizational units at one location. Isolated productivity programs will have trouble in persisting.
9. *Feedback and Correction.* One major characteristic of many productivity program failures we have studied was the lack of mechanisms by which the organization could judge how well programs were functioning. But they were either not being performed or not being performed well. A direct and accurate feedback mechanism for measuring performance of program activities is necessary if the change program is to adjust, grow, and remain viable.

SUMMARY

Many productivity and employee involvement programs, although initially successful, do not persist over time. We now know some of the critical processes that affect long-run viability or failure of these programs. The set of action plans presented here ensure the long-run viability of productivity programs, in general, and specifically for gainsharing.

Notes

1. P. S. Goodman, *Assessing Organizational Change: The Rushton Quality of Work Experiment* (New York: Wiley-Interscience, 1979).
2. P. S. Goodman and J. W. Dean, Jr., "Creating Long-Term Organizational Change," in *Change in Organizations,* ed. P. S. Goodman (San Francisco: Jossey-Bass, 1982); R. E. Walton, "Establishing and Maintaining High Commitment Work Systems," in *The Organizational Life Cycle,* ed. J. R. Kimberly and R. H. Miles (San Francisco: Jossey-Bass, 1980).

3. P. H. Mirvis and D. N. Berg, eds., *Failures in Organization Development and Change* (New York: Wiley-Interscience, 1977); Goodman and Dean, "Creating Long-Term Organizational Change," note 2, above.

4. Ibid.

5. R. I. Golembiewski and S. B. Carrigan, "The Persistence of Laboratory-Induced Changes in Organizational Styles," *Administrative Science Quarterly*, 15, 1970, 330–340.

6. J. M. Ivancevich, "Changes in Performance in a Management by Objectives Program," *Administrative Science Quarterly*, 19, 1974, 563–574.

7. Goodman, *Assessing Organizational Change*, note 1, above.

8. Goodman and Dean, "Creating Long-Term Organizational Change," note 2, above.

9. Ibid.

10. J. M. Ivancevich, "A Longitudinal Assessment of Management by Objectives," *Administrative Science Quarterly*, 17, 1972, 126–138.

11. Walton, "Establishing and Maintaining High Commitment Work Systems," note 2, above.

12. Goodman, *Assessing Organizational Change*, note 1, above.

13. Goodman and Dean, "Creating Long-Term Organizational Change," note 2, above; Walton, "Establishing and Maintaining High Commitment Work Systems," note 2, above.

14. Goodman and Dean, "Creating Long-Term Organizational Change," note 2, above.

15. V. H. Vroom, *Work and Motivation* (New York: Wiley, 1964); E. E. Lawler, *Pay and Organizational Effectiveness* (New York: McGraw-Hill, 1971).

16. E. A. Locke, D. Sirota, and A. D. Wolfson, "An Experimental Case Study of the Successes and Failures of Job Enrichment in a Government Agency," *Journal of Applied Psychology*, 61, 1976, 701–711.

17. Goodman, *Assessing Organizational Change*, note 1, above.

18. Ibid.

19. E. Trist and C. O'Dwyer, "The Limits of Laissez-Faire as a Socio-Technical Change Strategy," in *The Innovative Organization*, eds. R. Zager and M. P. Rosow (New York: Pergamon Press, 1982).

20. Goodman and Dean, "Creating Long-Term Organizational Change," note 2, above.

21. Walton, "Establishing High Commitment Work Systems," note 2, above.

22. P. S. Goodman, personal correspondence; R. E. Walton, "Teaching an Old Dog Food New Tricks," *The Wharton Magazine*, Winter 1979, 38–47.

23. Goodman and Dean, "Creating Long-Term Organizational Change," note 2, above.

24. Goodman, *Assessing Organizational Change*, note 1, above.

25. Goodman and Dean, "Creating Long-Term Organizational Change," note 2, above.

26. W. Crockett, "Introducing Change to a Government Agency," in *Failures in Organizational Development: Cases and Essays for Learning*, ed. P. Mirvis and D. Berg (New York: Wiley-Interscience, 1977).

27. Walton, "Teaching an Old Dog Food New Tricks," note 22, above.

28. A. Levine, *Why Innovation Fails* (Albany: State University of New York Press, 1980).

29. L. L. Frank and J. R. Hackman, "A Failure of Job Enrichment: The Case of the Change That Wasn't," *Journal of Applied Behavioral Science,* 11, no. 4, 1975, 413–436.
30. R. E. Walton, "The Diffusion of New York Structures: Explaining Why Success Didn't Take," *Organizational Dynamics,* Winter 1975, 3–21.
31. J. Fadem, "Fitting Computer-Aided Technology to Workplace Requirements: An Example" (paper presented at the 13th Annual Meeting and Technical Conference of the Numerical Control Society, Cincinnati, March 1976).
32. S. E. Seashore and D. G. Bowers, "Durability of Organizational Change," in *Organization Development: Theory, Practice, and Research,* eds. W. L. French, C. H. Bell, Jr., and R. A. Zawicki (Dallas: Business Publications, 1978).
33. S. A. Mohrman, et al, "A Survey Feedback and Problem Solving Intervention in a School District: We'll Take the Survey But You Can Keep the Feedback," in *Failures in Organizational Development: Cases and Essays for Learning,* ed. P. Mirvis and D. Berg (New York: Wiley-Interscience, 1977).
34. Walton, "Establishing High Commitment Work Systems," note 2, above.
35. Levine, *Why Innovation Fails,* note 28, above.
36. D. P. Warwick, *A Theory of Public Bureaucracy* (Cambridge, Mass.: Harvard University Press, 1975); Crockett, "Introducing Change," note 26, above.
37. E. J. Miller, "Socio-Technical Systems in Weaving, 1953–1970: A Follow-up Study," *Human Relations,* 28, no. 4, 1975, 349–386.
38. Goodman and Dean, "Creating Long-Term Organizational Change," note 2, above.
39. Paul S. Goodman, personal correspondence.
40. Goodman, *Assessing Organizational Change,* note 1, above.
41. Goodman and Dean, "Creating Long-Term Organizational Change," note 2, above.

Chapter 8

Nineteen Years of Experience with the Scanlon Plan: Southwest Corp.

Brian Graham-Moore

KEY ASPECTS OF SOUTHWEST'S PLAN

Traditional Gainsharing and the Three Basic Elements

Southwest Corp. no longer exists. It was once part of ABC Corp., a Fortune 500 company. Now, only remnants of ABC exist after a hostile takeover. Most of ABC's constituent divisions have been sold, assets liquidated, and employees released. Until this catastrophic change, its largest plant was Southwest, which operated with a traditional Scanlon Plan for almost 20 years. This case reveals a frank documentation of Southwest's history with traditional gainsharing. Interviews started before the plan was installed by a leading Scanlon Plan consultant, over 20 years ago. Interim interviews and surveys were conducted during a 19-year period. One year after Southwest's sell-off, interviews were conducted with former Southwest managers to collect their unconstrained views of how the Scanlon Plan fared during this 19-year period. Unfettered by loyalty and disillusioned by corporate's poor decision making that necessitated the selling of Southwest's leading plant, the managers provided information giving a balanced view of the Scanlon plan.

Before proceeding with Southwest's experience with the Scanlon plan, a clear description of their plan is necessary. Southwest's Scanlon plan is a companywide productivity improvement plan. It consists of three basic elements: A philosophy of cooperation, an involvement system designed to increase efficiency and reduce costs, and a formula that permits a bonus to be paid based on increases in performance.

Southwest's Philosophy

All managers believe that employer-employee cooperation is essential. Teamwork is promoted in the belief that both worker and manager have valuable information to share. This sharing of knowledge provides the worker with the means to collaborate and cooperate with management. Management leads, but the workers actively participate. It is important to value openness.

Southwest's Involvement System

The traditional Scanlon committee structure was established in the organization and thus became a new mechanism for communication. This structure facilitates the communication, evaluation, and disposition of suggestions. Two kinds of committees were organized. A production committee was formed in each department or working unit and consisted of carefully selected workers. The screening committee consisted of management and selected workers and one supervisor from the production committees. The functions and authority of both committees is covered in greater detail later in this chapter.[1]

Southwest's Formula

After 18 months of deliberation, Southwest Corp. management opted for a traditional Scanlon plan (see Chapter 3 for other choices), and a baseline measurement of productivity was developed. This baseline, or base ratio, was determined between (1) total labor costs, including factory and salary payroll, vacations, and holidays, and (2) sales value of production, including adjustments for such items as inventory fluctuations price variations. The formula relates total human resource costs to the sales value of production.

$$\text{Base ratio} = \frac{\text{Total human resource costs}}{\substack{\text{Value of sales including inventory changes} \\ \text{(finished and work-in-process inventories)}}}$$

This relationship between the human resource costs and the production value is the normal ratio of labor to output, or the base ratio. Any increase in the denominator (sales value of production) relative to the numerator (total human resource costs) represents an increase in labor productivity. This increase is a bonus to be distributed to everyone on the participating payroll. Therefore, with the entire organization focusing its attention on this relationship between human resource investment and performance, the formula encouraged employees to learn more productivity-linked behaviors in order to do better than the base ratio.

The philosophy of cooperation, the involvement system, and the formula make up what is generally known as the Scanlon plan at Southwest Corp. These three elements mutually reinforce each other in definitive ways as we shall see.

Southwest's experience with the plan is an example of a well-managed firm that successfully increases its productivity goals through continual improvement.

Productivity Outcomes at Southwest

Over the course of 19 years, Southwest Corp. has seen many changes to its ways of doing business. For example, in 1970, virtually all of their output went to one customer as private label business. In 1988, they did almost as much industrial trade as they did private label. In 1973, the first OPEC crisis hit all manufacturers using petro-chemical raw materials with a 400 percent increase in raw material cost. Without adjusting the Scanlon ratio for equity, that would have created huge Scanlon bonuses without any commensurate increase in labor productivity. Then, in 1976, Southwest Corp. increased their capacity with a huge capital investment that nearly doubled their ability to produce. In this expansion, the work force increased by approximately 25 percent. In the late 1980s their work force expanded an additional 13 percent due to acquisitions. Thus, in 1988, they could produce twice what they could produce in 1970 with a 38 percent increase in total work force. These kinds of changes can wreck a Scanlon bonus calculation if left unadjusted. Nevertheless, Southwest Corp. management was able to pay bonuses. Exhibit 8.1 represents the annual average bonus percent of pay from 1971 to 1989. The range of annual average bonuses for this 19-year period is from 2 percent to over 22 percent with the overall annual average of 8.8 percent. To understand this, take the sum of your own annual pay for the past 19 years and multiply it by 8.8 percent! *All* Southwest Corp. employees (except the plant manager) received this bonus on top of competitive wages and salaries.

Care must be exercised in the interpretation of any measure of productivity, such as Exhibit 8.1, since output per man-hour can be influenced by many factors. Obviously the gainsharing plan is one of these factors. Even after 19 years, it is difficult to determine just how great a role the gainsharing played at Southwest Corp. in increasing productivity. However, the intangible benefits provided solely by gainsharing were more than enough to justify its existence and provide a reason for its continuation.

While the overall history of the bonus is good, Southwest's single Scanlon ratio evolved into a modified formula to measure true increases in productivity while retaining equity for all. For example, beginning with the single ratio, management soon saw that the labor value added of produced goods was higher than those bought on the outside and merely passed through packaging and distribution. Therefore, they calculated two ratios separately (the split ratio discussed in Chapter 3). These ratios are then combined in order to value total labor productivity. This split ratio is more precise given the characteristics of their business. Also, Southwest Corp.'s management was able to adjust the denominator of the Scanlon single ratio due to the OPEC crisis in 1973 and still show a productivity bonus.

Exhibit 8.1 Average Annual Bonus Percent

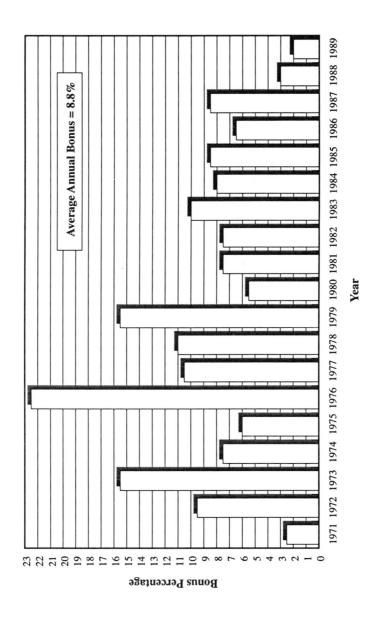

Through the years, other formula changes have occurred at Southwest Corp., yet trust in the fairness of management has been maintained. Clearly, if the objective of the formula is to reward cooperative efforts and true labor productivity, then equity for both the company and workers is important. The worker must trust management's construction and calculation of the formula. On the other hand, management must not feel that the formula is a give-away. Indeed, one of the concerns of Southwest Corp.'s management about the plan has been the efficacy of the formula. This proves to be more than an empirical problem, as corporate constantly challenged the level of bonuses paid.

Exhibit 8.1 shows that Southwest's best bonus ever was almost 23 percent of annual pay in 1976, but beginning in 1977, the effects of doubling plant capacity and the significant increases to the payroll caused these outcomes:

1. bonuses were lower, yet productivity was good (there were more people on the participating payroll);
2. 1970 was no longer a good historical base (it was until 1977); and
3. corporate's countervailing pressure against high bonuses became greater.

When those outcomes are combined with large changes in Southwest's product mix, management had to develop policies that would permit recalculation every six months, if necessary. This review by management compares each six month period to the previous six and then this is compared with the previous year. Gains in productivity are captured that permit the company to remain competitive. However, since 1977, bonuses have ranged from 2 percent to 15.5 percent and averaged 8 percent. The average for the years 1971 to 1976 is 10.6 percent. Thus, by careful adjustment management balanced the need for recalculating the productivity bonus while not reducing opportunities to achieve a bonus by working smarter.

Unfortunately, the running battle between corporate and plant management was exacerbated in 1976, the year of the best bonus. Strong beliefs held by corporate managers prevailed. They firmly believed that productivity increases greater than 15 percent were not possible. Therefore, they argued any bonus payout above 15 percent was a give-away. Since 1976 only 1979 approached such levels of payout. Most plant level Southwest managers felt compromised by corporate's leveling of bonus opportunities. 1979 was probably just as productive as 1976. The extra .5 percent was plant management's way of protesting the cap to the Scanlon formula.

To summarize, the purpose of the formula and its accurate formulation is equity—a fair share for all. As it has been stated:

> If the employees decide favorably and the formula is arrived at from the historical accounting facts, then the ratio is set at the most representative position consistent with current market and production demands. The ratio is subject to continuous study and evaluation to insure the optimal equity of everyone. If the ratio

jeopardizes the company's fiscal and competitive position, the deficiency in equity for all is recognized and the ratio is appropriately modified. If the ratio severely disadvantages the employee investors, the inequality is clearly defined and the appropriate change is made.[2]

THE INVOLVEMENT SYSTEM
AS STRUCTURE AND PROCESS

Often overlooked and sometimes overstated, the involvement system is the structure and process of the plan. There are few in-depth studies of this system in the gainsharing literature. Therefore, understanding the characteristics of the system, as exemplified at the Southwest Corp. plant, is the objective of this section.

Since the plan was introduced by a highly skilled Scanlon consultant, the introductory process at Southwest Corp. included the three steps basic to any Scanlon plan introduction:

1. presentation of the three components of the plan, i.e., the philosophy, the involvement system, and the formula;
2. election (companywide) to determine if the plan will be instituted for a trial year; and
3. installation of the productivity formula and the involvement system, assuming a positive vote.

These steps appear simple. But it is important to remember that each one of them is itself a detailed process requiring careful execution. Southwest Corp. management spent a great deal of time discussing exactly how these steps would be achieved.

After the presentation of the plan by the consultant a vote was taken. The next step was to staff the production and screening committees. A description of the production and screening committees, their governing procedures, and guidelines for handling suggestions was distributed to the work force in order to help them understand the plan. Management then decided on the number of production committees (eight—one for each department in 1971). This was the number of committee members needed to ensure balanced representation among departments, shifts, and job levels (three to five committee members per department depending on the size of the department and the number of night shift workers). A provision was made for the numbers to be changed at a later time if the circumstances warranted. After 19 years, 10 production committees were needed.

Southwest Corp. management felt that representation was essential to the success of the plan for two reasons. First, it guaranteed good representation of ideas. By making certain all functional units of the company were represented, the involvement system obtains input that could reflect the differing viewpoints of all employees. Second, good representation aids in the process of peer review. Critical evaluation of all suggestions on many different levels is made possible through adequate representation of the work force.

The purpose of the committee is to use workers' ideas to improve the performance of their jobs. The production committee consists of the departmental supervisor and at least two employee representatives. Suggestions for improved operations are presented to this production committee as they occur. At least once a month the production committee reviews the suggestions that have been submitted. Suggestions not affecting other departments and not exceeding a specified dollar amount are put into effect at the departmental level by the production committee. Originally suggestions costing up to $200 could be implemented without review. This amount grew to $500 in 1989. Also, any suggestion rejected at the production committee level always receives another hearing by the screening committee once a month.

The screening committee is made up of management and hourly representatives from the production committees. Its three main activities are to (1) review and evaluate suggestions, (2) announce the bonus (or deficit), and (3) discuss the business reasons for the bonus or deficit. These three activities are discussed further below.

- The purpose of reviewing and evaluating suggestions is to process all relevant information and to guarantee that collective points of view intersect at the point of decision. The ultimate decision, however, is the plant manager's in virtually all Scanlon plans.
- After five years Southwest's plant manager knew that immediate feedback was necessary for the Scanlon plan to remain effective. He believed that the announcement of the bonus or deficit provided some of this feedback. Each department or functional area had one representative who listened to the controller's Scanlon report. Then the representatives would leave the meeting and announce the bonus or deficit in their respective work areas. However, his strongest belief was that the most important feedback was the rapid implementation of suggestions.
- The third principal activity of the screening committee, discussing the reasons for the bonus or deficit, includes a discussion of how the bonus or deficit affects the company and its objectives in terms of production costs. Emphasis of this activity depends on the circumstances. At Southwest, this discussion could be anywhere from two minutes to half an hour. Within a mature Scanlon company, the discussion of why a firm can or cannot achieve its goals always surfaces within the screening committee meetings. As a result of these discussions, the screening committee becomes a task-oriented classroom for combining individual and corporate goals to achieve success.

THE SUGGESTION-MAKING PROCESS

Southwest Corp. developed specific procedures for handling suggestions. Explanation of these procedures should provide the reader with a global overview of the involvement system, and more importantly, how the production and screening committees make this system work. Although concrete procedures for handling suggestions are described below, it is the *process* of handling them that insures the involvement system. In other words, one should always keep in mind that these procedures are by no means absolute. The important thing is that Southwest Corp. managers made every effort to deal with co-workers face to face in all aspects of the suggestion-making process. By doing this, lines of communication were developed and expanded on at all job levels. The involvement system provided an employee not only with the opportunity to exchange ideas with his peers but, more importantly, to exchange ideas with his supervisors. In this respect most Scanlon plans offer the distinct advantage of increased communication that leads to increased employee participation in the overall attainment of company objectives. The following Scanlon procedures used by Southwest were not intended to become a bureaucratic device that interfered with or took the place of open communication.

1. Someone with a suggestion should submit it in writing to a departmental representative.
2. The supervisor or departmental representative should discuss the suggestion with the person making it, discuss it with others who may be affected, and take appropriate action as soon as possible.
3. At least once a month, both committees should review the status of previously discussed suggestions, should expedite delayed suggestions, and should discuss new suggestions.
4. Suggestions involving more than the specified dollar amount should be referred to the screening committee.
5. The production committee should assign the responsibility for following through on delayed suggestions to one of its members.
6. The production committee should keep records of its activities. These records should include all submitted suggestions and their status—action proposed, action taken, and so on.
7. By a certain day of the month, the production committee should submit all suggestions received during that month to the screening committee.
8. All suggestions and actions taken by the production committee should be reported to the screening committee monthly.

The production committee can take one of five actions on the suggestions it receives:

1. Reject the suggestion with carefully stated reasons.
2. Accept the suggestion and use it.

3. Accept the suggestion and place it under investigation. (A suggestion is normally placed under investigation when there is insufficient information to make a decision or when it is necessary to ascertain if net savings offset the cost of implementing the suggestion).
4. Accept the suggestion by recommending it to the screening committee. (Such a suggestion is usually one a production committee feels should be placed into effect but costs over the specified dollar amount).
5. If production committee members cannot agree on the acceptability of a suggestion, it is referred to screening committee.

In summary, the involvement system is a new committee structure superimposed on the organization to facilitate communication, evaluation, and disposition of suggestions. As mentioned, two kinds of committees are established—production and screening. Obviously, the involvement system is an integral part of the Scanlon plan. The production committee and screening committee coupled with employee participation and cooperation help determine the success of the plan. For this reason, it is important that all employees have a basic understanding of this system and how it operates.

The human resources manager developed these guidelines for production committee members. As they are elected to their positions, they meet with him to review and discuss these responsibilities:

As the Production Committee Representative you will have certain responsibilities in coordinating the Scanlon activities for your department. Since you were elected as the representative for your department by your fellow employees, it will be necessary for you to spend some time in soliciting suggestions, following through on suggestions, giving clear and accurate reports to your group as to the status of their suggestions, and also doing your homework for the Screening Meeting. Remember your fellow employees are counting on you!

1. *How much money can we spend to implement a suggestion?* Production Committees are authorized to spend up to $200; Department Heads up to $400; and the Plant Manager is authorized on expenditures up to $500. Any expenditure of more than $500 would require capital expenditure and needs to be budgeted.
2. *When should our Production Committee Meeting be held?* This meeting can be held any time prior to the Screening Committee Meetings. It probably would be helpful if you held the meeting two or three days before the Screening Meeting so you can do some last-minute checking. You may also wish to hold more than one meeting in a month, if suggestion activity warrants it.
3. *Where should our meeting be held?* The meeting can be held anywhere at any time. The most important thing is that we meet!
4. *How soon should a suggestion be put "in use"?* If a suggestion is made and has merit, don't wait for a Production Meeting or a Screening Meeting to implement. If the cost is within your expenditure guidelines, get it working.
5. *What should be covered at our meeting?* It is most important to review the status of all active suggestions. Be prepared for the Screening Meeting with

quotes, maintenance schedules, and the present status of the suggestion. The key is to act and keep the suggestion moving.

6. *If a suggestion needs to be investigated, what should we do?* On suggestions requiring an investigation, assign an investigation team, and list these employees so their names are typed on the minutes. It is very important that all investigation team members be notified and asked to investigate a suggestion and gather all pertinent facts concerning the suggestion. If members of other departments are concerned, be sure to notify the appropriate people.

7. *What should I report at the Screening Meeting?* At the Screening Committee Meeting, it is not necessary to read the entire suggestion, but only to refer to the suggestion and report on the disposition. It is most important to have as much information about a suggestion as possible in case it will be discussed. If you need to refer a suggestion for additional approval for expenditures, do so at this meeting. Remember your committee can spend $200, and department heads may approve $400 in expenditures.

8. *What should I report to my department after a Screening Committee Meeting?* At the Employee Information Meeting give the bonus disposition and the status of the reserve account. Also review the status of all suggestions, and be sure the individual who made the suggestion has an explanation of the disposition. This includes giving the reason for a rejection in the event the suggestion is not approved, or the status of the suggestion at the present time. This is most important to the suggestion maker since there is no suggestion as important as the one he or she made.

RESULTS OF THE SUGGESTION-MAKING PROCESS

After so many years, would the results of the suggestion-making process still be favorable? Would ideas dry up? Would everyone get tired of the Scanlon plan? Since the process of group problem solving involves the entire organization in new ways regardless of the prevailing organizational culture, can it sustain itself over time? One way to answer these questions is to look at the results of the involvement system across 19 years. Exhibit 8.2 graphs total suggestions made by year. They range from a low of 120 to a high of 360. Remember that the employment level in 1970 was 160 and, in 1989, it was 219. Nevertheless, the total number of suggestions by involved employees remained very healthy. Rejection rates of suggestions since 1981 range from 11 percent to 37 percent, or roughly *63 to 89 percent of all suggestions were accepted!* It is revealing to do an in-depth analysis of suggestions by their content. This analysis allows numerous inferences to be made and provides even greater insight into the plan and its overall effect on the organization. A management committee (consisting of the plant manager, the controller, and the human resources manager) was established at the Southwest Corp. plant for the purpose of evaluating suggestions. Also, the participation of the technical director of the plant was especially helpful. The results of these analyses are depicted in Exhibit 8.3.

Exhibit 8.2 Suggestions by Year

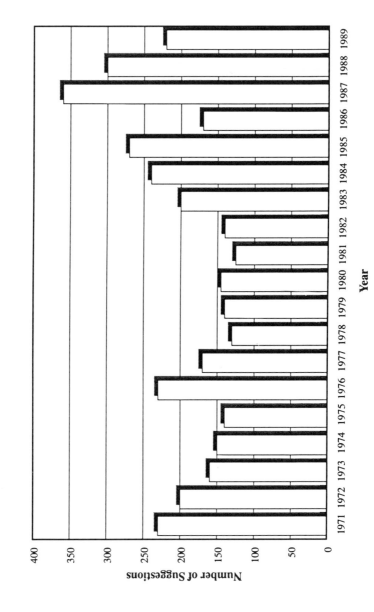

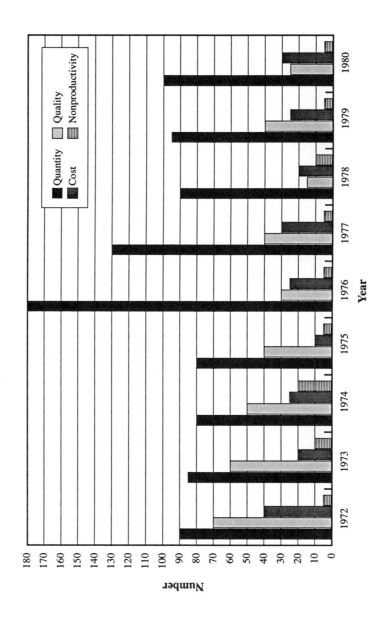

Exhibit 8.3 Type of Suggestion, 1972–1980

Exhibit 8.3 indicates that all suggestions analyzed from 1972 to 1980 fall into one of four categories (multiple-category suggestions were tallied in their primary category). The first category is irritants, i.e., suggestions that improve working conditions, but not necessarily the quality or quantity of the product being manufactured. Other categories represented in Exhibit 8.3 are quantity (suggestions that increase the number of units manufactured), quality (suggestions that increase the product value so that it will obtain a higher price or draw fewer complaints), and cost reduction (suggestions that increase the use of waste-reducing methods, the conservation of raw materials, and the conservative use of resources allocated for overhead costs).

During the first three months of 1971 there were 91 suggestions, which involved the majority of the work force. By the end of the trial year, 82 percent of the work force at Southwest Corp. had made at least one suggestion. These facts clearly indicate that the installation of this type of system does increase communication within an organization as measured by their suggestion making. The involvement and participation of most employees within the organization is a result of refining, processing, deciding, and feeding back the disposition of all suggestions. The involvement and participation required to process suggestions leads to more open communication.

In the first three months of operation under the plan, irritations with the working conditions at Southwest Corp. dominated the suggestions made by the employees. This situation is to be expected for two reasons: (1) suggestion making is a new activity, and common sources of ideas come from the irritants (the dissatisfiers that exist in the work environment); and (2) time is required for the consultant, management, and the committee system to determine which suggestions influence the bonus. Once all parties focus on the financial benefits, more suggestions should begin to relate to this outcome. Because production committees can implement some suggestions immediately, they are required to look at costs. It is at this time that employees, at all levels, become aware of the true effect of a given suggestion and priorities are established. This learning process helps reduce the flow of suggestions, since only productivity-improvement suggestions are sought.

If suggestions are not implemented, they may stop. A factor that seems to influence the rate of suggestion making is the ability of the organization to put good suggestions to work. When business conditions are not expanding, management may be reluctant to make a capital investment on worthy suggestions. Holding up a suggestion implies to the suggester that future attempts at suggestion making have a reduced probability of being accepted.

Exhibit 8.3 provides an extended look at suggestion-making activity over a nine-year period at Southwest Corp. Suggestion making that focuses on quantity represents the most common type of suggestion. Note that nonproductivity-related suggestions are still being made nine years into this Scanlon plan. Some nonproductivity-related suggestions are referred to the safety committee.

Remaining nonproductivity-related suggestions that could be classified as irritants are dealt with outside of the involvement system.

A careful review of Southwest's suggestion history has shown that periods of favorable economic activity, good markets, and other external environmental factors covary with the type of suggestions made. That is to say that increased productivity focuses worker attention on how to increase quantity, improve quality, and reduce costs. During slack periods there may be high rates of suggestion making, but productivity-related suggestions are more difficult to implement. Examples of the different types of suggestions made at different economic time periods are provided below.

Slack-period suggestions in mature plan organizations such as Southwest Corp. signify search behavior on the part of well-motivated employees. However, Southwest plant management believes it is often unrealistic to expect useful suggestions during this time. Problem-solving behavior requires problems that are immediate and solutions that are implementable. Conversely, the busy-period suggestion making exemplifies the immediacy of this type of problem solving. In slack periods, it does not matter as much how quickly the production cycle is turned around. However, when production picks up, the productivity-minded worker sees that a given suggestion would increase quantity and be useful. Obviously, a relationship exists between outside forces of demand and inside problem-solving focused on problems of immediacy.

Major developments within the organization are a second reason for significant changes in the suggestion mix. These developments include such things as an addition of a new department or work area, technological changes in production, and turnover in management or supervisory-level positions. Exhibit 8.3 represents this situation very clearly. Looking at the 1976 data, one can see that a significant increase in quantity suggestions occurred. This can be attributed to the addition of a new production department within the Southwest plant. This period also coincides with Southwest's highest bonus. Again this shows how the three components of traditional gainsharing mutually reinforce each other (philosophy of cooperation, involvement, and bonus).

A CHALLENGE TO MANAGEMENT

Southwest also discovered that dealing with the Scanlon plan over time provided management with both its greatest problem and challenge. The trial year is filled with much to learn, much excitement about this new organizational development, and much optimism about the bonus. However, time and familiarity diminish these factors significantly. Handling this situation as it occurs is a true sign of a successful firm. Successful plan firms like Southwest Corp. manage to rekindle the enthusiasm from that first year through a genuine interest in organizational development (OD). Another factor that aids the firm in keeping the plan fresh is the natural relation of the bonus to the firm's ability to meet its markets effectively. No bonus accrues automatically. The bonus exists only if all employees zealously pursue the goals of increasing quantity, improving quality, and reducing costs.

Southwest management worried that the number of suggestions could decline. This potential for continued suggestion-making did not decline. However, suggestions related to irritations with the work environment declined as suggestion-making behavior related to productivity was learned. Please refer to Exhibit 8.3. Over the 19-year period, 1987 was the best year for suggestion-making. This is after 16 years of the plan!

Four Key Roles

At Southwest Corp., four key roles emerge in support of the Scanlon plan: (1) plant manager; (2) controller; (3) human resources manager; and (4) departmental supervisor. Each of these roles has different duties, pressures, and opportunities that shape the quality of plan involvement and maintain this quality over time.

The most important role in the promotion and maintenance of the plan is the plant manager or chief executive officer. After 19 years of experience with Scanlon, the Southwest Corp. plant manager has clearly demonstrated his expertise in performing the duties necessary to sustain the initial enthusiasm and vitality surrounding the plan. He has been a catalyst for successful and realistic goal setting and an ardent proponent of quality communication. Based on interviews with his workers, he was viewed as a fair person and thus, he exemplified a truly successful Scanlon plant manager.

Another important role in promoting and maintaining the plan over time is that of the company controller. His role cannot be minimized. He has to more than adequately handle the ever-increasing responsibilities required of him under traditional gainsharing. He is available to the production committee meetings and reviews their ideas. By doing this, he provided the workers with a constant reminder of high-cost areas that could be remedied by increased suggestion making. In this sense, he is often viewed as the key to problem solving in the involvement system.

The third major role in the maintenance of the plan is the company human resources manager. His overall goal consists of communicating what Scanlon is and what it is not to all levels of personnel. The Southwest HR manager had successfully achieved this goal. He provided orientation to all new personnel regarding the plan and noted plan activity that could be useful for future training and promotion decisions. More importantly, he often served as a reinforcer of the policy that affected the other roles previously discussed. In other words, he not only provided training and discussion for where Southwest Corp. is but also where it wanted to be in the future with their gainsharing program.

Southwest Corp. departmental supervisors occupied the fourth key role in maintaining successful operation of the plan over time. Besides the fact that they influence many important decisions in terms of the acceptance or rejection of suggestions, departmental supervisors provide the essential link between management and workers. This link is necessary for the quality communication advocated by the Scanlon philosophy. In this regard, the departmental supervisors play an indispensable role in the overall operation of the plan. Southwest invested in additional training for departmental supervisors to facilitate Scanlon communication.

The Use of Task Forces

It takes more than these key people to successfully maintain or "feed" the program over time. Southwest developed task forces to stimulate the suggestion-making process. The task forces were formed at the departmental level and given assignments. The information obtained from these assignments was then used for determining areas needing improvement and this information was later referred to the appropriate department.

Feeding the system requires managers and workers to share their concerns, thoughts, and information on which production areas require attention. Southwest obviously possessed such people and it was these people who made the entire plan successful for 19 years.

INTANGIBLE BENEFITS OF THE PLAN AT SOUTHWEST CORP.

Observations of Management Personnel

As mentioned earlier, the plan provides the organization with both tangible and intangible benefits. Following 19 years of experience and observations, Southwest management was asked to cite the intangible benefits stemming from the incorporation of the Scanlon philosophy. These observations surfaced:

1. The plan provides the employees with the assurance that they will receive some degree of recognition by peers, by supervisors, and more importantly, by management. This is accomplished by the documentation and evaluation process required for all suggestions.
2. The plan increases the communication between all employees within the organization through their participation in the involvement system.
3. Increased representation and variety of ideas are provided by the plan since management receives suggestions from all levels of employees.
4. Many suggestions result in savings to management in terms of time, training, and development. Examples of these areas follows:

a. Scanlon helps develop employees at all levels. This is done by workers actively participating in the involvement system and thus becoming better acquainted with the entire production process.

b. The plan identifies employees with potential for supervisory or managerial positions. The production committees and screening committee provide a forum for the emergence and observation of leadership abilities.

c. The plan educates employees regarding the need to justify capital budget requests. The mutual sharing of information and constant feedback on suggestions between management and workers provides the workers with management's rationale for accepting or rejecting suggestions.

d. Where suggestions result in the addition of a capital item, the employees have a greater interest in getting the unit operating faster or overcoming start-up difficulties. Since the plan's emphasis is on productivity improvement, the workers want the production process to run as smoothly as possible.

e. Workers become better acquainted with the entire production process through increased communication with all employees. This can contribute to a fresh approach to improving plant safety and housekeeping.

f. Scanlon provides workers with the rationale for holding the total plant labor force to a minimum. Here again, this is the result of open communication between management and workers.

g. The plan provides a means of uniting two or more departments in a common project. The involvement system and increased communication makes this situation possible.

h. The plan is an important addition to the benefit package of the firm and provides the firm with a competitive advantage in the recruitment of new employees.

While tangible benefits are important in the assessment of the plan and its effect on the organization, the intangible benefits cannot and should not be ignored. They also influence company performance in a more subtle yet very important way. These benefits lend further support to the fact that the plan provides the organization and its workers with many advantages, thus making it a superior performance improvement program.

Long-Term Results

Until now, our discussion has focused on the initial short-term intangible effects of the plan at Southwest, i.e., the first year. While the net changes spanning the first year experience are impressive, most new programs do well in the first year. The ultimate question at the end of that first year was—could these nonbonus outcomes keep improving?

Survey data collected in 1980 is instructional. Our analysis was divided into two groups—managers and hourly workers. In terms of participation, 100 percent of Southwest Corp. managers surveyed believed participation had increased within the first year of the plan's inception. In the area of communication, 89 percent of Southwest's managers felt that communication had improved over the years. Regarding cooperation, once again 89 percent of Southwest's managers surveyed believed cooperation had improved.

Southwest's hourly workers were also questioned to determine their attitudes concerning changes in participation, communication, and cooperation over an eight-year period. With respect to participation, 63 percent of the hourly workers observed an increase in participation levels.

Eighty-eight percent of the hourly workers believed communication had improved since 1971. Regarding cooperation, 88 percent of the hourly workers perceived an improvement in cooperation by 1980. These significant increases in perceived improvements in communication and cooperation appear to be the result of the hourly workers' learning over time.

Factors Influencing Success

Overall, the social and psychological outcomes of the plan at Southwest can be classified as positive. However, these positive outcomes are not assured by the plan. In other words, the success of the plan is determined by many factors—some under the control of local management and some not. Those factors that helped determine the success of the plan were: (1) a clear understanding of the plan and how it works by all employees; (2) a supportive and optimistic attitude by all personnel in critical roles in the organization (managers and first-line supervisors); and (3) an overall organizational climate of acceptance and trust.

Clear Understanding

The first factor, clear understanding, was felt to be under management's control. The presentation of the plan is crucial to its successful operation. Therefore, Southwest's management paid close attention to the methodology used to introduce and familiarize the work force with the plan since it realized the effects would be felt for years to come. An example of this can be seen in the human resource manager's orientation program for Scanlon participants.

Supportive Personnel

The second factor, supportive personnel, was partially under management's control but was also dependent on the type of personality found in the organization's key roles. While all personnel in critical roles may appear supportive and optimistic, it is still possible for these key people to seriously undermine the plan. If these key people are unsure of their own abilities, autocratic in their interpersonal relationships, or threatened by change, their shallow support and optimism will soon be detected. Then, the plan may appear manipulative and spurious. So, it is imperative that all management be genuinely supportive of the plan in order to ensure its success. Southwest Corp. had only minor problems in this regard. Team building among managers and supervisors was viewed as an appropriate training technique to instill the Scanlon philosophy.

Trust

The third and final factor, trust, is also partially under the control of management but is also influenced by the personalities found in the work force. Management can and should counsel and reassure workers. This will help promote and foster a climate of both acceptance and trust. However, management does not solely influence the organizational climate. The success and, in a sense, the foundation of gainsharing rests on the work force made up of individuals who fit the following employee selection profile:

1. high on interpersonal trust measures
2. valuing prosocial, assisting behavior while being
3. motivated by extrinsic factors rather than intrinsic factors, i.e., pay for performance.

It is not mandatory that all workers fit this profile, but a majority of the Southwest work force did. If this is not the case, the goals of increasing participation, communication, and cooperation will be difficult to achieve.

SUMMARY

Performance at Southwest Corp. appeared to be enhanced by 19 years of the Scanlon plan. The bonus formula, which measures labor productivity, showed an average payroll bonus of 8.8 percent over the 19-year span. When output of 1970 is compared to levels at 1989, it increased by 78 percent.

Development and maintenance of the bonus formula over time raised special problems in fostering an atmosphere of equity and mutual trust. Forced to change the formula because of external demand, pricing factors, and increased capacity, Southwest Corp. management made their reasons clear. Some workers may not have understood this and if so, they could have seen the plan as manipulative. The decision to use a simple rather than comprehensive bonus formula helped in communicating the reasons for changing it. Southwest Corp. chose a simple formula to reinforce this worker understanding. The rationale for this choice is discussed in Chapter 3.

The analysis of the involvement system at Southwest Corp. revealed that irritants with the working environment are a common source of suggestions in the early stages of the plan. However, as learning occurs, productivity-related suggestions dominate—especially those that focus on quantity. Productivity also affected suggestion-making behavior. Slack-period suggestions reflect ideas not related to productivity. Feeding the system with accounting and technical information is especially helpful in overcoming this problem.

Costs associated with operating the plan, such as time spent in meetings, appear to be outweighed by the benefits, both tangible and intangible. Indeed, the benefits of gainsharing appear to be the reason it remained viable for 19 years at Southwest Corp. Had corporate handled the leveraged buy-out better and not meddled in the bonus calculation, the Southwest plant might have joined the ranks of Herman Miller and Donnelly Mirrors as very long-term Scanlon examples. As it is, 19 years is a long time and corporate's poor performance doesn't detract from gainsharing's impact on Southwest.

Notes

1. B .E. Moore and T. L. Ross, *The Scanlon Way to Improved Productivity* (New York: Wiley-Interscience, 1978).
2. C. F. Frost, J.H. Wakely, and R.A. Ruh, *The Scanlon Plan for Organization Development: Identity, Participation, Equity* (East Lansing: Michigan State University Press, 1974).

Part Two

Cases and Applications

Chapter 9

Gainsharing in Nonprofit and Public Sector Organizations

Brian Graham-Moore and James E. Jarrett

Can traditional gainsharing be utilized in nonprofit and public sector organizations? It has certainly been attempted. A review by Saggese in 1980 identified 12 gainsharing programs in the public sector.[1] Since that time, the states of Washington and Texas instituted programs permitting various forms of incentives for state employees which included gainsharing. Perhaps the most interesting municipal example reported was on the City of Loveland, Colorado.[2]

Begun in 1982, the Loveland program covers all of the approximately 400 city employees. Three tests must be met before employees may receive funds. First, city revenues must exceed actual expenses. Second, expenses must be less than or equal to the prior year's expanses *on a per capita basis.* Third, there must be acceptable satisfaction with city services as determined by a citizen satisfaction survey performed in May/June of each year (see Exhibit 9.1).

Loveland's program supports two elements of the city's mission statement: cost-effectiveness and high quality client service.[3] Each year since its inception, a bonus has been distributed per employee as shown below::

1987	$206
1986	310
1985	250
1984	353
1983	308
1982	100

Ongoing reinforcement is provided by monthly monitoring of the status of net income, and statements are placed in work stations throughout the city.

Exhibit 9.1   Gainsharing Pool

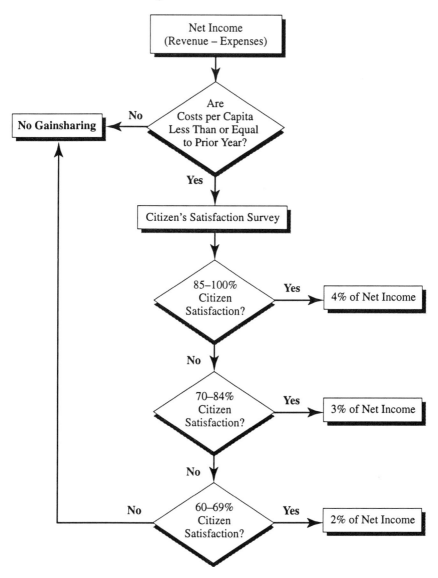

Bonuses are distributed the week before Christmas. There is no formal employee involvement program; nor is there an employee suggestion system. Some citizen reaction against the program has surfaced, but it has not been vehement.

The federal government has produced a number of demonstration projects where gainsharing was attempted. According to the General Accounting Office report of 1986,[4] three were ongoing:

1. a 36-person data transcription project at the Redstone Arsenal in Huntsville, Alabama;
2. a 90-person maintenance project at the Newark (OH) Air Force Station; and
3. a 230-person warehousing project at the Defense Logistics Distribution Center in Tracey, California.

Overall, early public sector examples of gainsharing have been unimpressive. Why? There are many reasons why gainsharing projects have not succeeded. Some reasons would apply equally to private sector organizations. However, some barriers seem unique to governmental organizations. Not all of the following factors apply to nonprofits, but many do. Nonprofits are freer, perhaps, to use gainsharing, but they are mission driven in the same way public sector organizations are. When nonprofits achieve cost avoidance (rather than cost savings) they are just as likely as public sector organizations to redirect the monies of budgets brought in under expected levels to other areas of the organization in order to further pursue their mission.

BARRIERS UNIQUE TO THE PUBLIC SECTOR

Traditional gainsharing has many hurdles to jump if it ever will have a chance to succeed. Consider some of the following barriers unique to most public organizations.

1. Legal barriers to public sector incentives still exist, but the bigger problem is the mistaken perception of many officials that incentives cannot be used.
2. More commonly, incentives are viewed as inappropriate, even if legal. This view has another more negative corollary. Public employees are viewed by taxpayers as already more than adequately compensated, given the amount and type of work produced.
3. Elected officials sometimes have ideological, antigovernment biases. A private sector parallel to this situation is infrequent—a CEO or Board whose members would rather destroy the organization than improve it. Operationally, actions are antiemployee and designed to keep the organization as small as possible.
4. Other elected officials, while not antigovernment, simply do not view government management as a high priority in comparison to the unmet service needs of citizens.
5. Appointed officials and agency heads, not only elected officials, often restrict progress. They rarely embrace new budgetary and operational initiatives suggested by elected officials. To them, promises that cost savings won't jeopardize future departmental requests pose credibility problems.

6. Existing budgetary practices can be a major barrier as well. If existing practices permit agencies to retain most or all of any savings, departments are unlikely to volunteer for a program that turns back funds for use by other governmental bodies.
7. The tendency toward overregulation in the public sector reduces the willingness to try such innovative methods as gainsharing. Fear of negative citizen reaction toward employee pay is rarely a consideration for private managers.
8. Regulations pertaining to spending practices can be a problem for governments. For instance, when funds are provided by another level of government, there normally are provisions and conditions that place limitations on their use. Local governments using state funds and state governments using federal funds have already encountered limitations to sharing any savings as bonuses.
9. Measurement of white collar outputs are thought to be more difficult to make. Generally there is a higher proportion of pure service activities in governments. Measurement of government service outputs, while improving, is still imprecise in many cases.

These are serious constraints. However, since the 1980s, privatization has become a reality. Many public organizations are losing their function to the private sector via outsourcing or outright competitive bidding. Some, such as the U.S. Postal Service, are simply losing market share via competition. Given these changes, innovation in management practices is occurring in the public sector at what is believed to be a faster rate. What follows is a case on traditional gainsharing in a medium-sized transportation authority. In some ways, this represents the first known attempt of traditional gainsharing in the public transportation industry.

GAINSHARING AT MID-WEST TRANSIT AUTHORITY

In the early part of 1987, after attending the Public/Private Cooperation Workshop sponsored by the Urban Mass Transportation Administration, the assistant general manager of the Grand Rapids Transit Authority (GRATA) began gathering information about gainsharing in various industries. The idea grew at GRATA and ultimately led to the development of a Scanlon plan that was presented to its employees, who are members of the Amalgamated Transit Union (approximately 130 in the bargaining unit). The Scanlon was offered to everyone in May 1990. It was the product of a union-management task force and was very detailed in its explanation of the involvement system. This proposal was submitted to the entire work force for ratification and it did not receive sufficient votes for acceptance.

At about the same time in 1989 the Board of Midwest Transit Authority (MTA) authorized managerial bonuses based on the good organizational performance during the fiscal year ending August 31. The sentiment of MTA's management was that everyone had contributed to organizational performance, not just the managers. The Board then authorized the first ever bonus to all employees. It was $250. Totally unexpected, virtually all MTA employees received this $250 in early December of 1989. Reaction was uniformly favorable, at first. MTA management started receiving input that a flat $250 was nice to receive even if it had no connection to organizational level and individual performance. The general manager tasked his assistant managers to research better ways to distribute future bonuses—if they ever occurred. One reason why the general manager was motivated to do this is found in the very public nature of his contract. This contract describes his base compensation as $100,000 annually and he could receive an additional $50,000 if he achieved improvements as expressed by this ratio:

$$\frac{\text{Cost/Vehicle Mile} \times \text{Complaints} \times \text{Accidents}}{\text{GM's Rating} \times \text{Passenger Miles} \times \text{On-Time Performance}}$$

This formula was a quantitative measure of those goals MTA held to be important. The denominator reflected the general manager's performance appraisal rating times Passenger Miles times the On-Time Performance measure. In effect, the denominator was an output that was impacted by the numerator of cost factors. Just as in gainsharing ratios, decreasing the numerator while increasing the denominator is how improvement occurs. Its purpose is to measure improvement over those same factors of the previous year. This very similar formula found in the general manager's contract, the granting of the first ever bonus to everyone at MTA, and the fact that GRATA in Michigan had begun an attempt to install a Scanlon plan, combined to bring together a gainsharing task force. A search for a qualified gainsharing consultant revealed that a nearby university professor indeed filled the requirement.

Two design teams were formed and met with the consultant. One team worked on the involvement system, the other (and smaller) team worked on formula construction. Exhibit 9.2 depicts the structure of the involvement system. Five Improvement Teams were to be created—one for each functional area of MTA, but two Improvement Teams for Fixed Route since there were so many operators in the department.

Appendix 9.1 is the final product of the employee involvement design team. Rules, roles, and functions are described in this design. It is not surprising that it appears very similar to the traditional Scanlon plan since the design team had knowledge of GRATA's design. They reviewed other ideas and designs, yet came back to this structure as being sufficient for MTA.

The design team finished their task months ahead of the formula construction team. This latter team was breaking new ground in formula construction since a traditional cost saving calculation would not involve everyone equally. Operators in the Fixed Route and Special Transit Services numbered about 500. For the most part, their work was performed with no other MTA employees

Exhibit 9.2   MTA Gainsharing Involvement System

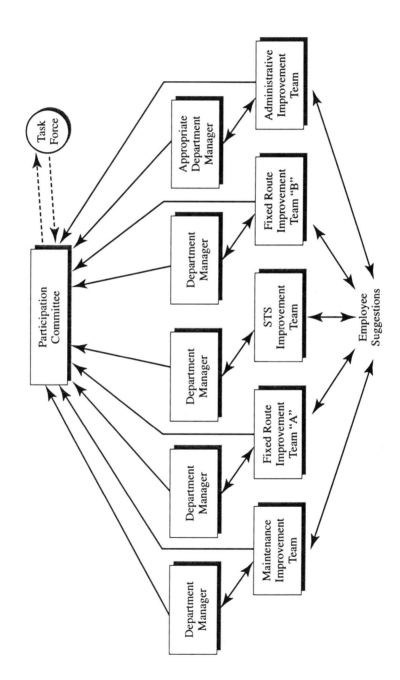

since most of their time was spent driving long and short buses, vans, and special cars. Traditional gainsharing works best when there is high task interdependency and line of sight communication. The technology of a transit authority works against this factor. Thus, would opportunities for problem solving, sharing of information, and cooperation be possible? The formula team searched for objectives that would involve the operators on more than one level. Therefore, the strategy from day one was to create a hybrid calculation. This calculation had to include goals that each individual operator had control over. The formula development team researched ten or so areas and finally chose:

- on-time performance
- accidents
- ridership
- customer complaints
- operating costs

Only operating costs had a basis in traditional gainsharing. Operators generally felt that the operating cost of their vehicles was the domain of maintenance. While this is only partially true, the maintenance department could contribute heavily to cost reduction. However, the other four factors in the calculation had generally positive, but varying levels of approval by the operators. For example, drivers of buses do believe that on-time performance is important and, for the most part, under their control. Heavy traffic, traffic accidents, etc. obviously affect on-time performance, but senior operators with years of experience knew how much their passengers clocked their performance. Conversely, operators felt they had less impact on ridership. They believed that advertising, fare price, and poor parking for private vehicles were greater factors influencing ridership. Some drivers were fatalistic about the goal of reducing accidents, but most agreed that safe driving was associated with lower accident rates. Most drivers disliked using customer complaints as a measure of customer satisfaction, because it operates the same way accidents do, as a negative measure. Thus, a reduction in complaints and/or accidents represents bonus opportunities.

The formula design team analyzed three years of data for all of the factors in the calculation. They presented suggested benchmark goals to senior management and, in some cases, negotiated these benchmarks for levels that would maximize bonus opportunities. This team had strong union representation and the commitment of a talented staff accountant. Most measurement problems and issues were resolved in the team. The consultant was able to point out measurement strategies that saved time, plus he continually sought consensus amongst union and management members of the team.

Exhibit 9.3 reflects goal definitions and payout scenarios for the first year. This exhibit brings together cost savings based on improvements in the operating budget plus goal performance incentives which were funded by the Board. The scenario, if achieved, would pay quarterly, but the annual average

Exhibit 9.3   Midwest Transit Authority Gainsharing Plan—
1991 Scenario

GAINSHARING INCENTIVES

	Gainsharing Baseline	Expenses if Savings = 3%	Potential Bonus Pool	As a % of Earned Wages	Avg Annual Pmt/Emp
First Quarter	$ 5,084,936	$ 4,919,547	$152,151	0.4%	$104.50
Second Quarter	$ 5,708,557	$ 5,415,816	$167,499	0.5%	$115.04
Third Quarter	$ 5,711,750	$ 5,653,162	$174,840	0.5%	$120.08
Fourth Quarter	$ 5,761,330	$ 5,610,008	$173,505	0.5%	$119.17
Annual Total	$22,266,528	$21,598,532	$667,996	1.9%	$458.79

The "Gainsharing Baseline" includes cost items within the control of employees, such as labor costs, sick leave, services, supplies, utilities, and miscellaneous expenses. Excluded are benefits, fuel costs, purchased transportation and most lease costs.

"Expenses if Savings = 3%" estimates 1991 expenditures if employees achieve a savings of 3% from the "Gainsharing Baseline".

If actual quarterly expenditures are less than the corresponding quarterly "Gainsharing Baseline", a bonus pool is created. Employees receive 50% of monies in the bonus pool at the end of each quarter. However, gainsharing bonuses are capped at 6% of earned wages.

PERFORMANCE INCENTIVES

	Goals for 1st Quarter 1991	Annual Bonus Pool	As a % of Earned Wages	Avg Annual Pmt/Emp
On-time Perf	86.0%	$ 55,000	0.3%	$ 75.55
Accidents	3.5/100,000 miles	$ 45,000	0.3%	$ 61.81
Complaints	0.264/1,000 passengers	$ 40,000	0.2%	$ 54.95
Ridership	32.21 passengers/hour	$ 35,000	0.2%	$ 48.08
Costs	$2.69/mile	$ 25,000	0.1%	$ 34.34
Annual Total		$200,000	1.2%	$274.73

On-time performance is a combined percentage of fixed route and STS performance, weighted by vehicle miles. The goal increases each quarter in 1991 by one percentage point.

The accidents goal is the current three year average of vehicular accidents per 100,000 miles for directly operated service. The goal will be adjusted each quarter to reflect the most recent accident experience.

Complaints per 1,000 passengers for systemwide service are included in this indicator. A unique goal is set each quarter that reflects the two year average for the quarter being measured.

Ridership is measured by passengers per revenue hour. The first quarter goal is a 5% increase over the current three year average. Each quarter thereafter, the goal is increased by an additional 5%.

Cost is measured by cost per vehicle mile, systemwide for all types of service. The goal is the current three year average, and will be adjusted each quarter to reflect the most recent cost experience. Annual Bonus Pool is funded by the MTA Board.

Gainsharing + Performance = Total Bonus

was $733.52 in the first year. This hybrid formula is an example of traditional gainsharing with goal sharing. Obviously, the most difficult part is convincing a board of unpaid directors that $200,000 for goals is a good investment—especially given the public sector barriers listed earlier in this chapter.

MTA: The First Year

Introducing gainsharing to MTA employees proved to be a difficult task because of the very nature of their work. Most operators work split shifts, which makes their total day relatively long. Evening meetings were planned and they were conducted by the consultant. Attendance was good and all attendees received printed handouts with information describing the bonus calculation and the involvement system (see Appendix 9.1).

The five Improvement Teams were scheduled for training immediately after the organizationwide educational effort. They required basic training in how to run a meeting and problem-solving techniques (see Chapter 13). To coordinate their activities, a permanent part-time gainsharing facilitator was appointed. Given the nature of MTA's work, this proved to be absolutely necessary. Again, due to the nature of the operator's work, the three Improvement Teams for Fixed Route and STS required more coordination and help from the gainsharing facilitator and the consultant than the other two teams.

The Participation Committee was chaired by the general manager. Each of the quarterly meetings in 1991 went smoothly as there were bonuses to announce and suggestions to discuss and process. For some of the employees, this represented the first time they had ever seen the general manager and his staff. Again, this is an indication of how low task interdependency is in the transportation industry. Drivers spent most of their time driving and the remainder in training. Line of sight supervision is negligible unless there are problems, such as equipment breakdowns, accidents, or complaints. Indeed, a central concern of operators is personal safety. MTA, as with most transit authorities, requires exact fare and operators and vehicles have little or no visible cash. Nevertheless, incidents occurring on fixed route buses were always discussed. Technically, safety suggestions belonged to the safety program, but they did surface in the gainsharing suggestion system and find their way to the Participation Committee.

The total number of suggestions was 230 in 1991, the first year of the gainsharing program. Exhibit 9.4 breaks these down by category. As with our knowledge of the gainsharing literature cited in Chapter 2, cost reduction suggestions were most often offered, some 112 of them or 49 percent. Almost all safety suggestions came from the drivers. Most were referred to the safety program. It should be pointed out that in 1990 there was no suggestion system and no known suggestions, which includes the safety program.

There was great concern about getting operators together for Improvement Team meetings and even greater concern about their ability to make

Exhibit 9.4   Suggestion Making by Department and Category for 1991

Category	Department						
	Maint[1]	Adm 1	Adm 2[2]	STS	FR 1	FR 2	Total
Cost	29	23	3	22	32	6	112
Quality/complaints	0	0	0	7	1	5	13
Quality/on-time perf	0	0	0	2	4	5	11
Quality/other	0	0	0	1	1	1	3
Safety	1	0	0	1	2	6	10
Efficiency	2	3	0	2	6	21	34
Irritants	2	0	1	11	8	24	46
Total	33	25	4	46	54	68	230

Note: Some suggestions cut across categories, but were forced into one category.
[1]Maintenance had no new suggestions as they were researching the initial batch of 33 from early 1991.
[2]Administration Improvement Team 2 existed for approximately six months.

meaningful suggestions. Exhibit 9.4 shows a total of 168 suggestions made by drivers or 73 percent of total suggestions made. While it is true that the maintenance department only made 33 suggestions, virtually all were of very high quality and implemented. One, in fact, saved over $20,000 in operating costs for 1991 and all future operating budgets since it impacted on an on-going technological process.

Suggestion making slowed down in 1992 for a variety of reasons. First, the rate of implementation was slow by management. Second, gathering information for investigating suggestions by the Improvement Teams (except for Maintenance and Administrative Teams) proved to be a difficult process. For example, operators did not understand the organizational structure of MTA. Many times communication was stymied as department head availability was lowest in the middle of the day. This is a normal time for meetings and coordination for MTA management. However, it was the only time that operators on split shifts had available. In spite of this, suggestion making produced better suggestions as organizational learning had taken effect in the second year of gainsharing. To improve this process, management appointed a fixed route driver to the role of involvement system coordinator. She replaced the part-time facilitator of 1991. She had high credibility with the other operators and she was given time to learn the culture and communication patterns of the MTA office. Suggestions totalled 168 in 1992 and were generally perceived to be higher quality than in 1991. Again, the maintenance department excelled in adding value through suggestion making.

Bonus History

Exhibit 9.5 shows the actual payout of bonus monies in 1991. Performance bonus payouts were over three times the amount earned via cost savings. The total bonus paid from this hybrid calculation was $152,351. Obviously, the total was less than the scenario offered in Exhibit 9.3. Average bonus received was around $300 per person. From the Board and management's point of view, this was better than 1990 where $250 was simply given to everyone. That bonus was the same amount given to all, i.e., flat. The gainsharing bonus was a percent of earnings per quarter (therefore it varied) and it was instrumentally linked to cost savings and measured performance goals. Thus, management expected those with higher earnings to receive higher absolute bonus amounts. Management also believed that MTA employees were making a connection between the performance goals and the behaviors associated with those goals.

The formula development team responsible for the 1991 calculation audited the calculation and it was working. Recommendations for 1992 were to delete the 6% cap to the cost saving calculation, but base the cost saving share on an 80/20 split. That is, $.20 out of every dollar saved each quarter from expected operating costs was to go into the bonus pool. The thinking was that operating budgets had a four year experience base and were considered quite accurate. If working smarter could create actual costs below expected costs, then $.20 of every dollar saved would be justifiable to the public at large.

At first, some MTA employees thought this split was unfair. However, first quarter 1992 cost savings were greater than the performance bonus payout. First quarter bonuses in 1992 were $99,905. Of that first quarter total, $65,763 came from the traditional cost savings calculation (the 80/20 split). Thus $328,816 was the true savings and 66% of the first quarter savings came from the cost saving side of the hybrid formula. By the second quarter of 1992, the bonus distribution was $98,979. Again, the cost savings contribution was greater by almost one half. At the third quarter of 1992, gainsharing cost savings were greater by three times, but total bonus performance was only

Exhibit 9.5   1991 Bonus History

Quarter	Gainsharing Savings	Performance Goals
1	—	$33,750
2	$32,305	$23,750
3	$ 3,796	$35,000
4	—	$23,750
Total	$ 36,101	$116,250
Grand Total	$152,351	

$73,141. However, total bonus performance across the first three quarters of 1992 was $272,025. The 1992 bonus pool exceeded $300,000 and MTA entered its third year of gainsharing in 1993.

SUMMARY

Was gainsharing successful at MTA? The answer is mixed. Did it pay bonuses based on savings and improvement in performance, there are many unanswered questions. Just as we proposed at the beginning of this chapter, there are barriers unique to the public sector. Taking a second look at them and contrasting them with MTA is fruitful.

Are the bonuses large enough to motivate? Even with the tremendous improvement of 1992 bonuses over 1991 bonuses, private sector gainsharing payouts are usually larger and easier to achieve. Why? True cost savings are difficult to prove when cost avoidance might require returning unused funds to the source from which they originated. That is, if a public transit authority can operate for less by working smarter, then shouldn't it receive fewer subsidies? In addition to this, the formula was a hybrid, i.e., complex. Therefore, employee understanding and trust are hard to achieve.

MTA is luckier than many public sector entities in that it can charge for its services. Many, if not most, public sector organizations can't do this. Therefore, improvement programs may ultimately be demotivational if the goal is to reduce budgets. Yet, we want our nonprofit and public sector organizations to operate efficiently as well as effectively.

Legal barriers to public sector organizations are all but gone; however, perceptions of the public at large and of many officials can still be a barrier. In the MTA case, many citizens and even officials do not value public transportation. Given that, they may be critical of any plan helping public transportation operate more efficiently.

Existing budgetary practices were not a barrier at MTA. In fact, they made it easier to establish factual, audited data bases of cost history. The MTA Board was able to justify its decision to try traditional gainsharing because budgetary practices laid the groundwork for benchmarking cost and performance improvements.

While governmental regulations did impact on spending at MTA, management worked legally with all funding constraints in order to establish bonuses. This proved to be less of a problem than initially thought because of the liberalization of rules in this area combined with state laws permitting incentive programs.

Did MTA compromise any gainsharing measurement standards? Perhaps it is too early to know, but all their performance standards reflected goals that management and the Board would accept. Goals of improvement for each performance standard were negotiated, but the past performance history was empirically assessed and, therefore, known. In every case, improvement in on-time performance, customer satisfaction, and reduction of accidents was expected to be better than previous periods. Normatively, this makes sense yet many of these goals were not achievable due to changes in the environment, technology, and even strategy. The board and management reserved the right to change the goals every year. In the private sector, traditional gainsharing, even goal sharing, has a greater stake in continuity. Long-term gainsharing plans may adjust the formula for fairness, but rarely change the overall goal, which is to reduce the cost of the good or service.

Can results such as MTA's be achieved without an employee involvement program? The honest evaluation after three years seems to be that traditional gainsharing was easily adapted and quite successful in the maintenance department. Large, actual savings are documentable. This was less true in the other departments. The fixed route and special transit drivers did indeed have more trouble getting involved. It took extra effort by the consultant and the gainsharing coordinator to schedule and work with them. Special attempts at communication, such as stories in the MTA newsletter and attachments to their daily route orders, were necessary to remind them of the involvement system. Many drivers were only casually involved after two years. Suggestion making was low among drivers as well. Interest in the bonus announcement was high at each quarter, but feedback on interim progress before a quarter was low. Indeed, the great risk and challenge concerning employee involvement was constantly there. That is, how could MTA involve people who don't interact with one another very often? The teams could overcome this problem since they met on a regular schedule, but they often felt powerless when it came to seeking out other drivers. Overcoming this barrier to employee involvement remains a task for the gainsharing coordinator.

As we move to more purely service areas, goals valued by managements, boards, and constituents require that a monetary value be established in order to make gainsharing work. Consider this. Management perceives that on-time performance will build ridership. Management may be wrong, but on-time performance is a reasonable goal to increase ridership and revenue. If on-time performance, as a goal, is achieved with empty buses, then bonuses still have to be paid. Thus, the classic problems of most of the nonprofits and public sector surface very quickly. Can traditional gainsharing be adapted to answer these problems? In MTA's case, it did improve service, but not uniformly. Traditional gainsharing did involve employees, but did it best when task interdependency was high and information sharing was more easily achieved, as in the maintenance department. MTA was able to pay bonuses, but had chosen to adjust the formula each year in ways that made understanding it difficult for employees.

On balance, MTA was reasonably successful, but more adjustment and modification of gainsharing will be required to make it truly successful. One would like to revisit MTA at the end of, say, five years to evaluate how well traditional gainsharing fits into their culture and organizational goals.

Notes

1. M. Saggese, "Shared Savings Programs in the Public Sector," manuscript, 1980.
2. First edition of this book.
3. J. Winters, "Productivity Improvements in Loveland, Colorado," in *Management Science and Policy Analysis Journal-Letter* (Washington, D.C.: American Society for Public Administration, Section on Management Science and Policy Analysis, Vol. 2, No. 3, Winter 1985), 11–15.
4. U.S. General Accounting Office, *Gainsharing: DOD Efforts Highlight an Effective Tool for Enhancing Federal Productivity* (Washington, D.C.: General Government Division, GAO/GGD-86-143BR), 15.

Appendix 9.1

The MTA Involvement System

Objectives

To increase the level of employee involvement and participation to improve productivity.

To improve all lines of communication within the organization, horizontally and vertically.

To improve the level of trust between labor and management.

To equitably share any improvements in productivity through a financial bonus.

Recommended Employee Involvement System

Please see the diagram (Exhibit 9.2) which lays out the design of our structure. Four components make up the Employee Involvement System. These are:

1. All employees as suggestion makers
2. Five Improvement Teams with 10 to 15 members, depending on the size of the area they represent.
3. A Participation Committee
4. Occasional task forces

All Employees as Suggestion Makers

Everyone is a source of information on how to make MTA run more smoothly. This intelligence is founded on the fact that the person closest to the job is the one who knows it best. Therefore, this represents a tremendous source of productive knowledge—especially when we see how other organizations have successfully improved their systems by involving everyone. The evidence that we have reviewed strongly suggests that all employees have highly relevant information to improve organizational productivity, but an appropriate culture and structure are needed to facilitate their involvement. Encouragement for suggestion making is the first step. Then help in developing, investigating, and evaluating suggestions is appropriate.

Improvement Teams

In all, five permanent Improvement Teams are needed. There will be two for Fixed Route and one each for STS, Maintenance, and Administrative Areas. Their job is threefold: (1) to help in the development and processing of suggestions, (2) to create an environment of problem solving and decision making at all levels of MTA, and (3) to give a sense of stability, structure, and permanency to the Employee Involvement System. Improvement Teams should meet at least once a month or more if their work demands it. Membership is voluntary, but people are to be selected with those characteristics conducive to making the Employee Involvement System a success. They are to be paid regular rates for time spent in Improvement Team meetings.

The Improvement Team should elect a leader. This person automatically serves on the Participation Committee. The team leader will call the Improvement Team meeting and the purpose of the meeting will be to develop, investigate, and evaluate suggestions for final sign-off by the Division Manager. The size of the Improvement Team may need to be adjusted up or down, depending on tasks pursued. The Improvement Team can recommend changes in their size, but the Participation Committee should approve these changes.

Improvement Team members will be established so that no more than 50 percent of the members are being rotated at one time. The rotation system will begin after the program has been in operation for one year.

The Improvement Team has these specific responsibilities:

1. Encourage MTA employees to submit suggestions or ideas that improve productivity, improve customer satisfaction, or improve the quality of working life.
2. Assist MTA employees in developing and writing suggestions.
3. Review all suggestions for cost and scope on a regular basis.
4. Implement, with Division Manager's authorization, any suggestions costing less than $250 and affecting their division only.
5. Maintain a log of all suggestions submitted to the Team.

The Participation Committee

The Participation Committee has overall responsibility for the conduct of the Employee Involvement program in order to assure it functions smoothly and effectively. To do this they will meet at least once a month to review suggestions costing more than $250 or having such scope that they affect more than one area of MTA. The Participation Committee will appoint occasional task forces to investigate suggestions of merit when technical complexity or time constraints require. In addition, the Participation Committee will review and announce the gainsharing bonus. The reasons for a bonus or a deficit should be a regular part of the Participation Committee agenda.

Specifically, the Participation Committee has these responsibilities:

1. Coordinate Improvement Team activities.
2. Recommend action on all suggestions and improvements referred by the Improvement Team and appoint task forces as necessary.
3. Analyze the performance of the gainsharing formula. (A special formula task force should report to the Participation Committee to facilitate this.)
4. Coordinate improvements to assure they do not conflict.
5. Assure that a participative environment is being created by the Employee Involvement System.

The Participation Committee will be made up of ten persons:

5 Leaders from the Improvement Team (to serve one year, then rotate)
1 Union President (or designate)
1 General Manager (or designate)
1 Manager of Maintenance (or designate)
1 Manager of Administration (or designate)
1 Manager of Fiscal Services (or designate)

The Suggestion Process

The structure described above is designed to facilitate the flow of ideas and suggestions that will result in the gradual and consistent improvement of MTA. The suggestion flow is summarized as follows:

Step 1—Suggestion Development

Any employee wanting to submit a suggestion would write it down, seek help in its development, if necessary, but submit it to the Improvement Team on a Suggestion Form.

Step 2—Suggestion *Review and Input*

The Improvement Teams review all suggestions, solicits input from appropriate resource people, including Division Managers. Division Managers will have ten working days to respond to a request for input. When all input has been received, the Decision Step is initiated.

Step 3—Decision Step

Three decision paths are possible:
a. If a suggestion costs $250 or less to implement and affects only one Division, the Division Manager may implement.
b. If a suggestion costs more than $250 or affects more than one Division, it would go to the Participation Committee for a decision. The Participation Committee has two options: it can recommend to implement or not implement to the General Manager; or it can establish a Task Force if it feels further study and input is needed.
c. If a suggestion is rejected at any level the primary responsibility for feedback to the suggester is an Improvement Team member. Ideally, a face-to-face discussion as to why a suggestion was rejected is best. This should be backed up with a written note to the suggester.

When the decision to approve is made, it moves to the Implementation Step.

Step 4—Implementation Step

This step requires development of an implementation plan in cooperation with the Division Manager. This plan describes key activities, timetables and responsibilities, as well as development of an evaluation plan so that the effectiveness of the improvement can be monitored.

Built into this flow is an appeal procedure so that if a Division Manager rejects a suggestion that the Team supports, it may be sent to the Participation Committee for a final recommendation.

Gainsharing suggestion-making policy should clearly state that no lay-off should occur from productivity suggestions. Management should promise to let attrition account for reduced level of employment caused by working smarter. This policy includes the offer of retraining MTA employees displaced by methods improved by gainsharing suggestions.

The Gainsharing Principles that precede these recommendations serve to guide policies and procedures not fully specified in this memo of recommendation for an Employee Involvement System at MTA.

Authors' Note: For suggestions on Gainsharing Principles, see Chapter 16.

Chapter 10

Gainsharing and Unions: Current Trends

Timothy L. Ross and Ruth Ann Ross

In order to fully understand the relationship of all parties within a gainsharing framework, the role of unions, one important institution, needs careful attention. Should unions like gainsharing? Should they learn more about the company, get more involved, get complaints resolved, perhaps make more money, and ensure more long-term job security through gainsharing? Or should they attempt to preserve the status quo and oppose the institution of gainsharing plans? Walter Ruether of the United Auto Workers was famous for his goal of increasing the pie and then sharing the benefits with members through profit sharing, a trend the UAW often continues today. Theoretically, the employee involvement component of many gainsharing plans should appeal to many union leaders because it emphasizes workplace democracy.

But, in reality, unions have generally been less than enthusiastic supporters of gainsharing. Unions have offered active support for these plans primarily in situations in which wage concessions are sought and gainsharing is part of an integrative package. That is, the unions are forced to accept no increases or actual decreases in a contract with the possibility of making up some of the difference through gainsharing. Broadly speaking, contracts negotiated by the steel and automotive industries are examples of this approach. These plans are normally negotiated and do not usually include employee involvement as an integral part of the system. In effect, they are really variable compensation plans. Union leaders frequently support implementation of gainsharing and then subsequently decrease their active involvement.

Why do industries encounter opposition or less than enthusiastic union support and what can be done to overcome it? This chapter will discuss research dealing with these questions. We will outline the concerns of high-ranking union officials about gainsharing plans. We will discuss what aspects of the plans they find objectionable and what they find attractive. Finally, we will recommend how to address the union's concerns in a manner that is straightforward and ultimately in the best interest of the company, the employees, the union itself, and most important, the United States as a competitor in international trade. Interestingly, unions in many other countries, such as Japan, actively support variable compensation and other bonus systems.

GENERAL UNION POSITIONS

In their study on worker participation and American unions, Kochan, Katz, and Mower described four stands taken by national unions on employee participation processes in general.[1]

1. *General opposition.* The general opposition to such plans is clearly stated by national union leaders. Local unions are discouraged, but not prevented, from participating. Several unions take this stand, although such opposition is probably found less frequently today.
2. *Decentralized neutrality.* National leaders do not take a stand either for or against such systems and leave the decision to the local unions. They do not provide significant staff support to locals that do get involved, but may offer guidelines on how to respond when employers discuss gainsharing plans. Probably the majority of unions are in this category.
3. *Decentralized policy with some national union support.* National union officials other than the president advocate such systems. These officials support and advise interested locals. At this time, the United Steel Workers and the United Auto Workers appear to best represent this position and at times position 4.
4. *Support from the president.* The union president goes on record as advocating such systems. Staff support is available to assist and train local officers, and movement is made toward integrating worker participation with collective bargaining and other union activities. Few unions fit this mold.

It is significant that most unions probably take a position of decentralized neutrality. Supporting a new form of labor-management cooperation can involve risks for high-ranking union officials; their predisposition to delay or to avoid taking a stand is understandable. They have sometimes been "stung" by supporting such systems in the past. The idea of contingent or variable compensation in which gainsharing is the only or primary way for union members to increase their economic standing has obviously made this a much more complex issue for unions. Previously, gainsharing was always above negotiated wages and was not discussed as part of a contract. Many consultants in the field still strongly support such a total separation, although if it is part of the contract, such a stand is perhaps unreasonable.

The recent increase in the number of gainsharing plans being implemented has provided considerable information as to how the plans will influence the unions involved. A survey of unions sought to identify the specific aspects of gainsharing that unions will favor, as well as those that unions will likely oppose.

A discussion of why consultants thought employee involvement gainsharing should be separate from the union contract, a belief shared by most union officials who really understand employee involvement gainsharing, is probably appropriate. The most commonly cited reason is so that the company will not substitute it for normal negotiated wages–that is, so that management will not say "you are earning good bonuses, you don't need a raise." If the pay structures are kept separate, this possibility should decrease. Another reason is so that management will not be held hostage by the union on minor aspects of the plan, especially the employee involvement part. Thirdly, if the union is actively involved as is typically the case, the gainsharing segment is separate, the union can take significant credit if it is successful, but they can still be in a position to blame management if it does not fulfill expectations. Finally, from a practical standpoint, if the union seriously opposes the system, then the employee involvement portion of the plan will *not* be installed successfully. The results are outlined below.

THE SURVEY

The respondent could evaluate, using a four-point scale, the importance of nine reasons why unions may favor gainsharing systems and nine reasons why unions may oppose such systems. Additional items could be added, if necessary. Other items obtained information about the respondent and assessed the respondent's familiarity with various gainsharing plans. The survey was kept as simple as possible in hopes of increasing the response rate.

Responses were obtained from 17 of the larger American trade unions out of 50 surveyed, including the UAW; the United Rubber Workers; the International Ladies Garment Workers Union; the United Brotherhood of Carpenters and Joiners of America; the International Union of Tool, Die, and Mold Makers; the International Brotherhood of Boilermakers; the International Association of Machinists; the Teamsters; and the International Union of Bricklayers and Allied Craftsmen, as well as other smaller unions. In most cases, the director of research and education for the union or a research staff member completed the survey. First and second requests were sent to numerous other unions, but even an inducement of a book on gainsharing could not generate a response.

Why Unions May Support Gainsharing

Most unions are either neutral toward or "mildly" in favor of gainsharing plans. In the survey, even if they can see many positive aspects of such a system, for each item, the percentage of respondents indicating that the reason was "important" or "very important" to support was determined. They can see a number of positive attributes in such systems. Exhibit 10.1 describes the relative importance of nine reasons why unions may favor gainsharing. Let us discuss briefly the first five reasons.

1. *Increased recognition.* A gainsharing plan can provide many opportunities for employees to receive special recognition for their contributions to company performance. Through being elected to or selected for team positions, seeing their ideas implemented, and other means, the workers find that their extra efforts are noticed and appreciated, not only by management but also by coworkers.

2. *Better job security.* Although some fear that improved productivity will result in the need for fewer employees, other unions have taken the position that a successful plan means a successful company and therefore greater job security. Raymond Majerus, deceased secretary-treasurer of the UAW, stated:

   > Thus it's vital that the basic job security needs of workers are addressed when these programs are designed. We've tried to do this in a number of situations—without success I should add—by proposing that profit sharing and productivity sharing bonuses be distributed in the form of increased paid time off the job rather than cash. In this way, productivity gains can be used to increase employment and enhance job security rather than reduce it.[2]

   Most national union officials probably accept the contention that productivity is important for long-run job security. Unfortunately, local leaders often fear that productivity increases will reduce job security in the short-run, and therefore they may resist such plans. Many plans today also emphasize quality and/or other variables more than labor performance as necessary to ensure job security.

3. *Increased involvement in job activities.* Although a popular line of thought holds that unions are clinging tenaciously to outdated beliefs that workers really are interested only in getting more pay and better benefits, the survey results suggest otherwise. Respondents seem to recognize that many of the employees they represent want more control over the way they do their jobs. A gainsharing plan may be effective in helping to achieve this goal.

4. *More money.* One advantage offered by a gainsharing plan that is not found with most other TQM or employee involvement systems is the potential of earning a financial bonus. A bulletin published by the

Exhibit 10.1 Reasons Why Unions May Favor Gainsharing
(Percentage Making "Important" or "Very Important")

	Percentage
1. Increased recognition	95
2. Better job security	94
3. Increased involvement in job activities	94
4. More money	94
5. Increased feeling of achievement of contributing to the organization	86
6. Increased influence of union	70
7. Greater contribution to nation's productivity	69
8. Compatibility with union goals	64
9. Fewer grievances	47

United Brotherhood of Carpenters and Joiners of America (UBC) had this comment about quality circles, a system which normally does not pay a bonus:

> We recommend that if a Quality Circle Program is accepted, it be combined with some form of Gainsharing plan for employees. The savings resulting from the Quality Circles must be shared with employees for two reasons. First, it is only fair that savings achieved as a result of employees suggestions and participation in the Circles directly benefit employees. Otherwise the program becomes a means of manipulating workers for the benefit of the company. Second, employees rapidly lose interest if there is no incentive involved for them.[3]

The article went on to recommend the use of a Scanlon Plan and noted that this type of plan has been used successfully in UBC locals. A company may find it easier to begin with a Scanlon plan or some other "pure" gainsharing plan in concert with a system such as TQM as long as people see each part as an assist and support to the other.

5. *Increased feeling of achievement of contributing to the organization.* This certainly doesn't suggest that the era of adversarial relationships between labor and management is over, but it does imply that unions are aware that many of their members want to have an impact on the success of their companies. A gainsharing plan, if designed with the union's concerns in mind, can be one vehicle to help meet these needs. Informal discussions with a number of local union members confirm this finding.

Why Unions Would Oppose

The findings reviewed in the previous section represent just one side of the story. Results tabulated in Exhibit 10.2 show the relative importance of nine

Exhibit 10.2   Reasons Why Unions May Oppose Gainsharing
(Percentage Marking "Important" or "Very Important")

	Percentage
1. Management may try to substitute it for wages	94
2. Management cannot be trusted	88
3. Peer pressure to perform may increase	77
4. Bonus calculations are not understood or trusted	76
5. Union influence is undermined	66
6. Increased productivity may reduce need for jobs	64
7. Grievances may go unprocessed	64
8. Gainsharing is incompatible with union goals	57
9. Employees really do not want more involvement	20

reasons why unions may be opposed to employee involvement gainsharing. Let us examine the five most important reasons for opposition.

1. *Management may try to substitute it for wages.* A basic traditional principle of gainsharing is that the gainsharing bonus should serve as an extra incentive for improving productivity, separate from the basic compensation package. It is generally recommended that the gainsharing plan be kept out of collective bargaining negotiations on pay. As the survey responses reveal, most unions are not interested in replacing any part of their members' paycheck with a bonus that can vary in amount, as some recent experiments such as DuPont and Saturn have shown, unless economics force such action. Gainsharing is generally used openly for this reason only when it is part of a concessionary package. Most gainsharing firms increasingly offer wages that are competitive for the geographic area.

   Variable or contingent compensation based on gainsharing will continue, especially in companies where union wages are considerably higher than those prevailing in the area and the company is in severe financial difficulty. Otherwise, gainsharing will be separate from negotiated wages in most situations.

2. *Management cannot be trusted.* Much of the writing on union and management cooperative efforts expresses the concern by the union that it is not being dealt with in good faith. Unions fear that management will violate the spirit of cooperation by laying off employees after productivity gains are made, will manipulate the bonus calculation to suit its needs, or will attempt to change the rules of the plan at some later date. If management adopts such actions, the plan is likely to be short-lived. Normally, before the plan is installed, specific ground rules are established to decrease such possibilities.

3. *Peer pressure to perform may increase.* In a typical gainsharing firm, all jobs are "on standard" in the sense that performance during the base period or a goal must be exceeded to earn bonus. This means that anyone who performs inadequately hurts everyone's chance of earning a bonus. Some unions fear that workers will complain when others are not doing their jobs properly, creating divisiveness in the work force and placing unfair pressure on employees too old to perform at top levels. It has been our experience, however, that the pressure exerted to correct substandard performance is focused not so much on fellow workers as on management. Also, in most cases the plan is not based only on labor productivity. Of course the same argument could be made for quality improvements.

4. *Bonus calculations are not understood or trusted.* In addition to a concern that the company will juggle the figures, some unions hold that gainsharing bonus calculations are inadequate measures of employee performance. According to an International Association of Machinists' research report:

> The relationship between a worker's productivity and the bonus . . . is very remote. Not only that, but many factors beyond the worker's control, including production processes, demand, management efficiency, and quality of materials, help determine the extent of savings. Total sales, for instance, may be affected by seasonal demand for the product or by the marketing skills of the firm. Since most low to middle income families budget their income to the hilt, it is difficult to make adjustment for unexpected declines in income.[4]

One way to minimize lack of trust in the bonus calculations is to have them tied to the factory's or company's financial reports so that the same figures are used for bonus calculations as are used for tax and corporate report purposes. These figures can be attested to by the public auditors. The marketing skills of the firm can be sharpened by including the sales and marketing force in the gainsharing plan, as many firms have done. Some firms do make the plan open to audit by the union.

5. *Union influence is undermined.* In one scenario, the union could lose power if the workers come to see the employee involvement system (for example, the teams that review employee ideas) as a more effective way to handle issues that are normally channeled through the union's grievance procedure. Management gets credit for bettering the workers' condition, and the union is increasingly bypassed. Research, however, has shown that involvement in such plans typically does not cause members to evaluate their unions more negatively.[5] In most installations, a strong attempt is made to preserve the union contract provisions and keep union issues outside of employee involvement gainsharing.

6. *Additional reasons for opposition.* Although not included as an item on this survey, one of the major obstacles to gainsharing may be the view that such employee involvement plans are used as tools against the organized labor movement. Two laid-off UAW members noted: "Quality of Work Life (QWL) programs are quickly becoming the single most important management technique being used to thwart unionization. In addition to greater productivity, nonunion firms see QWL as being decisive in keeping unions out."[6]

Labor leaders see managerial opposition to union organizing efforts in America as a major force limiting cooperative efforts and experimentation in the workplace. Unions will not embrace such plans openly until they feel that their right to represent workers is accepted. We know of no unions that have been decertified after gainsharing was installed. But, unfortunately, the fear may still be there.

Many union officials also say that they are turned off by some forms of employee involvement. For example, many unions supported quality circles only to have management withdraw its support at a later date, which then resulted in failure of the program. Unions have generally been supportive of Total Quality Management (TQM) concepts to date but that can change for the same reasons as mentioned above.

WHAT'S IN IT FOR UNIONS?

Up to now we have discussed ways in which a plan can benefit individual employees. But an equally important issue is the extent to which the union as a third party can profit from its role as a joint partner in developing and supporting the system.

First, only the most productive and competitive firms will grow and hire more employees as dues-paying members. Japanese and European companies are still in many cases producing better quality products at lower costs. Unionized U.S. firms, which have been adversely affected by these pressures, can be strengthened by gainsharing. Most Japanese firms also have bonus plans.

Second, the union benefits by association with a plan desired by the rank and file. Charles Hecksher, research economist for the Communication Workers' union, observed:

> In such cases, for unions to oppose QWL is simply a suicidal strategy. It puts us in the position of opposing something which the workers see as good. It may, if anything, be worse to do what many unions have done, which is to sit on the sidelines and play a "watchdog" role. That approach lets management get all the credit for improvements resulting from QWL while the union is seen as negative, weak, and irrelevant to a process which directly benefits workers in their daily lives.[7]

By being actively involved in the gainsharing plan, the union can also raise its visibility among the 80 percent of the membership that is less active in union affairs. These members should come to see the union as a more powerful force in issues that directly influence their work life. In this way their solidarity and identification with the union are enhanced.

Often, the union's effectiveness in negotiations and grievance-handling is hampered because of a lack of detailed information regarding company finances, decision-making processes, and plans for the future. The improved communications developed under a gainsharing plan should provide the union with better knowledge. In addition to allowing the union to better serve its members, this new sharing of information is also helpful in developing trust in management and in helping the union to see business conditions as they truly are.

Firms with gainsharing systems are likely to take a longer view of employment than many other firms. That is, they have some ability to reduce wage costs (by reducing bonuses) and, thus, decrease the need for disruptive layoffs during seasonal or cyclical business downturns. Surely such policies satisfy the union's long-term interests at both the local and international levels. Certainly, such bonus systems allowed the Japanese to much better survive a very nasty 1992–1994 recession.

Gainsharing also promotes extra pay when performance makes it available, but the firm is not saddled with a permanent higher wage level during times of economic downturns. The adjustment process is automatic; the union does not have to negotiate difficult wage concessions.

Finally, a union that has actively supported a successful gainsharing plan probably will find itself in a better bargaining position during negotiations. If the plan has in fact resulted in greater productivity, less scrap, and higher quality, and if these improvements can be tied to the union's participation, then the union will likely be better supported in its own demands. Frankly, the more successful the company, the more ability it has to pay higher wages.

HOW TO GET COOPERATION

Rather than recommending outright rejection of gainsharing plans, some national unions are finding it more advantageous to take an active part in the plan, provided that certain conditions are met. These conditions include assurances that the union's power will not be threatened, that the union members will not be hurt by the plan, and that management is being honest in stating reasons for implementation.

Job Security

Often, the union's greatest concern will be that streamlined operations and other productivity improvements could result in layoffs—doing the same work with fewer people. The union is likely to demand some assurance that this will not happen.

To maintain employee job security, management will have to see that the cost savings generated under the plan are not wasted. Part of the money saved should be invested in the marketing and sales organization so that sales volume keeps pace with production. Ideally, gainsharing plans should be installed in sites where there is a potential for an expanding market.

Although a successful plan should result in more jobs in the long run, it is essential that management and the work force be flexible and imaginative in finding ways to maintain employment levels in the short run. While waiting for sales volume to develop, a firm may find it possible to reassign production workers to maintenance or some similar function. One manufacturer of industrial electrical products sent some of its production workers out with salesmen to help demonstrate products during times when they were not needed in the plant. Another problem arises when, during times of rapid growth, some companies hire new workers for temporary bulges in production. During such volatile periods, it may be best if at all possible to subcontract some work, thus affirming the company's commitment to retain the employees it takes on. This is obviously a sensitive issue.

Involvement of Participants

All involvement should be voluntary. This condition is easily met because a gainsharing plan is by its nature voluntary. Employees support the plan because they see it as being in their best interest.

Union representatives should be involved in all phases of the plan development, implementation, and evaluation. This will satisfy the union's need to see to it that there are no hidden tricks up management's sleeve. More important, it should help ensure the plan's success. Research has shown that systems in which the union has served as a visible and joint partner are most likely to result in improvements in the workers' views of their jobs and of their union's performance.[8]

Keeping the Plan Out of Union Contracts

There should be some assurance that the plan will not affect the collective bargaining agreement. Keeping the plan out of the labor agreement will avoid complications and generally make life easier for management as well as the union. Most plans have a memo of understanding, which specifically states what items will continue to be decided by management and which items are part of the union contract. Tying into wage negotiations obviously makes this separation difficult. Bonus payments have always been in the gray area of labor contracts and will likely continue to be so.

Most unions will not accept scapegoating of the workers as a major cause of poor productivity. Support of the plan eventually should lead to changing those rules that obstruct the employees' attempts to work more efficiently. To earn a bonus under gainsharing, employees should not have to work harder or longer, but smarter and more consistently.

Sharing of Information

Finally, some unions will expect management to open its books to some degree. Management must be willing to be more open and continue to share with the union relevant information about the organization's business. This will be especially important when presenting monthly or quarterly bonus results. Sharing information on the company's performance and walking union representatives through the calculation will be basic to building and maintaining cooperation. Successful firms are normally those most willing to share this information.

Winning Unions' Support

In many instances, the items discussed thus far will constitute necessary but not sufficient conditions for gaining the cooperation of the union as a joint partner in the plan. Responsibility still falls on management to convince the union that such a system is in its own best interest and, more important, in the best interest of the employees. Management must take the initiative in most situations. Additional steps will have to be taken to create an environment that will generate enthusiasm and make the plan a success, but ups and downs with regard to support should be expected. These steps will vary depending on the company and union, but a few general idealistic recommendations can be made.

1. *Pick the right facility.* If a company's long-range goal is to establish plans in several locations, it is important that things go well in the initial site. There are a number of variables to consider when making this selection, but a central one should, of course, be a good relationship between management and the union.
2. *Be frank in discussing the costs and the payoffs.* No union will risk a workplace experiment until it fully understands its advantages— financial and otherwise—for the workers. At the same time, the plan will ultimately be harmed if the potential benefits are exaggerated. Even if the plan is successful, the union's expectations could be raised to a level that cannot be satisfied. All parties involved must understand that large amounts of effort and support are required to make the plan work, and that much time may pass before they see financial rewards.
3. *Visit other gainsharing companies.* Key union representatives should be taken to firms—both union and nonunion—with active plans. (Nonunion installations are probably somewhat more common.) They should tour the facility and, if this is allowed, talk to anyone in the plant. It may be possible to arrange a meeting with the local president,

who can tell what gainsharing has meant to the union. Most important, they should talk to the gainsharing plan coordinator, if available, who holds a key position in nearly all successful gainsharing plans. Obviously, some care must be exercised in site selection.

4. *Be responsive to the union's inputs.* The union will be looking for evidence that its concerns are being taken seriously. In this regard, nothing is more effective than timely feedback. Raymond Majerus of the UAW observed:

> Management has to do more than simply listen to the union and its workers; it has to understand what is being said, react quickly to suggestions/proposals, and implement changes when they are warranted. In a worker's eyes, quick feedback and follow-through are perhaps the most telling yardsticks of management's commitment to an incentive program.[9]

5. *Seriously consider formation of a labor/management steering committee.* This group can be selected by both management and the union and can develop broad ground rules and a plan outline. When properly used, such a group is extremely effective in opening lines of communication and laying the groundwork for a plan that both sides can live with. This group can be permanent to maintain integrity of the system.

6. *Don't use gainsharing against the union.* Gainsharing could be used to exert negative pressures on the union in such instances as undermining provisions in the contract or pushing for decertification. This will quickly undermine support from any union.

SUMMARY

Are we on the brink of a new era of union-management cooperation? Probably not, although employee involvement gainsharing plans offer much promise for improvements in this area. In general, management will continue to pursue its goals of creating a profit, providing a reasonable return for shareholders, and improving employee relations. Unions will continue to strive for higher wages, benefits, and job security, and will still work for better conditions and for workers' rights.

The desires of employees, however, remain to be considered. Items of concern for this group include interest in expanding their roles, acquiring more control over their jobs, having a more direct impact on the company's performance, and sharing in the benefits. A study dealing with a large sample of workers found that four out of five wanted substantial say over the way the work is done and the quality of the work produced. Even more surprising is the list of things which fewer respondents indicated that they wanted to influence: when the work day begins and ends, who should be fired or hired, pay scales or wages, how complaints or grievances are handled, and who gets promoted.[10]

Such findings would indicate that employees are at least as concerned about how they do their jobs as they are about traditional bread-and-butter issues.

The trend toward contingent compensation further complicates this process, but the trend is not likely to change. However, it is unlikely that U.S. firms will endorse the system as actively as has Japan, where up to 41 million employees are on bonus plans which average around 25 percent of their pay.

Employee needs will not be easily ignored, either by the company or the union. The key is to develop systems that serve the needs of all parties, systems that currently are being devised by the country's more progressive firms and labor organizations. Such cases demonstrate that cooperative efforts can work when the different sides communicate openly, show an honest regard for the other side's concerns, and are cognizant that the goals of employees, management, and unions are essentially the same.

Because of its emphasis on establishing common goals, gainsharing has played an increasingly important role in this effort. That trend will accelerate as more firms and unions become familiar with the concepts that form gainsharing. The attitudes of union officers regarding gainsharing are not likely to change, however—some will support the idea, some will oppose it, and others will not know what position to take.

Notes

1. T. A. Kochan, H. C. Katz, and N. R. Mower, "Worker Participation and American Unions: Threat or Opportunity?" (Cambridge, Mass.: Sloan School of Management working paper No. 1526-84, Massachusetts Institute of Technology, 1984), 24–25.

2. R. Majerus, Secretary-Treasurer, UAW, "Incentive Plans: Why They Work and Why They Don't," address to the Conference on the Economics of Incentive, Cooperation and Risk Sharing, New York, N.Y., March 29, 1984, 5.

3. "Quality Circles: How Should Unions Respond?" *UBC Organizing—Industrial Bulletin,* United Brotherhood of Carpenters and Joiners of America, January 1983, 4.

4. "Profit Sharing and Group Incentive Plans," IAM Research Report, Vol. 7, No. 2, International Association of Machinists and Aerospace Workers, Spring 1979, 3.

5. T. Kochan, "Worker Participation," note 1, above, 15–20.

6. M. Parker and D. Hansen, "Using Quality Programs to Thwart Unions," *Workplace Democracy,* Winter 1984, 8.

7. C. Heckscher, "A Union Response to Quality Programs," *Workplace Democracy,* Winter 1984, 9.

8. T. Kochan, "Worker Participation," note 1, above, 21.

9. R. Majerus, "Incentive Plans," note 2, above, 7.

10. T. Kochan, "Worker Participation," note 1, above, 8–9.

Chapter 11

Integrating Quality and Customer Service into Gainsharing Calculations and a Case Study

Timothy L. Ross and Ruth Ann Ross

Throughout its 50 to 60 year history, traditional gainsharing in such various forms as the Scanlon and Rucker® Plans has long integrated quality and customer service into their measurement systems. Unfortunately, the integration was often quite weak. However, today's gainsharing plans have taken a much more proactive role in emphasizing quality and customer service in their employee involvement and bonus measurement systems. TQM, Statistical Process Control (SPC), and other systems have helped with this emphasis. This chapter reviews the changing emphasis and outlines a case study with major quality improvements.

THE HISTORY OF TRADITIONAL GAINSHARING QUALITY AND CUSTOMER SERVICE MEASUREMENT

Traditional gainsharing plans were very simple in their approach, particularly in how they considered quality and customer service. Most calculations related inputs or costs to such outputs as sales or value of production in dollars or units as discussed in Chapters 4 and 5.

With the traditional calculations such as single ratio of labor, multicost, value added, and allowed labor, practitioners attempted to integrate quality and customer service in a variety of fairly simple ways. First, through education and communication, firms tried to emphasize the importance of quality and customer service. Second, they started to deduct from the calculation for problem areas at two or three times the actual cost of returned products. That is, if actual returns were $40,000, firms started deducting two or three times that ($80,000 or $120,000) as a penalty against the plan. A similar approach was used for Improshare® or allowed labor. The employees were also told that only good production was rewarded. Scrap and rework were considered just a penalty on the plan, which was certainly true. These systems probably worked well from the 1940s to the late 1980s. It was then that quality and customer service gained importance, especially in manufacturing where most gainsharing applications occurred. The customer service and quality aspects were linked with the primary calculation, but the emphasis was not strong nor well focused in most situations.

Some of the plans also integrated a structured employee involvement system with the bonus system, especially Scanlon-oriented plans. These systems often used an overlapping team concept to push decision making down to the lowest level when possible as discussed in Chapter 3.

CURRENT TRENDS OF INCLUDING QUALITY AND CUSTOMER SERVICE

As companies have moved toward more emphasis on internal and external quality and customer service, they have used a variety of approaches to integrate these issues directly into the calculation. Some of the most common of these are outlined below.

Broader Calculations

The easiest way to include quality and customer service is to broaden the calculation to include more costs and complete the integration with education and communications. That is, tell and show participants how the calculation is influenced positively by improving internal (e.g., scrap, rework, overtime) and external (e.g., returns, complaints, premium freight) quality and customer service. Using this approach requires a major commitment to education and identity building. This approach is excellent if the firm is committed to long-term employee involvement.

Creating a Separate Pool for Quality and Customer Service

This common approach separates all quality and customer service costs into a separate pool, in addition to, say, a labor productivity pool. All the costs related to scrap, rework, overtime, premium freight, and returns for example are combined into a single pool. This becomes a cost of quality pool. It is then necessary either to develop some measure of output against which to measure these items or to base them on targets. Some companies increase the weight of this pool compared to the weight of other pools or give employees a different percentage of this particular pool in order to emphasize the importance of this performance criterion.

Goal Orientation

This approach is very simple in concept—"if you do this, you get this." For example, if scrap is reduced by $200,000 over the previous year as a result of a set goal, the participants would get so much of the savings. A substantial number of separate goals could be established not just for quality and customer service but also for other factors. (We once saw a plan with 27 separate goals or pools of costs or performance measures.) Although not normally grouped into gainsharing terminology or writings (gainsharing plans are normally considered to be organization- or plant-wide systems), the goal approach has been used extensively in developing small group incentive plans.

Another point should be made here. A goal approach often allows a firm to somewhat "control" how much bonus is paid. One can actually specify how much will be paid for what, if appropriate. This allows even a new start-up company to install a gainsharing plan.

An important note should be made here. Each of the previous three approaches are generally considered to be self funding. That is, costs have to be reduced in order for the company to pay a bonus. Some firms have the requirement that costs have to be reduced in some area before a bonus is paid, and will not pay for improvements such as improving upon shipping schedules, because they are not self funding. Finally, using a pool approach also allows an organization to include a variety of other factors in the calculation, such as inventory control and safety.

Indexing Approach

Two approaches are often used here. First you just create a ratio of where you were or some desired state, and where you are today. For example, if on-time shipments are 90 percent and you believe that this is a good target, then you would develop a ratio for calculating gainsharing of 90 percent divided by the percent of current performance. If current on-time deliveries are at 94 percent, then the index would be 94 ÷ 90, or 104.4 percent. This can be used to adjust any other calculation such as multicost or allowed labor, by plus 4.4 percent or some multiple of it (for example, increase 4.4 percent improvement times 3 if you want to increase the weighting).

A second "index approach" is to establish an acceptable level of performance that is then converted to a percent (e.g., for 1,000 deliveries, 10 customer complaints equals 10 percent; 5 equals 20 percent). These performance levels often include a series of items, such as customer complaints, quality, and customer service, and then convert them to a weighted index for all the factors to be included. The index can be paid by itself or can be used to adjust a more financial, self funding component of the calculation.

Points Approach

This could be considered an example of a goal oriented approach but it is based on an accumulation of points rather than dollars in total or a bonus percent. That is, each activity or performance level is worth so many points. A value is then assigned to the points and paid to each employee as a percent of their wage or some other method as long as the Fair Labor Standards Act regarding overtime is complied with.

Each of these approaches can be used for a wide variety of situations. If you have something you want to improve, have a measure of it, and can decide how much you want to reward the employees for the improvement—be it organization wide or in a specific group—you can develop a gainsharing calculation. Playing around with the different options is really fun. One caution is in order, however. When designing the calculation, thoroughly research the options before implementation. Changes made to the calculation later may create mistrust, particularly if the participants are not aware that this can/will happen.

A CASE STUDY OF GAINSHARING DRIVING QUALITY IMPROVEMENT

Flying high on the flagpole in front of the Evart Products Co. in Evart, Michigan, is a flag designating the company as a winner of the Chrysler Corp. Quality Excellence Award. This much-coveted award goes only to facilities in which defect rates are less than .04 percent—that's four defective products per 10,000 shipped.

It wasn't long ago, however, that the company—which supplies automotive assembly plants with exterior signal lighting, high-mount stop lights, dashliners, pads, trims, and other plastic products—was flying in the face of disaster. Just ask Larry Roman, Evart's plant manager--he can remember when the defect rate was a whopping 4.37 percent, or 437 defective parts per 10,000.

"Four years ago, I received complaint calls—and sometimes multiple complaint calls—every week from managers at assembly plants because we were rated as one of the five worst suppliers in almost every plant. I'm talking about out of *all* their outside suppliers—hundreds or thousands of suppliers. We were shipping them junk," says Roman.

Knowing something had to be done to turn the company around, a task force of corporate- and plant-level managers, including the personnel manager, Mike Critchfield, was formed to explore the organization's options. In late 1986, this group concluded that gainsharing offered the greatest potential for addressing the firm's many problems in a rapid way. The pros and cons of this approach were discussed with all employees in large town meetings in late 1986 and early 1987. In June 1987, more than 90 percent of the employees voted to implement a gainsharing plan for a trial period of one year. (The trial period later was expanded to 18 months.)

The gainsharing plan worked. In just four years, Evart has pulled off an impressive turnaround. For example:

- The 1991 defect rate stood at just .02 percent, or two defects per 10,000 parts shipped and improvement continued.
- The company has earned numerous awards for its achievements in product quality.
- Evart's much-improved reputation has allowed it to capture business from other facilities, making it the largest supplier of nonheadlight lighting systems to Chrysler.
- The company has achieved a level of management and nonmanagement cooperation and employee involvement that's unheard-of in most automotive plants and progress continues.

Quest Plan is a High-Involvement System

Quest Plan, Evart's gainsharing system, can be described as a high-involvement gainsharing plan because it consists of two parts: 1) a bonus calculation that pays employees regular bonuses for improved company performance; and 2) a structured employee suggestion system that facilitates employee participation through the involvement of nonmanagement employees in work decisions; the system is similar to that discussed in Chapter 3.

What the Quest Plan does is link the bonus and the involvement system so that they work in tandem to create organizational change. The bonus gives workers the *motivation* to improve productivity and quality, while the involvement system gives them the *power* actually to make these changes. At the same time, the interlocking nature of the three-tiered framework of committees included in the suggestion system fosters better communication, coordination, and working relationships.

With Evart's bonus calculation, the amount of actual production taking place is assessed each month, and the allowed costs associated with this level of production then are determined. The allowed costs are an estimate of how much it should have cost to produce these goods, based on the way the plant has performed historically. Quality is heavily emphasized with a separate pool.

Employees achieve a gain (improve the overall performance of the company) when the actual costs of production are lower than the allowed costs for that month. This is accomplished by increasing output, cutting labor costs, cutting material costs, decreasing waste, or improving the overall performance of the plant in other ways.

Everybody Likes the Checks

Employees at all levels believe that organizational effectiveness has improved since the Quest Plan was implemented. Some of the more frequently mentioned areas of improvement are:

1. *Product Quality.* A number of indicators of product quality showed dramatic improvements under the Quest Plan. For example:
   - Evart's rate of defective products shipped to its main customer (Chrysler) decreased from 4.4 percent in 1986 to 0.02 percent in 1991 and decreases continue today.
   - The firm's Supplier Quality Assurance Survey scores increased from 78 percent in 1986 to 96 percent in 1993.
   - Evart received the Acustar Quality Council Award in 1989 and the Chrysler Quality Excellence Award in 1989, 1990, 1991, and 1992 model years. The company received the Volkswagen Quality Excellence Award in 1990, and other awards followed in 1992 and 1993.

   Why would a gainsharing plan contribute to quality gains? "Everybody likes that check when it comes from the gainsharing plan," says one first-line supervisor. Although the supervisor admits that there's a certain percentage of people who remain by choice uninvolved in the program, he says that there's a larger percentage who actually take more pride in the parts they produce. "They realize that, if the part is defective, it hurts the contributions to the payout. It's as if the money is coming out of their own pockets."

   Quality improvement also can be attributed to Evart's success in linking the Quest Plan with its Quality Improvement Process, an eight-step quality assurance system used at Evart. Says Roman, "We were able to get management at Acustar to agree that Quest would be our Quality Improvement Process. So we now have all eight Quality Improvement Process steps assigned to the people on the Quest board as their steps. We then follow the steps and turn them in just the way the rest of the Chrysler plants do."

   Roman points out, however, that quality isn't achieved by gainsharing alone. There are many other processes involved. For example, Evart hired a quality control manager with solid background in statistical process control and other areas. Roman says this helped the company implement the system of controls needed to ensure quality. "With the proper implementation of our quality principles—our statistical process control methods—we were able to augment the efforts of Quest and make those improvements in quality."

2. *Cost Savings.* According to Rick Christner, Evart's controller, the performance improvements enjoyed by the firm weren't limited to just gains in quality. "Before, it was management's problem. But now, people are interested in how much parts cost, how much waste is in the operation, how much power we waste and whether utility usage is excessive." As a result, employees often have suggestions on ways to cut costs.

3. *Improved Sales and Employment.* According to Jim Walker, coordinator of the Quest Plan, the gainsharing plan also has paid off with

increased sales and job security. "We've increased sales to the point that we're back to full employment here," says Walker. "We've picked up business from a lot of companies that have gone under. It's because of our quality rating—we can achieve things that they can't." Based on the volume of work coming in, Walker predicts Evart's sales will more than double by 1995. This means that the company will need to hire an additional 100 to 200 employees.

4. *Employee Involvement.* From August 1987 through November 1991, Evart employees contributed 4,329 performance-improvement suggestions by way of the Quest Plan. More than 90 percent of the workers have become involved with the plan in some way, either by contributing ideas or by serving on one of the plan's many teams. The rate of involvement as well as the rate of implemented suggestions continues to increase.

When asked what they liked most about the Quest Plan, the overwhelming majority of employees talked about the new power they enjoy under the plan's involvement system. Says one hourly, nonmanagement employee, "If you have an idea to change the whole setup in your area, all you have to do is write a suggestion. And if it's feasible economically, it will be done. The next thing you know—sometimes within 30 days—it's already changed around and operating. It almost sounds too good to be true. If it's that easy, then it can't be right, actually to have that much say in what goes on around here, I mean, to have a voice that management listens to."

Early in the Quest Plan's implementation, the nonmanagement employees proved that they could generate useful ideas for improving inefficient work methods and quality, many of which have been in place for years. The next logical step was to get these employees involved in the design of new jobs so that they could be engineered for maximum efficiency before they went on line. According to Nelson J. Morren, manager of manufacturing engineering, that's just what the company did.

"We consistently appeal to the people for their ideas when launching new product/programs. And they're very participative along those lines. They're involved with the launch of new products. They're brought into the picture. They voice their concerns about things they see that we, from an engineering standpoint, would miss. The whole philosophy is that we're not the only ones who are going to be doing the engineering—it isn't a case in which the only people who can think of engineering things are engineers," says Morren.

5. *Improved Self-Management.* Some employees felt that the involvement system has led, not only to better ideas for work design, but also to nonmanagement employees' becoming self-managed; that is, they're becoming more concerned about company performance and are more

conscientious when performing their jobs, and this has taken some of the pressure off management to provide close, continuous supervision.

"If you have involvement, you have a whole source of new ideas, improvements and cooperativeness that you don't have if everything keeps coming down from the top," says Roman. "Now the ideas come from the employees themselves. Lots of them I don't even know about. All I know is that there are improvements, and they're working better out there. And because they're the ones to come up with the ideas, investigate them, and implement them, they're the ones who make themselves keep at it; I'm not. From the top, I can't say to that many people: 'You must do this every day. This is your job,' I don't have the time to do that. I don't have the awareness. I'm not smart enough. I can't wear all those hats," Roman explains.

6. *Communications and Employee Relations.* The Quest Plan's involvement system, with its procedures for handling suggestions and its hierarchy of interlocking teams, was designed to open new lines of communication and foster improved interpersonal relations within the firm. Nearly all of the employees we spoke with felt that it had succeeded in this regard. "I think the [Quest Plan] has done a lot for this company, mainly in the form of better communications," says one supervisor. "Years back, the management portion of this company was off-limits to the hourly people. An hourly person wasn't allowed in the front office unless he or she was escorted. Now there's kind of an open-door policy, and everyone's encouraged to become involved and creative."

These sentiments also were echoed by an hourly employee. "I think people feel free to come in and talk to a manager if they need advice or input, or even if they want to tell about a suggestion. Before, you'd rarely see an hourly person in these offices; now you're liable to meet almost anybody in here. As a matter of fact, before Quest came in, a lot of the people out on the floor didn't even know who the managers were. You know, there was this wall right here, and you just didn't cross it. They didn't come out and we didn't go in. It's just like a revolving door now. Communication is 100 percent better."

The Transition Created New Concerns

The introduction of the gainsharing plan at Evart involved a transition to an entirely new philosophy of management, so it's no surprise that this transition has brought with it a number of new difficulties and concerns. The areas of difficulty discussed most frequently include:

1. *Helping Supervisors and Managers Adjust.* Perhaps more than any other group, supervisors and managers can feel threatened and vulnerable when gainsharing is implemented. Almost overnight, their

company expects them to allow a greater amount of employee involvement in work decisions, forcing supervisors into a more participative management style for which they may possess few skills. Even worse, supervisors often fear that they'll look bad when employees submit performance-improvement ideas. After all, if it was such a good idea, why hadn't the supervisor already thought of it?

Supervisors may experience problems in the early stages of a gainsharing implementation, but these difficulties tend to fade as time passes, and they begin to feel more comfortable with their new roles. One hourly worker described the supervisors' transition in these terms: "I think that they're the ones who have dragged their feet. I worked second shift, and there were a lot of disbelievers—or whatever you want to call them—when they started out. But once they started to change over, they went whole-hog. And they wound up being the models before they got done. It just took a while for some of them."

2. *Staffing Problems*. It takes time to run a gainsharing plan—time to research ideas, hold meetings and perform the other activities necessary for organizational change. It's assumed that any inefficiency caused by pulling employees off their jobs for these activities will be outweighed by the long-term gains in performance eventually achieved by the plan. Nevertheless, employees often report concern about the short-term staffing problems that can be caused by a gainsharing plan.

"The problem that it creates for me as supervisor is that three or four employees on my crew are involved in it, and for hours out of the day, when I could use them on the floor repairing equipment or machinery, they're gone," says one supervisor. "It's difficult to maneuver the work load and still allow everything to be done that needs to be done as far as the gainsharing plan is concerned. Actually, I have one employee who works one hour a day, because he does seven hours of work on Quest. It's a problem that's bothersome for me, because I could use him, I'm short-handed a lot of times anyway." On the other hand, the supervisor agrees that it pays off. "I can see the benefits that are derived from it, so I just work around it one way or another," he explains.

3. *Mistrust of the Calculation*. During 1988, the average employee earned gainsharing bonuses totaling $1,012. During 1989, these bonuses totaled $1,058. But in 1990, Evart employees saw nothing in the way of Quest bonuses. Walker attributes the lack of bonuses to broader problems with the national economy and auto sales. "It has just shut everything down," he says. Many nonmanagement employees agree.

Despite this sentiment, our interviews did *not* suggest that the majority of workers actually distrust the calculation. The plan again began to pay bonuses in 1991, and it's hoped that this, along with con-

tinuing training and education, will lead to greater understanding and trust. In 1993, bonuses increased to over 5 percent.
4. *Union Concerns.* Four officials of the United Auto Workers (UAW) local at Evart were interviewed, and they expressed mixed feelings about the Quest Plan. They discussed the following positive features.
   • Quest allows employees a voice in making changes at the company,
   • has improved working conditions in some cases,
   • has improved job safety,
   • has opened lines of communication, and
   • pays financial bonuses.
   On the other hand, the UAW representatives also stated that the plan had the following negative features.
   • Some suggestions have caused jobs to be overloaded with operations.
   • Some suggestions can eliminate jobs.
   • Some important cost factors aren't included in the bonus calculation.
   • Standards were raised after the plan began, making it more difficult to earn bonuses.
   • After being voted in permanently, the plan stopped paying bonuses (temporarily).
   To some extent, the union has taken on a watchdog role, looking for Quest suggestions that could eliminate positions, load jobs, or create safety hazards. When necessary, it can grieve objectionable suggestions. The union representatives advise other companies considering a plan to keep the gainsharing plan and the union contract separate, and to look constantly for ways to improve the system. Says one union official, "You've got to fine-tune that baby every year, just like a car. You've got to move with the times. Times change, and I think this program has got to move with them, too. It has to be flexible."

This case illustrates the benefits to be derived from an employee involvement gainsharing plan, especially one focusing on quality. Gainsharing can help speed the process of change since in a situation like this, closure was quite probable if rapid change didn't occur. Employment has also grown significantly as is often the case with a good employee involvement gainsharing plan over a multi-year period in both good and bad times.

SUMMARY

The need for improved quality and customer service has resulted in more emphasis being placed on these factors in gainsharing calculations. Innovative approaches continue to be added with increases in gainsharing flexibility in its application to different situations and emphasis. Evart is an example of a firm that used the system for quality and other improvements.

Chapter 12

Managerial Perceptions of Employee Involvement Gainsharing: A Case Study and Survey

Timothy L. Ross and Ruth Ann Ross

Although employee involvement gainsharing plans have grown in popularity in recent years, we still need to understand them better. Why do they work or not work? Can they be used to foster organizational change or should they only be installed after changes have been made and employee involvement has evolved? That is, should they be used to lead organization change, which was the traditional approach, or lag it? Do managers gain or lose control with more employee involvement, and how does adding a bonus affect the change process? Would managers continue their plans or drop them? Can they work well in both autocratic and participative management situations or only in participative ones? These are a very few of the questions that concern gainsharing. Without any doubt, the consultant/practitioner/innovator has led the researcher in gainsharing development and implementation.

To delve into a small portion of the research questions, we surveyed 108 managers in eight firms that have gainsharing plans. We will review the managers' evaluations of how their jobs were affected, how their subordinates behaved, and how satisfied they were with their plans. In addition, we will review other studies documenting the organizational benefits that can be expected from such plans and will present a case example of one company's experience with a plan. All of these plans have fully developed employee involvement systems. None are just bonus plans.

A SHORT CASE EXAMPLE

Ross Manufacturing (a fictitious name), a 480-employee manufacturing company in Ohio, has operated since 1983 under a gainsharing plan typical of many being implemented today. The plan has two basic features: (1) an idea system that solicits and implements employees' ideas on improving performance, and (2) a bonus formula that measures performance and pays employees a financial bonus when performance exceeds a targeted level.

The idea system is the heart of the plan, because it opens lines of communication, builds team spirit, and channels workers' energy and creativity toward productivity and quality goals. It is a way to get things done and, although different firms use different types of idea systems, Ross Manufacturing's will be used as a typical example.

The process begins when an employee writes down an idea on a simple form and turns it in to the department's team. Ross has 16 such teams. Each consists of a supervisor and from one to four elected nonmanagement representatives. Team members often help employees refine their ideas and prepare them for submission.

The departmental team investigates an idea to determine cost, feasibility, and likely benefits. The team may implement an idea if it costs less than $200, the team members all agree that it is a good idea, the idea does not affect another department, or if the team can get another department to agree to implement. If a department is seriously affected or does not agree, the idea goes to a plant-wide council consisting of management and one elected nonmanagement person from each department team. The council reviews ideas costing more than $200 and acts in an advisory capacity to management. Cross-functional groups are formed as needed for larger, more interdependent problems.

Ross employees have contributed ideas touching almost every aspect of its business. Employees have made suggestions on ways to simplify jobs, improve quality, reroute work materials, reduce material handling, eliminate unnecessary operations, reduce set-up time and down time, order office supplies, and other ways to improve the organization's effectiveness. Over 800 suggestions were made during the first two years of the system, resulting in more than $500,000 in estimated cost savings.

In most organizations, involvement systems like the one just described are designed by both nonmanagement and management personnel. At Ross, a cross section of employees from all levels of the organization met over a two-month period to develop their idea system and design other plan policies.

The second major feature of the plan, the financial bonus, was developed so that employees could share in the gains made under the new system of management. Gainsharing differs from most other employee involvement plans, such as TQM, because of the bonus component of the system. The basic philosophy in employee involvement gainsharing is equity: all employees should benefit financially for their creativity and extra effort just as the company benefits financially.

In simple terms, the company's performance—labor costs, material costs, sales value of production, and so forth—is assessed every two months.

When performance for a current term is above the performance for the historical base period of the preceding several years, 40 percent of the improvement goes to the employees and 60 percent is retained by the company. Any bonus is paid to all employees as a percentage of wages earned for that term. Fifty percent of the employee's share is held in a reserve pool to be paid, if positive, at the end of the year. The reserve encourages positive attitudes toward long-term improvements in performance. The larger the reserve, the more long-term emphasis exists in the plan.

It should be noted from previous chapters that this is only one example of a bonus calculation and that most companies will tailor formulas to their specific needs. Some companies pay bonuses more frequently, on a monthly or even weekly basis. Some firms define productivity narrowly, such as work output per direct-labor workhour; other calculations include so many indices of performance that they resemble formulas for profit-sharing plans. A primary distinction is that most gainsharing plans require performance to exceed some historical level before a bonus is paid. This is not so with many profit-sharing plans. Some gainsharing plans are also based on goals or targets. More plans are incorporating penalties against poor quality.

Results at Ross Manufacturing

A successful plan requires adjustment from almost everyone in the firm, and many organizations appoint a full-time coordinator to administer gainsharing activities and facilitate the change process. At Ross Manufacturing, Bob Gibson was plan coordinator during the first two years of their plan. Gibson remembers that during the early period of implementation there was some concern about how staff and middle-level managers would adjust to the more participative management style. Said Gibson:

> I think the middle-level managers felt a little bypassed because suddenly we had an open channel from the bottom of the organization right to the top. Care must be taken not to bypass these managers, but to keep them involved.
>
> We have people with professional degrees—I'll use an engineer as an example—who thought "that guy out there running that machine doesn't know as much about that as I do." We've had to deal with the attitude not to belittle or insult either one, but to bring them closer together. To make them see "By golly, maybe he does have something to add. And maybe I did overlook this when I designed it." And I think we've gained a lot.
>
> The object is to build teamwork, to get everyone involved. In part, this requires working with managers who may feel threatened when subordinates make suggestions for productivity improvement. Some will see such suggestions as thinly veiled criticism of how they were managing their work units. There is sometimes fear that others will say, "If you are such a good manager, why didn't you think of that idea?"

This may be an especially sensitive issue for first-level managers or supervisors. Some supervisors fear that they will lose their authority, their control over the work unit, when their people are given a say in work decisions. Gibson recalls:

> Initially, the supervisors thought they were going to be undermined. The non-management people had a tool whereby they could go around their supervisor and get something done. I was so anxious to get involvement from the nonmanagement people on the floor that I overlooked the supervisors. I set the departmental teams up with the people from the floor as chairmen. I think I really hurt the supervisors when I did that. They said, "Everybody's talking about my department, but I don't have the say." And that wasn't my intent. I was so anxious to grasp all the involvement I could that I bypassed the supervisors.
>
> Now, however, the supervisors are the chairpersons and the system is working much better. Because they know their way around. They know who to ask and how to get things done.

Ross Manufacturing's experience shows that when more participative management is introduced, it can cause apprehension among managers at all levels. The success of their plan also demonstrates, however, that sensitivity and responsiveness to the managers' legitimate concerns can ease their adjustment and help make a plan even stronger. More will follow on Ross Manufacturing later in this chapter.

A SURVEY OF MANAGERS IN GAINSHARING FIRMS

Of course, Ross Manufacturing is only one firm, and its experiences with managers under a participative productivity plan may not be representative. We wanted to learn about the experiences of managers from a variety of organizations with similar systems.

To this end, we distributed a survey to 145 managers in eight gainsharing organizations. Completed questionnaires were returned by 108 (74 percent) of the managers. Of these, 4 percent were upper-level managers, 33 percent were middle-level managers, 59 percent were first-level managers, and 4 percent did not indicate a classification.

All of the organizations were production firms, with products including waste-disposal trucks, industrial pumps, hydraulic equipment, valves, wood products, industrial monitoring equipment, and information processing equipment. Each firm employed between 100 and 450 employees (with an average of 288) and had been managed under a gainsharing plan for between one and six years.

The survey allowed the managers to evaluate various aspects of their jobs. Each area was rated with a five-point scale, ranging from "very poor" to "very good." For each area, the manager made two ratings. The first evaluated the area as it was before the gainsharing plan and the second evaluated the area as it was at the time of the survey (after the plan was in effect).

Managers' Adjustment to Participative Management

One group of questions was designed to assess the managers' perceptions of their own jobs. We wanted to know whether a manager's role becomes more difficult under the participative gainsharing philosophy. Of particular concern was whether managers felt they still had control in the work unit, whether they still understood their role as managers and felt they could not get things done.

These questions dealing with role adjustment, along with a summary of responses, are presented in Exhibit 12.1. It indicates that the managers, as a group, perceived improvement under gainsharing in every area.

Items 1, 2, and 3 reveal that, after plan implementation, managers felt that they had greater influence over their jobs, had greater ability to get work done, and were better able to handle crisis situations. This change in their general capacity to make things happen probably has much to do with improved cooperation from the people they directed. As item 4 reveals, the percentage of managers rating such subordinate cooperation as good or very good jumped from 48 percent before the plan to 80 percent after. A later section of this chapter will deal with subordinate performance in greater detail.

Item 5 shows that an alarmingly large number of managers do not consider their work load to be reasonable. Despite this fact, the average manager felt the situation had improved after gainsharing was adopted, even if not by much. This perception is especially encouraging in light of the fact that gainsharing adds new tasks to most managers' role: leading meetings, soliciting ideas, and helping to research and implement employee ideas. These findings may suggest that the increased teamwork, work effort, and cooperation in the work unit sufficiently lightened the managers' work load to offset the extra duties required by the plan; this hopefully always happens in the long run.

Items 6 and 7 reveal that, under a gainsharing plan, the average manager developed an even greater understanding of his or her job duties, goals, and objectives. The greater clarity of managerial goals and objectives probably results from the new lines of communication and the increased emphasis on goal setting. For example, employees at Ross Manufacturing meet (in groups of 80) once each month to review the company's performance. After opening remarks from the president, the company controller provides a detailed account of the factors influencing company performance. Time is spent identifying such areas as warranty costs or direct labor costs that are helping or hurting the employees' chance to earn a bonus. A question and answer period follows. When the meeting ends, managers and nonmanagement personnel alike leave with a better understanding of the goals that should be pursued in the following month.

These common goals, in large part, contribute to each work unit's sense of teamwork and cohesion. While the monthly meetings at Ross have been suc-

Exhibit 12.1　Survey Responses, Managers' Adjustment to Gainsharing

	Percentage Indicating "Good" or "Very Good"	
	Before Gainsharing	**After Gainsharing**
1. Your influence over what happens on your job	41%	66%
2. Your ability to get work done	64	75
3. Your ability to deal with "crisis" situations	56	77
4. The extent to which your subordinates do what you want them to do	48	80
5. The reasonableness of your work load	25	36
6. Your understanding of what your job duties are	60	71
7. Your understanding of the goals and objectives of your job	58	84

Note: Percentages are based on 108 completed questionnaires received from managers in companies with gainsharing plans.

cessful in this regard, other gainsharing firms choose to post company performance data on a more frequent—even daily—basis.

In summary, the survey presented no evidence that the managers lost control of their work settings or experienced major adjustment difficulties when their plan's more participative management style was adopted. It should be remembered, however, that these changes did not come about automatically. In most of the surveyed companies, the organization supported its managers by giving them a realistic appraisal of what to expect, seeking their input along the way, and providing education and training as to how to manage under the plan. Such positive results cannot be expected when these safeguards are overlooked.

Managers' Evaluations of Subordinates

A second group of questions on the same survey allowed the respondents to evaluate changes in the behavior of the employees they managed. This was necessary to test one of the major assertions of the gainsharing philosophy: that employees behave differently under a plan. That is, a plan should not only open up lines of communication and accelerate the implementation of good performance improvement ideas, but should also lead to more team-oriented behaviors in a majority of the employees. With common goals, the average employee should be more concerned about keeping costs low and output high without sacrificing quality. The surveyed managers were in an excellent position to provide these evaluations.

The summary of item responses in Exhibit 12.2 suggests that the managers felt that the average employee showed substantial improvements in all of

Exhibit 12.2   Survey Responses, Managers' Evaluations of
Subordinates' Performance

	Percentage Indicating "Good" or "Very Good"	
	Before Gainsharing	After Gainsharing
1. Your subordinates' concern for controlling costs	24%	70%
2. Your subordinates' concern for increasing the amount of work accomplished	25	69
3. Your subordinates' concern for maintaining/ improving quality	40	84
4. Your subordinates' willingness to accept change	20	58
5. Your subordinates' feeling of involvement in their jobs	27	72
6. Your subordinates' commitment not to be unnecessarily absent	36	67

Note: Percentages are based on 108 completed questionnaires received from managers in companies with gainsharing plans.

the areas assessed. Items 1, 2, and 3 indicate that while employee concern about costs, outputs, and quality had been somewhat low prior to gainsharing, major improvements were seen afterward. The remaining items reflect similar gains with regard to employee willingness to accept change, job involvement, and absence rates. In short, most managers believed that their people were performing more effectively under their plans.

It should be emphasized, however, that an employee involvement gainsharing plan should not be designed as a "speed-up" device. A gainsharing plan should result in a work unit that performs more intelligently, with employees using their know-how to cut waste, shorten delays, and remove obstacles to higher efficiency. When everyone pulls in the same direction, performance improvements follow. Although some firms encourage gains in output quantity, the company using a plan primarily as a speed-up mechanism is likely to encounter strong and ultimately fatal resistance; this approach can probably not survive in the long term.

Satisfaction With the Gainsharing Plan

A final group of questions allowed the managers to indicate general satisfaction with their organizations' gainsharing plans. Responses were made on a seven-point scale ranging from "strongly disagree" to "strongly agree," and are summarized in Exhibit 12.3.

Exhibit 12.3   Survey Responses, Managers' Satisfaction With Their
Gainsharing Plans

	Percentage Indicating "Somewhat Agree," "Agree," or "Strongly Agree"
1. You are satisfied with your bonus plan.	77%
2. Your company should continue with the plan.	91
3. Would you advise others to install a plan like yours?	82
4. The plan is good for nonmanagement employees.	89
5. The plan is good for supervisors.	74

Note: Percentages are based on 108 completed questionnaires received from managers in companies with gainsharing plans.

It can be seen that over three-fourths were at least somewhat satisfied with their plans, and over nine-tenths felt that their companies should continue under gainsharing. Informal conversations with individual managers revealed that, while they were generally pleased with the gainsharing concept, there was often some specific aspect of their company's plan that they found disagreeable. These "bugs" in the system varied from manager to manager, and comments ranged from "I don't like the paperwork" to "I don't like some of the costs included in the bonus formula." Such individual objections are, of course, to be expected from any diverse work force. On the average, however, managers liked the gainsharing idea, and 82 percent said they would advise others to install a plan similar to their own.

Interestingly, respondents were somewhat more likely to agree that their plan was good for nonmanagement employees (89 percent) than for supervisors (74 percent). This is probably because nonmanagement participation in plan activities is voluntary—workers can be as involved or uninvolved as they desire, and even the disinterested employee will share in the bonus if the plant earns one. On the other hand, supervisors must of necessity put out extra effort, actively participate in the plan to make it work, and assume a broader role as manager. As was discussed earlier, however, this new role should eventually lighten the supervisor's work load, as the work unit develops as a team and assumes more responsibility for managing itself.

THE CASE OF ROSS MANUFACTURING

The impact that gainsharing has on management and nonmanagement personnel can be better understood by reviewing further the case example. Ross Manufacturing's experience is useful in that it shows how firm commitment to the plan from top management, along with openness and teamwork, can be effective in turning an unprofitable company into a profitable one. We will review the organization's unfavorable conditions existing prior to implementation, follow the actions taken to maintain employee involvement during the first year when no bonuses were paid, and summarize the improvements in organizational effectiveness that were ultimately achieved.

Declining Profitability

The late 1970s had been good times for Ross. Markets were strong, and plant employment soared to a high of 700. But as the economy declined, cities and private haulers cut back on orders for truck bodies and garbage truck units. By the early 1980s, the company was failing to show a profit in most months. Layoffs followed, trimming employment to around 300 by 1982. Remaining employees listened to the news of the closing of other manufacturing plants in the area, and rumor had it that Ross' closing was not far off. John Miller, president of Ross at that time, agrees: "That's true. . . . I don't think there's any question about that," he acknowledged. "You're on a collision course when management and the hourly personnel—the people who make it happen—don't communicate with one another and refuse to listen to each other's ideas and suggestions. That's really what was causing our problems more than anything else."

Worsening the division between management and nonmanagement personnel was an outdated individual incentive system that served as a constant source of conflict. The company averaged 160 grievances a year, many of them involving rates established under the old incentive plan. Because the old rates had not kept pace with changes in technology, some workers could reach their daily quota in only a few hours' time. Miller saw this as a major obstacle to productivity: "When you put an incentive system in and you are forced to put a cap on it that says an employee can only earn X number of dollars, that says that you have totally lost control. And that's what had been going on here for a long while. Let's face it, we had no incentive system. We had a giveaway system that said 'whatever you want to run, you run, then go sit in the corner or do whatever you want.'"

Turning It Around

Miller arrived at Ross in mid-1982, when morale was at its lowest. Poor product quality and resulting warranty and product liability claims were draining profits. In troubleshooting this problem, Miller wanted input from the employees on the production line. His goal was to reduce the number of inspectors on the payroll, and instead give employees responsibility for inspecting their own work. "You can't inspect quality in," he stated. "I don't care if you put on 50 inspectors. That won't get it done. People in the plant out there know when they're producing a quality part. They know when they're producing a part that will withstand the strains that it's required to withstand. And if you refuse to listen to their ideas, they'll tell you a couple of times and then they'll say 'OK, fine. The hell with it. If that's what you want, I'll produce all the junk you want.' And that's kind of what we were doing."

After buying out the old incentive system, the company began to develop the group gainsharing system that would replace it. From the beginning, it was understood that the new plan would encourage the participation of all employees. Management and nonmanagement personnel worked together on a developmental task force that hammered out plan details: Who would be eligible to earn a bonus? How would nonmanagement members on the departmental teams be elected? What kind of ideas would be acceptable as being "performance-related?" What would be included in the bonus calculation?

The goal was to promote employee ownership of the plan. To this end, management openly discussed the company's bleak situation with the employees and sought the union's input and recommendations. It was understood that without openness and trust, the attempt at participative management would fail.

The implementation was further supported by preparing managers for the transition to the new management style. Prior to the actual plan start-up, and continuing throughout the year, managers (including supervisors) received dozens of hours of education as to how to be more effective under the new system.

Employees were told that the system would not work without their commitment. To ensure this, a vote on the plan was held. The plan was to be adopted only if 80 percent voted in its favor; it was approved by 89 percent.

From the beginning, a variety of factors worked against the plan's success. The market for trucks and truck bodies had dried up, and low sales volume made it impossible for employees to earn a bonus during the first 12 months after implementation. One might have predicted that such events would cause employees to believe that the promise of a bonus was a management lie and subsequently lose all interest in the gainsharing plan, called PEP (Program for Employee Participation). This did not happen, however. President Miller attributes this to the new atmosphere of mutual respect developing in the firm. "It's a matter of trust and communication," he said. "We had monthly meetings where I got everybody together and poured out my soul: 'Here are the problems we're facing, and here are the opportunities we have. Here are the things which have gone right, and these are the things that have gone wrong. Here's where I think we are, and here's how long I think it will take us to get a bonus. Now what do you think?' And we continued to talk and we saw progress—not a lot of progress— but progress on a monthly basis."

Employees' ideas continued to come in and be implemented. New ways were found to cut costs—from the welders on the shop floor to the secretaries in the office. Finally, in the fourth two-month period, a $92,278 bonus was announced. Bonuses have been earned fairly consistently in subsequent periods, even if they are not always large.

Results for the Company

Ross was quite profitable after nine years under the PEP plan. Miller says that the big gains were in the area of quality control, with warranty costs based on sales now about half of what they were the preceding year. Product recalls have dropped to about 3 percent of sales. In keeping with Miller's objective, in-plant inspectors were reduced from sixteen before the plan to two after six years. Miller further adds, "I had nine people on the road. And those nine service people were out repairing junk. I mean things that are ridiculous; things that should not happen. Like someone on the production line forgot to put in some bolts or whatever. And that number of service people has now gone from nine to one."

In a recent year, less than 30 grievances were filed, down from an average of 160 annually in preceding years. In a recent year, 98.3 percent of the employees voted to continue with the PEP plan, up from 89 percent at the original vote.

SUMMARY

The results of our managers' survey suggested that the majority of managers in gainsharing companies had adjusted well to their new roles, had seen improvement in the behavior of their subordinates, and were generally satisfied with their plans. But, as the Ross Manufacturing case demonstrates, adjustment problems can occur, and managers must be given understanding, support, and training if they are to adapt to life under a plan. At Ross, this was accomplished in part by recognizing the needs of the managers and adjusting the plan's idea system accordingly.

Winning the support of managers in this way paid off at Ross Manufacturing. The company managers implemented their plan under the worst of conditions and held fast to its philosophy of participative management, even as months passed with no financial bonus. Ross has turned around and is making inroads in new markets both here and internationally. Many of the managers we talked with, however, felt that the plant would have simply become another entry on the list of unionized midwest companies forced to close had it not been for the PEP plan and the changes it introduced.

Chapter 13

Some Education Recommendations for Successful Employee Involvement

Timothy L. Ross and Ruth Ann Ross

As the use of employee involvement gainsharing and gainsharing in general expands into a variety of different situations, education needs for all levels of employees will also expand. For example, if gainsharing is being used solely as a form of contingent or variable compensation, education needs may be minimal. However, if gainsharing is installed to change significantly the way employees are managed or as a replacement for individual incentives, education of both management and nonmanagement employees may be extremely important to the plan's long-term success. Likewise, if gainsharing is installed with significant employee involvement, education may make the difference between long-term success and failure.

Although each organization must evaluate its own needs, internal/external resources, and ability to pay for such activities, what follows is an outline of perhaps a minimum amount of education that an organization should provide for the typical installation when considerable formalized employee involvement is included in the system. The approach used here is for a more generic, customized approach as opposed to a more "packaged" one. An outline is found on Exhibit 13.1.

STAGES OF EDUCATION

Stage 1

This stage represents preliminary top management education, which is always necessary. In some cases, training could include the union officials if applicable. The purpose at this stage is to investigate whether gainsharing is appropriate for the particular organization. Education may take the form of

213

Exhibit 13.1 Recommended Education With Major Employee Involvement

Stage	Audience	Timing	Typical Content
1	Top Management	First session of exposure: public seminar or consultant	Various gainsharing approaches Key decisions Different involvement approaches Different calculations Expectations Study and implementation strategies Evaluation of current system/need to change
2	Top Management	Early in study phase	Decide on calculations Develop a working plan Evaluate comprehension of plan
3	All Employees	Before introduction of gainsharing concept	Typical employee survey assessing need to change; must have feedback. Probably infrequently used in actual practice; some assessment of conditions is needed, however.
4	All Employees	After closure on calculation and after corporate approval; to help develop a task force for completing the plan document	Introduction to gainsharing General principles/philosophy Typical employee involvement Typical calculations (few details) Possible benefits to company and employees Plan of action Need to develop a task force to finalize plan
5	All of Management/ Supervisors	After introduction but before plan is finalized by a task force (3 to 5 hours)	Principles of gainsharing Implementation steps Typical involvement systems Typical calculations Differences in management styles How to achieve a more consultative/participative environment How to maintain it Common reactions to change and how to overcome
6	All Employees (1 to 1 1/2 hours), and	Immediately before implementation	All Employees: How the plan will operate All Managers/Team Representatives

	six hours for all Managers/ Supervisors/Team Representatives		Key mechanisms Purpose/goals Involvement system Bonus calculation/quality issues Policies Calculation simulations Agendas for meetings Mechanics of flow of information/ideas Planning and holding effective meetings Evaluation of meetings Responsibilities of everyone Handling change
7	All Employees	On a regular basis, at least monthly	Bonus results for period Current business/economic conditions Involvement activities Goal attainment
8	All of Management/ Supervisors/Team Representatives	After two or three months with gainsharing	Assessing plan's effectiveness with a simple survey on key issues, brainstorm good and poor areas Highlight plan's principles and procedures Group sensing Dealing with problem situations Key communication responsibilities Getting people involved Handling problem situations
9	All of Management/ Supervisors	Various after three months depending on needs; could be three six-hour modules developed for each topic	Managing in a participative environment/integration processes Planning and organizing skills Delegating Communication effectiveness Motivational systems Identifying and correcting problem situations Creativity/problem-solving techniques, such as brainstorming, Pareto analysis, cause/effect analysis Team building techniques Special calculation education Specialized statistical and other education

attendance at a seminar developed internally, which is perhaps most commonly conducted by an outside consultant. It is introductory in nature and frequently covers the topics outlined in Exhibit 13.1. A one-day session can provide a fairly thorough introduction. Many firms are exposed through a one or two day external education program.

Stage 2

This stage includes more in-depth discussions and work on a calculation. This is a key stage of development and, unless major issues are resolved at this point, the rest of gainsharing will not proceed. Material covered on formulas and measurement issues in Chapters 3 and 4 should be of significant help in this stage. Key issues are orientation (broad vs. narrow measures(s)), base periods, reserves, percentage to employees, and so on. Guidelines and key decisions must be narrowed fairly early. This stage typically involves just top management and top union officials if applicable.

Stage 3

This stage often consists of an all-employee survey, which is frequently considered optional but should not be. The survey can help assess the need to change, the level of employee knowledge, and the level of trust within the organization and in management, as well as other factors. Standard surveys that assess need to change and an evaluation of current conditions could be used. Feedback could then lead to gainsharing; the whole process is in itself educational provided feedback does occur.

Stage 4

This stage can be a brief half-hour to an hour presentation to all employees discussing what gainsharing is and the need to develop a task force to finalize the plan. One could use the feedback survey mentioned above as a lead-in to the gainsharing concept at this time. That is, use the survey results to help reinforce the need for such a system.

Stage 5

Pre-Implementation Education

If a major increase in employee involvement is desired, general managers'/supervisors' education about gainsharing should begin shortly after the company announces it is considering gainsharing. Usually this education takes place while a developmental task force is working out details of the company's plan. Within weeks the company will tell employees what those details are, so managers should be able to answer questions their people are sure to have. Three to five hours of education are usually adequate for this stage.

At first managers who are not used to gainsharing's consultative-participative approach may feel uneasy about its emphasis on teamwork, cooperation, and communication. They'll need to understand the difference between traditional supervision and supervision under a gainsharing plan. To help them develop that understanding, the trainer should introduce the principles of managing under gainsharing early, then assess, reteach, and reinforce those basics at each subsequent stage.

The session should include an initial preview of the plan's implementation steps and should give managers a detailed picture of how gainsharing will influence their jobs and the people in their work units. In addition to items covered in Exhibit 13.1 for stage 5, one could discuss the following:

- a supervisor's typical gainsharing-related responsibilities;
- what will take place in departmental gainsharing team meetings;
- how performance-improvement ideas may be implemented;
- how employees and the company should benefit under the plan;
- how the organization's communication and management systems might change;
- how to have effective consultative or participative management;
- how to motivate workers under group bonus systems;
- reasons employees sometimes resist change and don't want to become involved.

When these sessions are completed, managers will have an idea of what to expect from the plan and of what will be expected from them. Trainers will have the chance to identify managers who may need extra help in adjusting to the new way of life. This additional support can be provided either by a good inside manager or by an outside consultant. Obviously, much more extensive team building and financial analysis education would be desirable but these are not required. If an individual incentive system has been eliminated, managers typically need help with their management skills and requirements. Managers have often let the incentive system do their job of managing.

Stage 6

Education for Plan Start-Up

By this time the developmental task force will have completed its work, and managers need to become familiar with plan details decided by that group. This means managers should understand the plan's long-term goals; how production costs and other factors influence the bonus calculation; how bonuses are determined; who is eligible under the plan; and other technicalities of bonus distribution and team operations. These all must be somewhat customized to meet the needs of the organization.

Before implementation, the organization probably needs to conduct a series of meetings to explain the gainsharing concept to all employees, along with the specific plan, now finalized. Managers will soon have to move into this second stage of training. Five to six hours of training will probably be adequate for managers/supervisors and all team members; perhaps an hour should be allotted for the remainder of the employees. Some firms do much more.

The key word is "detail" because managers must quickly develop an understanding of everyone's individual gainsharing responsibilities as outlined in Exhibit 13.1. These include the responsibilities of—

- managers, supervisors, nonmanagement representatives, and the plan coordinator, if one exists;
- departmental versus plantwide teams, council (if applicable);
- management versus nonmanagement employees' responsibilities;
- the union, if applicable.

At the same time, managers should receive instruction as to how they will contribute to plan start-up, including:

- steps they must follow during start-up;
- how to begin with effective departmental team meetings, and what they should and shouldn't cover in them;
- how to evaluate gainsharing meetings;
- the importance of giving employees prompt feedback on ideas they contribute.

Obviously, many more sessions can be added.

Stage 7

This stage consists of ongoing education, which may be accomplished through meetings or through written communication or a combination of the two. Activities would include discussions of bonus results, how the involvement is going, problems and possible resolutions, surveys, and so on. Some firms make a major effort in this area, while others offer only limited training at this time. Regular organization-wide education/communication sessions should be held along with employing various written communication approaches.

Stage 8

Problem Sensing and Problem Solving

Two or three months after the plan is under way, managers and team members will have a sense of what is and is not going well. This is the time to review basic principles of gainsharing, identify positive aspects, see what problems have developed, and provide help in solving those problems. Six hours of education are usually necessary for all management and team representatives at a minimum.

One good way to begin the problem-sensing process is to review the gainsharing plan objectives outlined by the developmental task force and to assess the company's success in meeting them. Various organizations have also had success by—

- asking managers, representatives, and others to complete surveys to evaluate their plan's success on key areas;
- interviewing managers and representatives in groups to identify problem areas;
- brainstorming about solutions for typical difficulties encountered;
- administering a quiz to test everyone's knowledge about aspects of the plan.

Other possible topics are outlined in Exhibit 13.1, stages 8 and 9.

Groups must spend time discussing each problem and working together to come up with solutions. Drawing on each other's experiences is often useful and helps drive home the message that everyone's "in this" together.

Problems uncovered during these sessions frequently center on supervisory relations with nonmanagement personnel who are uncooperative or apathetic to the gainsharing plan. It can be worthwhile to have managers agree on correct ways to handle such employees and then role-play through several predictable confrontations.

While you'll have to focus a lot of energy on unresolved problems, you also should spend time promoting successes achieved under the plan. This helps "stir the pot" and maintain interest in gainsharing. Obviously information on the gainsharing calculation formula and other financial education should be part of this along with commitment building sessions.

Stage 9

Integrating gainsharing concepts with good management practice can be a time-consuming activity. If there has been a major commitment to employee involvement, organizations should plan for an additional 20 to 30 hours of general management education during the first two years under gainsharing. Additional training is particularly appropriate if a major change in management philosophy and practices is to be expected as outlined in Exhibit 13.1. This education will be necessary in part to deal with the system changes already discussed. Education also may be necessary because employees often demand better management under gainsharing. If the plan is successful, employees will be concerned about the organization's performance, and will see the central role managers play in improving it.

At this stage trainers should tailor programs to help managers integrate the gainsharing plan's structures and mechanisms into their everyday activities. At this point they'll likely appreciate the difference between "just managing" and managing under the gainsharing philosophy of cooperation and common objectives. The goal should be to help managers see how they can use the plan to improve their effectiveness at *planning work, delegating, communicating, motivating, correcting performance problems,* and *handling other management difficulties.* A team building program is often used at this point. Cross-functional team training is also often used in stages 8 and 9.

Managers may also find it easier to implement such tools as statistical process control once the plan is in place. The gainsharing bonus provides a common objective for all employees and gives managers a powerful lever for winning employee acceptance of performance improvement techniques. Specialized problems, such as elimination of individual incentives, may require specialized education in that specific ground rules must be developed as to how to manage in a nonincentive environment.

SUMMARY

A gainsharing plan's success or failure depends on managers' ability to adapt to the new approach, especially if extensive employee involvement is an integral part of the system. If upper management suddenly installs a plan on an unready organization, managerial frustration, resentment, and ill feelings may follow because employee involvement in work decisions often threatens a manager's sense of control over the work unit. The result may be managers who not only fail to contribute to the plan's success, but even work against it. This problem occurs more often when the work force is unionized.

Eventually most managers do well under gainsharing plans and evaluate them positively—but only when they are adequately prepared for the change and receive support and encouragement during the transition. When a plan succeeds, it's a safe bet that the foundation was thoughtfully designed and includes a comprehensive management/employee education program.

Chapter 14

Gainsharing Application in
the Service Sector

Timothy L. Ross

Will gainsharing and variable compensation be applied increasingly in the service sector as predicted by the 1992 and 1994 updated ACA studies.[1] Certainly so, but the pace may not be as rapid as predicted. Contrary to some individuals' perceptions, there are often fewer measurement problems in service sector firms than in some manufacturing organizations, although there may be fewer options. Actual applications in the past were more limited, apparently because of lack of interest in performance/productivity improvement, less competitive pressures, and the lack of awareness of the various systems. But all of that is changing. In this chapter, the types of service industries are discussed, then the different traditional gainsharing formulas as applied in the service sector are reviewed. The chapter concludes with a discussion of some approaches that have been used by various service sector firms and possible future trends along with goal-oriented approaches. All of the goal-oriented variables and approaches on quality and customer service discussed in Chapter 11 are applicable here. All organizations can use the employee involvement systems discussed in Chapter 3 or other systems. Chapter 9 discusses an actual application.

SERVICE SECTOR CLASSIFICATIONS

The activities commonly described as services cover a far-ranging group of organizations that share some common characteristics: output that cannot be stored and transactions that usually require direct interaction between an employee and a customer. Some people remove from the services category activities that are capital intensive and large in scale, but are not the airlines really service organizations even if capital intensive? This categorization divides the economy of the United States into the following three sectors, generally based on the nature of the inputs involved and the resultant outputs:

1. agriculture—agriculture, fisheries, and forestry;
2. industry—manufacturing, construction, mining, transportation, communications, and public utilities;
3. service—wholesale and retail trade; finance, insurance, health, travel, entertainment, and real estate; professional, personal, and repair; and federal, state, and local government including education. Utilities, communications, and transportation may really be toss-ups, fitting under either industry or service.

A review of the service group above suggests one common characteristic: generally labor-intensive operations. When this facet is combined with the need for direct interaction with the customer, it becomes possible to evolve a more precise service classification system that uses the potential for rationalization and control. Such a classification system has been devised by Chase.[2] The following four categories are based on the extent of customer contact, roughly defined as the percentage of the total transaction time that the customer must be in the system.

1. manufacturing—no customer contact during the production process;
2. quasimanufacturing—possible identifiable physical units of output;
3. mixed service—significant exposure to direct customer contact;
4. pure service—maximal exposure to direct customer contact; possible intangible units of service.

These categories become quite useful when managers attempt to use gainsharing as a means of achieving improvements in performance. Needless to say, increased competitive pressures have also confronted the service industries in recent years, encouraging the search for ways to improve quality and performance. This new factor is unlikely to change.

MEASUREMENT FOR GAINSHARING IN SERVICE SECTOR—A GENERAL REVIEW

In quasimanufacturing operations within the service sector of the economy, the availability of identifiable physical units of output and the minimal amount of customer involvement in the transaction tend to make productivity measurement relatively easy. (In fact, manufacturing firms with much indirect labor—e.g., engineering, material handlers, and maintenance—may be more difficult to measure.) Within the mixed category, such as bank tellers, fast food employees, or hospital nurses, who have a fair amount of customer or patient contact, productivity becomes more difficult. One reason for this is the relatively intangible dimension of quality that is included in the teller-customer or nurse-patient relationship. The closer one moves toward pure service organizations, the more difficult it becomes to devise "productivity measurement pure" gainsharing calculations. "Pure" in this sense is a physical output-per-hour calculation, such as Improshare®, rather than broader measures, such as multicost, or even prospective forms of gainsharing, such as beating budgets, which will be discussed later. Obviously, many such firms can use broad, financial calculations fairly easily.

Also involved is the customer influence on the level of resources (inputs) required to provide a satisfactory service as perceived by the customer (outputs), as well as the difficulty of identifying and measuring these productivity components. Until recently, another factor that has limited efforts to make effective use of performance measurements in the mixed services category has been the managerial preoccupation with other aspects of the overall operation. For example, managers have been mainly concerned with marketing of services and effectiveness of services, rather than with the efficiency of the service rendered. This obviously will have to change in the future as organizations such as hospitals and public utilities are likely to discover.

MEASUREMENT

In attempting to measure the performance of a mixed services unit, such as a hospital, it is difficult to separate productivity from other factors because hospital output is so heterogeneous and hospital charges may not be reliable guides to the relative costs needed to develop an overall output measure.

One suggested approach to an output measurement system requires the use of different weights for different illnesses, operations, accidents, and other service requirements. However, hospitals do have revenues, payroll costs, and operating expenses. Reimbursing agencies (third-party payers), which represent the major portion of hospital receipts, require detailed accounting for costs. In addition, statistical records such as MONItrend reports provide administrators with a considerable amount of information about the hospital's operations. Therefore, despite the many problems that exist, the data required for most of the performance gainsharing calculations are available for service sector calculations at a hospital. Gainsharing has been applied at many hospitals and interest is likely to grow in the future.

In banking, there is also significant information to draw on for performance measurement. The proper measure of banking output for use in this case can be narrowed to a choice between two concepts: the liquidity approach, which is based on deposits and the transactions approach, which is based on transactions. The transactions approach is the form most accepted by the banking industry. One can develop factors that might be considered for multiple weighting among different types of activities, such as number of accounts; number of checks handled; value of accounts and checks; savings and checking accounts; loans and size of loans. Some recent research dealing with productivity of bank branches indicated that suitable weights for transactions could be developed from the relative average times required for various logical groupings of transactions. Such times need to reflect the technology in place and any other site-specific factors. The most significant inputs related to these outputs are teller labor and other branch-related payroll and fringe costs, which are discussed later as an example.

Consideration also needs to be given to various other costs that are inputs, such as rent, depreciation, and cash variations and losses. While the decision as to which accounts to consider for inclusion in the calculations must be based on a site-specific review of historical data, it is highly likely that only a few will have significant impact.

The above two examples (medium-sized general-care hospitals and bank branches) represent extremes of the mixed services continuum; that is, organizations oriented to altruism and organizations dominated by finance. It is possible to develop the raw data needed to evolve one or more alternative measurements suitable for each type of organization. Suitable creative analysis of other industries on the services continuum is very possible. The nature of the useful alternative calculations is described in the following section. The nominal group technique has been found to be extremely useful in developing performance measurements in service sector environments. Regardless of perceived measurement problems, goals and other budget oriented systems can always be used. If activity takes place, one can pay for some improvement in the activity in its simplest terms. It could be simply cost or budget reduction.

ALTERNATIVE CALCULATIONS

The needs of individual service organizations and the availability of data required for various calculations can differ to a considerable degree. Fortunately, the calculations available for use in firms considering the use of gainsharing plans cover a wide range of options. A review of some of the most commonly used calculations as discussed in Chapters 4 and 5 is helpful in understanding the differences as applied to service organizations.

Allowed Labor

Allowed Labor calculations, such as Improshare®, are based on the use of work measures for tasks defining the amount of time required to produce a specific unit of output. These calculations are adjusted upward to allow for related unmeasured work associated with base labor that generates the output. Because of the requirement that some detailed measures be available for use, Allowed Labor calculations tend to be more applicable to quasimanufacturing operations, such as hospital laundries and bank check-processing operations. However, other firms, such as repair shops, general laundries, schools, and fast food organizations can use such calculations quite easily and can incorporate considerations for quality. These types of calculations have been used extensively in government situations. These calculations, such as meals per hour and so on, are frequently used as one measure of a broader or multiple pool calculation. Hospitals have developed detailed measures for each of their activities and then combined them into one bonus; some pay bonuses for department improvements.

Single Ratio of Labor

The single ratio of labor calculation is based on the simple relationship of total labor costs for the period to the total revenue. As shown in Exhibit 14.1, it may be calculated for a typical medium-sized general-care hospital as follows:

$$\text{Single ratio} = \frac{\text{Total labor}}{\text{Total revenue}} = \frac{\$295,000}{\$500,000} = 59\%$$

If the actual costs are less than 59 percent of revenue, a bonus is earned. The major advantages of the single ratio calculation are its ease of calculation and simplicity of understanding. Most manufacturing firms would have an allowable percentage lower than 59 percent. As previously noted, the labor intensity of mixed-service operations permits this calculation to represent a majority of the input costs, which can be broken out separately by department and/or function.[3] Indexing can be used to adjust for the inflationary impact on revenue and wages. However, the single ratio does ignore the impact of capital and/or energy inputs on changes in output. So adjustments may have to be made for say capital improvements.

For the typical hospital being used as an example, capital expenditures frequently involve the adoption of new technology, which is often embodied in new services that are additions to, rather than replacements for, existing services.

One problem that can occur with the single ratio is a variation in product mix over time. A common method of overcoming that problem is the use of the split-ratio calculation, which is discussed below. The single-ratio calculation could be used in hospitals, appraisal services, consulting firms, distribution centers, government services, security services, restaurants, car washes, educational institutions, and computer service firms, to name a few.

Split-Ratio Expansions

Essentially, the split-ratio calculation is two or more single ratios, which are aligned according to the labor intensity of the services that generate the total revenue. Each of these ratios would include the directly associated labor costs and a rational allocation of the other payroll and fringe costs as shown in Exhibit 14.1. In general, the split ratio has the same advantages and disadvantages associated with the single ratio except that it does help resolve the product mix problem. Many of the other problems that exist can be overcome by the

Exhibit 14.1   General Care Hospitals: Typical Financial Details for Use in Calculating Traditional Performance Gainsharing Ratios

Output

Gross revenue	$527,000	
Loss on medicare	−25,000	
Other adjustments	−23,000	
Net revenue	$479,000	
Interest (may be excluded)	15,000	
Misc. income (may be excluded)	6,000	
Total Revenue (TR)		$500,000

Inputs

Payroll	$250,000	
Fringes	45,000	
Total Labor (TL)		$295,000
Supplies/fees and materials	$125,000	
Adminis. & Misc. costs	55,000	
Other Costs (OC)		$180,000

Calculations

$$\text{Single ratio} = \frac{TL}{TR} = \frac{\$295,000}{\$500,000} = 59\%$$

$$\text{Multicost ratio} = \frac{TL + OC}{TR} = \frac{\$295,000 + \$180,000}{\$500,000} = 95\%$$

$$\text{Value-added ratio} = \frac{TL}{TR - OC} = \frac{\$295,000}{\$500,000 - \$180,000} = 92\%$$

use of a more comprehensive ratio—one that incorporates a greater percentage of the inputs required to generate the total revenue. Organizations that would find the split ratio more applicable include advertising agencies, architectural firms, and insurance firms based on different types of activities.

Multicost Ratio

The inclusion of other costs (OC) essentially converts the single ratio into the multicost ratio. As shown in Exhibit 14.1, it is calculated in the following manner:

$$\text{Multicost Ratio} = \frac{TL + OC}{TR} = \frac{\$295,000 + \$180,000}{\$500,000} = 95\%$$

While the resulting percentage will vary among service sector industries and depends on decisions concerning the specific costs to be added, the expansion normally results in a ratio that is 70 percent to 95 percent inclusive of the total revenue. This large percentage of the revenue reduces the problems of inflation and product mix. A problem that it creates, however, is a potential conclusion by the participants that they have little control over some of the factors included in the ratio. This calculation does have a major advantage over profit sharing in that management does not have to disclose profits. However, the more costs are included, the closer one gets to profit sharing.

The multicost formula can be applied to banks, employment agencies, executive search firms, hospitals, hotels and motels, restaurants, theaters, and many other types of establishments. It has been used in many manufacturing firms with major success when the orientation is toward overall organization performance.

Value-Added Ratio

As suggested above, this ratio is a modification of the multicost ratio. Using the data for medium-sized general-care hospitals found in Exhibit 14.1, the value-added ratio is calculated in the following manner:

$$\text{Value-added ratio} = \frac{\text{TL}}{\text{TR} - \text{OC}} = \frac{\$295,000}{\$500,000 - \$180,000} = 92\%$$

Research into the use of this ratio—which is the common basis of the Rucker® plan—indicates that it does not need to be changed for wage rate increases, changes in charges for services rendered, material cost changes, or variations in the portion of work subcontracted, all of which frequently test the single ratio. It would tend to give erroneous readings, however, following the installation of cost-effective technological improvements. Such changes would undoubtedly require a new or modified calculation for an equitable measure and/or related bonus plan.

This calculation can be used in sites where product mix is a problem, such as retail stores, job shops, theaters, and airlines, or when multicost is not selected for disclosure reasons.

Nontraditional Gainsharing Calculations

In service sector companies one could always utilize a goal-oriented system, such as those discussed in Chapters 4 and 5. If something can be measured, it can be included in a calculation. Quality related approaches are covered in Chapter 11.

Even broader-based measures of performance, such as those that include profit and return on investment, can be developed. Such ratios deal with the return achieved on assets or stockholders' equity. The calculations required under these measures closely resemble the multicost ratio supplemented by a factor to reflect the contribution of capital assets. Such plans require a major commitment from management, lack a direct relationship to performance productivity, and require a significant communications effort.

Some organizations attempt to overcome these problems by modifying one of the calculations discussed above in a manner that emphasizes one or more important areas of their business rather than very broad-based calculations. The variety of input data and output data available within an organization can be creatively combined to develop a tailor-made hybrid calculation. This can involve the use of a series of weights to give recognition to levels of service quality, generation of incremental revenue (cross-selling of available services), or other important factors for the long-term success of the firm. Multiple pool approaches discussed in Chapters 4 and 5 can also be used. Budgeted performance is sometimes used. The exact nature of the service sector industry and the site-specific, time-related situation will guide the choice of the best calculation for use by individual mixed-services firms.

Numerous governmental units have used gainsharing in a variety of situations. Most of the applications have used specific measurement formulas such as Improshare®. The U.S. General Accounting Office has published a report describing some of these experiences.[4] Most of the comprehensive applications are in civilian portions of military facilities.

APPLICATION—ACTUAL AND POTENTIAL

Many different calculations have been used by service organizations. Unfortunately, the calculation is often perceived by managers or owners as more important than the behaviorally oriented variables. This is seldom true, but this misperception works against gainsharing success. From a purely pragmatic standpoint, the objectives of the measurement system are more important than its form. For example, if one wants an overall improvement in performance (such as return on investment or return on sales) to coincide with bonuses, then one should adopt one of these measures or, preferably, the multicost or value-added formulas. Other firms could tie the amount of payment made to employees for improvement in, say, labor costs and quality measurements, to organizational profitability as discussed in Chapter 5. Looking at other options, gainsharing can always be based on reduction in budgeted costs or a whole range of targeted performance.

In actual practice, gainsharing can be applied in many service organizations, as the partial list given below indicates. Many service organizations also have profit-sharing programs, which in a very broad sense could be considered gainsharing, provided some hurdle is included. Some gainsharing plans that have been brought to our attention as actual or potential applications include the following:

1. allowed labor/Improshare: repair shops, laundries, schools, government applications;
2. single ratio: appraisal services, consultants, distribution centers, government services, security services, restaurants, car washes;
3. split ratio: advertising agencies, architects, insurance firms;
4. multicost ratio: banks, employment agencies, executive search firms, hospitals, hotels and motels, property management firms, publishing firms;
5. multiple pool: various pools for day labor, other costs, quality, customer service; can be applied about everywhere;
6. value-added ratio: dental clinics, retail stores, funeral homes, nursing homes, photographic studios, restaurants, theaters, printers;
7. standard labor ratio: captive service operations, data processing services, dry cleaners, libraries;
8. profit sharing or return on investment: TV and radio broadcasting, newspaper publishing, investment companies, law firms, accounting firms, medical clinics;
9. budgeted or goal oriented systems: normally based on improvements in some variables rather than just a percentage of profits. These have far ranging applications.

In the years to come, we expect many other service firms to install gainsharing.[5] Gradually, more firms will become familiar with its principles and with both behavioral and measurement data shown from real-life experiences. These service firms will normally start with the simpler calculations based on the criteria of understanding, administrative ease, and so on, and will move to increasingly more complex calculations. In fact, much of gainsharing's future growth will probably center on service sector firms because of limited past interest and applications and because of the increased emphasis on employee involvement in service oriented firms.

Notes

1. J. L. McAdams and E. J. Hawk, *Capitalizing on Human Assets* (Scottsdale: American Compensation Association and Maritz, Inc. 1992), and McAdams and Hawk, *Organizational Performance & Rewards—663 Experiences in Making the Link* (1994).
2. B. Chase, "Where Does the Customer Fit in a Service Operation?" *Harvard Business Review*, November–December 1978.
3. W. C. Hauck, "Measuring Effectiveness in Banks and Hospitals," *Industrial Management*, 28, March–April 1986, 26–27.
4. "Gainsharing—DOD Efforts Highlight an Effective Tool for Enhancing Federal Productivity," No. 86–143 BR (Washington, D.C.: U.S. General Accounting Office, 1986).
5. B. E. Graham-Moore, "Productivity Gainsharing in the Service Sector" in *Personnel Management: Compensation Service* (Paramus, N.J.: Prentice-Hall, 1987).

Chapter 15

Attitude Change Versus Performance Improvement: One Look at the Long-Term Results

Timothy L. Ross, Larry L. Hatcher, and Ruth Ann Ross

Gainsharing case studies typically emphasize the role of the average worker in reducing costs, increasing production efficiency, and improving product quality. If the organization is employee involvement oriented, a system of teams solicits and acts on employees' suggestions and subsequently develops goals.

Gainsharing plans have traditionally been discussed in terms of their impact on productivity, and many published case studies describe the resulting improvements. This emphasis on productivity is understandable since many of the early plans were implemented to save companies in serious financial difficulty.

In addition to productivity, worker attitudes have also received major attention in the gainsharing literature as discussed in Chapter 2. Various authors have suggested that a successful gainsharing plan can result in higher levels of cooperation, participation, and job satisfaction. The majority of the evidence regarding attitudes, however, is more qualitative in nature. Many of the case studies providing quantitative information on improvements in productivity provide only anecdotal evidence regarding changes in employee attitudes.

Representative of such studies is one reported by the U.S. General Accounting Office.[1] Financial data were obtained from 24 firms with gainsharing plans, and it was reported, for instance, that companies with annual sales of less than $100 million averaged work force savings of 17.3 percent. Savings averaged 16.4 percent at those firms with sales in excess of $100 million.

In contrast, the report provides data regarding attitude change, which is more subjective. It discusses interviews held with plant employees, concluding "climate between labor and management was said to have improved over what had existed before the productivity sharing plan was implemented." The conclusion is interesting, but without information on the sampling technique used, the interview format used, or the procedures used to analyze the responses, it is difficult to evaluate the accuracy of the finding. The 1992 American Compensation Association (ACA) study noted improvements in attitudes as well.[2] Again the results were informative but lacked the information needed to allow accurate evaluation.

Bullock and Bullock[3] reports the results of a survey that was administered to employees before a gainsharing plan was installed and then again one year later. Improvements were reported in work-group functioning, openness, trust, communication, goal setting, and a number of other areas. Unfortunately, statistical significance was not reported. The research reported in this chapter is based on longitudinal survey data in an attempt to begin filling this void in the literature.

A survey was administered to employees of a manufacturing company before a gainsharing plan was implemented, and again after 18 months under the plan. Care was taken to insure the reliability of the scales, which assessed employee satisfaction with the company, satisfaction with the work itself, cooperation, opportunity for participation, productivity, satisfaction with supervisor, and satisfaction with working conditions. Observed changes in attitudes were tested for statistical significance with the results reported below.

ASHLEY MARCH: A CASE STUDY

Background

Ashley March (a fictitious name) is a medium-sized midwestern company producing industrial equipment, with sales of around $30 million annually. Nearly two thirds of the 200 or so employees are in a union, and three-fourths are male.

The years 19X1 and 19X2 were particularly bad for the firm. Inventories reached an all-time high in 19X1, and high interest rates subsequently caused a substantial drain on profits. Production was cut to lower inventories, and layoffs resulted.

In addition to these difficulties, relations between management and non-management employees were strained. Mutual mistrust and poor communication existed throughout the organization. Many employees were resentful of the layoffs and felt that favoritism was also a problem. There was little, if any, sense of teamwork, and productivity and other performance measures suffered accordingly.

Gainsharing seemed an appropriate choice since it would address Ashley March's most pressing problems: lack of cooperation, low productivity, and poor worker attitudes. The need to change was very evident since survival was at risk. As is often the case, gainsharing was to be used to lead organizational change.

Details of the Gainsharing Plan

In developing a gainsharing plan, a company must deal with two basic questions: (a) How much employee involvement is desired? and (b) What type of bonus calculation is best? The system at Ashley March was designed by a developmental task force comprising a cross-section of employees from all levels of the company. The task force met over a three-month period to design the objectives, involvement system, rules, and policies and procedures, and to critique the calculation. In other organizations, the time period for this process has been shortened. Both a departmental and a higher level team system discussed in Chapter 3 helped to ensure that actions and communications occurred as necessary.

Research Questions

Much has been conjectured regarding the impact of a gainsharing plan on worker attitudes, but little has been demonstrated with carefully developed measures and statistical analysis of longitudinal data. Hypothesis testing is difficult in this area, because predictions made are often broad and nonspecific. For example, Frost, Wakely, and Ruh,[4] Moore and Ross,[5] and O'Dell[6] have each suggested that a plan can result in improved job satisfaction, but do not note which aspects of job satisfaction will be influenced: satisfaction with the company, job, work environment, and so forth.

The present study was designed to assess employee satisfaction in several areas and identify those showing a significant improvement under the plan. Proposition 1 stated that postimplementation satisfaction with the company, with the work itself, with the supervisor, and with working conditions will be significantly higher than preimplementation satisfaction in these areas.

There is less ambiguity in predictions made regarding other aspects of change. All three sources discussed earlier predict improvements in cooperation, employee participation, and productivity under a successful gainsharing plan. Although the chapter does not report behavioral indexes, it is possible to assess the change as perceived by the employees. Accordingly, Propositions 2, 3, and 4 state that there will be a significant improvement in employees perceptions of cooperation, opportunity for participation, and productivity, respectively.

Development of the Attitude Scales

Approximately one month before the gainsharing plan began, an attitude survey was administered to all company employees. This 78-item survey assessed their satisfaction, needs, and perception of various attributes of the company. Eighteen months later, another survey was administered. Forty-one items were common to the two instruments. Scales were constructed from these common items.

On an *a priori* basis, items dealing with similar constructs were grouped together. The homogeneity of these items within scales was assessed and questions displaying poor item-total correlations were sequentially dropped. All item analyses were performed using data from the preimplementation survey.

Seven scales were developed. These scales, and their items, are presented in Exhibits 15.1 and 15.2. All items used a 5-point response format, with 1 the most negative and 5 the most positive response. An employee's responses to the items were averaged to obtain his or her score on each scale for discussion purposes here.

Responses to Research Propositions

Proposition 1: Satisfaction

Employee satisfaction with the company was significantly higher on the postimplementation survey than on the preimplementation survey. The preimplementation mean average for this scale was 2.96, while the postimplementation average was 3.39, as indicated on Exhibit 15.1.

Similarly, satisfaction with the work itself improved significantly under gainsharing. The scale average on the initial survey was 3.22, while the average on the later survey was 3.46.

Although the score on the satisfaction with supervisor scale was more positive postimplementation than preimplementation, the difference was not significant. Similarly, the increase in satisfaction with working conditions was also insignificant; this fact was surprising to everyone since major improvements had occurred (the feeling was that expectations had increased after the installation).

In summary, the scales measuring satisfaction with the company and satisfaction with the work itself reflected significantly more favorable attitudes after gainsharing had been implemented. There is, however, no evidence that employees were more satisfied with their supervisors or with their working conditions after 18 months under the plan.

Proposition 2: Cooperation

From Exhibit 15.2 the mean for this scale increased from 2.20 to 2.69 after 18 months under a gainsharing plan. This improvement was statistically significant.

Exhibit 15.1   Items Comprising the Satisfaction Scales

Scale and Items	Survey Results	
	Pre-Mean	Post-Mean
Satisfaction with company		
1. All in all, how satisfied are you with your company?		
2. How do you feel about your future with your company?		
3. How are employee complaints dealt with by the company?		
4. Your feeling of loyalty to the company (is now). . . .		
5. Your feeling of trust and confidence in management (is now). . . .		
Average (1–5 scale)	2.96	3.39
Satisfaction with the work itself		
1. All in all, how satisfied are you with your job?		
2. Your interest in the work itself (is now). . . .		
3. Your being informed about performance measures for your job (is now). . . .		
Average (1–5 scale)	3.22	3.46
Satisfaction with supervisor		
1. To what extent do you have confidence and trust in your supervisor?		
2. How well does your supervisor know your work record?		
3. How well does your supervisor do the planning and scheduling of your work?		
4. How well does your supervisor do the people side of his/her job (giving recognition, building teamwork, giving feedback, etc.)?		
5. To what extent is your supervisor free to take independent actions that are necessary to carry out his or her job responsibilities?		
6. To what extent does favoritism exist in the treatment of employees at your level?		
Average (1–5 scale)	3.46	3.61
Satisfaction with working conditions		
1. Overall, how would you describe the physical working conditions (noise, lighting, temperature, etc.) of your location?		
2. How do you feel about the equipment and materials available to you to get your job done?		
3. How well does the company minimize safety hazards to you on the job?		
Average (1–5 scale)	3.14	3.26

Exhibit 15.2   Items Comprising the Cooperation, Participation, and
Productivity Scales

Scale and Items	Survey Results	
	Pre-Mean	Post-Mean
Cooperation		
1. How would you rate cooperation between departments in general?		
2. How would you rate communication between departments in general?		
Average (1–5 scale)	2.20	2.69
Opportunity for participation		
1. Is management willing to accept suggestions you make?		
2. Does your supervisor ask your opinion when a problem comes up that involves your work?		
3. Your opportunity for participating in the setting of goals, methods, and procedures (is now). . . .		
Average (1–5 scale)	2.83	3.23
Productivity		
1. How would you describe the level of productivity in this plant compared to what it could be?		
Average (1–5 scale)	2.42	3.05

Proposition 3: Opportunity for Participation

Before the gainsharing plan began, the average for this scale was 2.83. After 18 months under the plan, it increased to 3.23, which represented a significant change.

Proposition 4: Productivity

The most powerful effect in their study was seen with regard to this single-item scale. Employees felt that their plant was much more productive after the gainsharing plan was implemented, with the scale average increasing from 2.42 to 3.05. The improvement was significant.

Discussion

Satisfaction

A considerable number of studies, including the 1992 and 1994 ACA large scale ones, have demonstrated a positive relationship between employee involvement in decision making and overall satisfaction. In the present investigation, however, improvements in satisfaction were demonstrated only with regard to the company and the work itself.

One possible explanation for significant positive results in these two areas relates to a discussion by Bowers on control. He outlines numerous benefits resulting from employees' increased sense of control over their jobs. Under gainsharing, employees' sense of control over their jobs is expected to increase as the worker assumes a more active role in eliminating inefficient procedures and redesigning less effective aspects of their jobs. Bowers found that as control increased, so did satisfaction with both the company and the job.[7] These results suggest that gainsharing may provide one appropriate setting for researching such control techniques.

Unexpectedly, employees' satisfaction with supervisors did not significantly improve under the gainsharing plan in this one example, although the pre-average of 3.46 was already quite high. Previous research has shown that employees in a participative environment tend to be more satisfied with their supervisors than those in a more authoritarian situation; perhaps the change was not that major in this situation.

What remains is the present finding that employees did not become more satisfied with their supervisors after the gainsharing plan began. Subsequent longitudinal studies may provide an explanation for these unexpected results. Perhaps expectations have also increased in this area.

The lack of a significant improvement in the results measuring working conditions was unexpected by many employees at Ashley March. When this finding was presented at a meeting of the overview team, some workers and managers disputed it, arguing that the physical appearance of the plant had improved dramatically since the plan had been in operation. They felt that the employees had more pride in the company and were making an effort to keep walkways clear, dispose of scrap properly, and keep the area cleaner. They were convinced that expectations had increased since gainsharing had been installed.

Cooperation

Employees' perceptions of cooperation improved significantly under the gainsharing plan. This improvement probably was due to the work of department teams and other teams, work which involved meeting, discussing issues, solving problems, and working together. The formal structure of these teams and the suggestion process strongly encourages cooperation.

Opportunity for Participation

To evaluate the employees' perceived opportunity for participation involves little more than looking at actual results: if workers do not feel they are participating more, then the plan is not doing what it is supposed to do. In this case the employees did indicate on the postimplementation survey that they had a greater opportunity for participation since it was certainly true (i.e., team activities, meetings, submitting ideas).

Productivity

Evaluations of productivity made after 18 months under the plan were significantly more favorable than those obtained prior to implementation. While the scale measured overall performance, objective data gathered at the time of the survey revealed the specific areas of company performance showing improvement. For each of these measures, the 12-month period preceding implementation of the plan was used as a base, and was compared to the 18-month period following implementation.

Analysis revealed a 17 percent improvement in efficiency. Indirect labor was down 6.6 percent, scrap costs were down 49.0 percent, and warranty costs decreased 14.5 percent. Annual sales volume was approximately the same across the preimplementation and postimplementation time periods.

Virtually all personnel who were interviewed at Ashley March attributed these improvements to the plan. Unfortunately, research to date has been unsuccessful in determining which components of a gainsharing plan were most responsible for the improvements in company performance, a frustrating situation in organizational research. One line of reasoning attributes these changes to the motivating influence of participative decision making (PDM).

At least three processes may account for improvements in performance obtained in a participative environment. It may be that under a gainsharing plan, employees make more effective use of goal setting. In the departmental meetings at Ashley March, team members reviewed the ideas of their peers and set deadlines for either obtaining additional information or actually implementing the acceptable suggestions. Because these assignments were made in a participative manner, a team member was accountable to his or her colleagues for meeting deadlines. In this way, the participative structure of the plan provided the opportunity to set goals as well as a mechanism for monitoring success in reaching these goals. Research has shown that goal setting typically leads to higher levels of performance than admonishing people to do their best.[8]

With this in mind, goal setting is incorporated into many aspects of the plan. Goals are set regarding the number of suggestions to be obtained, reductions in warranty costs, improvement in various quality measures, and other areas affecting organizational performance. It should also be stressed that this goal setting is done in a participative manner. Studies have shown that goals arrived at in this way can be more difficult than assigned goals but sometimes lead to higher levels of performance.[9]

Another process that may explain the observed performance improvement is the cognitive component of participative decision making. This refers to the way a gainsharing plan taps the know-how of the average employee. It assumes that the employee operating a machine for a long time is in an excellent position to contribute ideas on how to cut scrap, improve output, streamline operations, and so on. By allowing this worker the opportunity to participate in job-related decisions, more intelligent decisions can be made. The result is improved operations and higher levels of performance.

Unfortunately, little is know about this cognitive aspect of participation. Many studies in the area of participation have subjects performing simple or unfamiliar tasks that do not lend themselves to employees working smarter. Future research should involve settings in which the contribution of worker knowledge in PDM is given a more fair test.

In addition to PDM, it is likely that productivity improvements at Ashley March may be attributed to the presence of a financial incentive. During eight of the first eighteen months of the plan, employees earned a bonus for having improved performance.

Although much has been written regarding the impact of financial incentives on performance and satisfaction (see Lawler[10]), a number of questions remain regarding the motivational attributes of a gainsharing bonus: Do employees see a relationship between their performance and the bonuses earned? Is it necessary that they understand the bonus calculation? How frequently must bonuses be paid in order for them to have a motivational impact? How large a bonus must be earned for it to be motivational?

The answers to these questions will have major implications as to how future gainsharing plans will be structured.

SUMMARY

It can be seen that the success of a gainsharing plan presents more questions than it resolves regarding organizational outcomes. Conditions at Ashley March improved, but why? Future research should identify those components of a gainsharing plan which most directly affect worker attitudes and performance. Researchers cannot keep up with the practitioners/innovators.

With regard to employee attitudes, these components may include the improved levels of communication between management and nonmanagement, the recognition of employees as an important resource in improving operations, and the increased amount of control employees are given. While it may be that some of the above components are more important than others, the possibility that their combined influence is responsible for the change should also be considered.

With regard to performance gainsharing, companies should provide useful sites for addressing some of the issues under debate in the motivational literature. Research should be directed toward understanding whether participation in decision making results in employees working harder, working smarter, or both. Work should also be done in understanding whether the financial bonus motivates performance, how its motivational attributes may be enhanced, and how it affects nonproductivity-related outcomes such as worker attitudes. These questions will become increasingly important as an even wider range of firms, from the troubled to the highly successful, install gainsharing.

It is hoped that more attitude- and productivity-oriented studies of gainsharing plans will follow. When larger numbers of studies documenting successes and failures from a behavioral point of view are accumulated, we will be in the best position to guide organizations toward the type of results enjoyed by Ashley March.

Notes

1. U.S. General Accounting Office. *Productivity Sharing Programs: Can They Contribute to Productivity Improvement?* (Document No. AFMD-81-22; Gaithersburg, Md.: U.S. General Accounting Office, 1981).
2. J. L. McAdams and E. J. Hawk, *Capitalizing on the Human Asset* (Scottsdale: American Compensation Association and Maritz, 1992).
3. R. J. Bullock and P. F. Bullock, "Gainsharing and Rubik's Cube: Solving System Problems," *National Productivity Review*, 1982, 1, 396–407.
4. C. F. Frost, J. H. Wakely, and R. A. Ruh, *The Scanlon Plan for Organization Development: Identity, Participation, and Equity* (East Lansing, Mich.: Michigan State University Press, 1974).
5. B. E. Moore and T. L. Ross, *The Scanlon Way to Improved Productivity: A Practical Guide* (New York: John Wiley & Sons, 1978).
6. C. S. O'Dell, *Gainsharing: Involvement, Incentives, and Productivity* (New York: AMACOM, 1981).
7. In A. S. Tannenbaum, *Control in Organizations* (New York: McGraw-Hill, 1968).
8. D. L. Dossett, G. P. Latham, and T. R. Mitchell, "The Effects of Assigned Versus Participatively Set Goals, KR, and Individual Differences on Employee Behavior When Goal Difficulty is Held Constant," *Journal of Applied Psychology*, 1979, 64, 291–298; G. P. Latham, T. R. Mitchell, and D. L. Dossett, "The Importance of Participative Goal Setting and Anticipated Rewards on Goal Difficulty and Job Performance," *Journal of Applied Psychology*, 1978, 63, 163–171; G. P. Latham and L. M. Saari, "The Effects of Holding Goal Difficulty Constant on Assigned and Participatively Set Goals," *Academy of Management Journal*, 1979a, 22, 163–168; G. P. Latham and L. M. Saari, "Importance of Supportive Relationships in Goal Setting," *Journal of Applied Psychology*, 1979b, 64, 151–156.
9. Latham, Mitchell, and Dossett, "The Importance of Participative Goal Setting," note 8, above.
10. E. E. Lawler, *Pay and Organization Development* (Reading, Mass.: Addison-Wesley, 1981).

Chapter 16

Gainsharing and the Future

Brian Graham-Moore and Timothy L. Ross

Throughout this book, we have attempted to encourage the serious reader to critically evaluate the theory and evidence underlying gainsharing, with an emphasis on traditional gainsharing. In some ways, the theoretical development of gainsharing is still limited, but we are hopeful that this book will provide a significant new contribution upon which to build. In the years to come, the field needs more work in both basic and applied theoretical gainsharing research.

Little doubt exists that many firms will find it difficult to adopt gainsharing. Quite simply, some firms shouldn't try it. Some organizations will explore modified gainsharing, which is a new area requiring more research. Pay for performance is and will continue to be popular in these competitive times. This book, however, is concerned heavily with the success of traditional gainsharing. Chapter 1, Understanding Gainsharing, provides a basic introduction necessary for comprehension. Throughout the rest of this book many of the conditions and variables associated with gainsharing success and failure have been delineated.

Any decision maker who wishes to pursue gainsharing may find the path difficult. What follows is our discussion of attitudes and opinions of managers who revealed some of their deepest concerns about adopting gainsharing.

IMPEDIMENTS TO GAINSHARING

As part of a small study project, we asked top plant, group, and corporate managers in two firms who were knowledgeable about gainsharing why they did not believe more of their peers were actively studying gainsharing as a formalized strategy. Their response is condensed in the following nine sections.

We believe these opinions are indicative of true managerial concerns and probably illustrate why gainsharing will not be applied in all firms.

1. *Why Pay for Something We Can Get from Good Management?* Clearly, there are multiple ways to manage and firms are exploring a wide range of options. Adding financial rewards links in fairness at all levels, not just at the top and probably makes change easier.
2. *Union Resistance.* Unions traditionally have not been strong advocates of gainsharing, probably because they lack knowledge, fear loss of control, or fear the program will be used in lieu of wage increases. This resistance is slowly giving way and gainsharing is being discussed in union negotiations.

   The United Auto Workers' union has long sought industrywide profit sharing as a wage supplement and has accepted performance gainsharing in many locations, and in some years, its members have been handsomely rewarded. Obviously, union leadership must be heavily involved in most situations for a plan to be successfully implemented.
3. *Risk of Failure.* This is perceived as a particular problem for some firms. Firms of this type often focus only on the bonus aspect of gainsharing but, if conditions are not right, bonus earning opportunities may be limited or even nonexistent for some time. Unless a significant need to change exists because of poor performance or unless a very successful firm wishes to share the fruits of that success with employees, these firms are unlikely to be drawn toward traditional gainsharing. Firms can go years with limited bonuses or even no bonuses and the system will still be viewed as successful.
4. *Lack of How-to Knowledge.* The relative lack of knowledge of gainsharing has been a problem, particularly in systems in which measurement is difficult (e.g., pure service organizations). Until experiences are more widely shared and research expanded into new areas, there won't be any ready answers. Nevertheless, the major improvements which have been made in accounting and information systems in recent years should help in this area. Electronic spreadsheets are a significant tool in gainsharing calculation assessment.
5. *Management Style.* The type of management found in a firm can have a positive effect on installations of some systems, while it can hurt others. For example, control-oriented firms might look upon Improshare® very favorably but may reject a Scanlon orientation because of discomfort with employee involvement systems. Many other managers, although they do believe that employees at all levels contribute more to organizational success, do not believe that they do so unless forced into such a position. Supervisors often feel most

threatened by gainsharing when employee involvement is required. This fear can be overcome through education and through favorable experiences resulting from gainsharing programs. Changes in supervisors are sometimes required. Many supervisors will come to view gainsharing favorably when a better departmental team results, and the supervisors find they have not lost control. After all, gainsharing committees are no different in appearance and function as the quality improvement teams which are in use today. Needless to say, firms are into employee involvement today as never before.

6. *Lack of Divisional and Corporate Support.* Lack of support is a major problem in some firms. These firms do not want to establish a precedent for other units by allowing one to install gainsharing. Other firms, however, actively encourage the installation of these systems with white papers, corporate task forces, staff support, seminars, references, and so on. Very few have a corporate position paper on gainsharing, but more are developing such a document. Some firms require several layers of approval, making it difficult for lower units to propose such plans. Chapter 8 provides a vivid reminder of corporate involvement in gainsharing.

7. *What to Do With Existing Incentive Systems.* These can range from individual, factory incentive systems to sales commissions. Generally, upon the installation of a gainsharing system, these individual incentive programs are eliminated through some form of buyout. Sales commissions and managerial bonuses are continued, although bonuses are typically not paid on the incremental portion, or a cap may be placed on sharing.

Individual incentives are thought to be somewhat inconsistent with gainsharing because they emphasize what the individual can do for himself or herself; gainsharing systems, in contrast, emphasize what can be gained by working better together as a team. Rarely are individual incentives equitably maintained. If part of a union contract, the union must be involved in the elimination of individual incentives since it normally negotiates part or all of the incentive system. If individual incentives exist at the time of installation, they can present thorny issues to be resolved. Some firms do mesh the systems without major difficulty, but this is rare.

8. *Inadequate Preparations.* Still weak in our research methodology is the way to establish whether a firm is a good candidate for installation and ultimate success. The ideas presented in this book should help significantly in this evaluation process. But what about the firm that considers itself inadequately prepared but still wants to proceed? How does it prepare for installation? Each of the major problem areas addressed in this book must be carefully reviewed. These can include broad areas of management commitment, employee identification

with problems, and financial system sophistication. Adequate preparation for each of these may take considerable time and resources. The more the employee involvement in the design, implementation, and operation of the plan, the more time it takes.

Frankly, many managers are unwilling to make such an investment and will drop investigation. The full implementation time is probably around one to two years, with impatient managements losing interest before the preparatory work is completed. Time lags are not necessary, but they normally occur. If a shorter time period for installation is necessary, the reasons for this rapid implementation must be fully understood before gainsharing is undertaken. Some plans are installed very rapidly even with employee involvement.

9. *Difficulty with Devising Calculations.* Obviously in some situations calculation alternatives will be limited. Rarely is it impossible to develop a viable calculation if management is determined. The first seven chapters offer more total information on gainsharing than exists anywhere else. An optimal calculation will normally result if key decision makers truly want to achieve organizational goals compatible with those discussed in this book. The key is to accept the relevant behavioral philosophies found in the optimal conditions for traditional gainsharing that are listed at the end of this chapter.

THE FUTURE AND GAINSHARING

Even given the present level of theory development, we believe that the accelerating growth trends in gainsharing will continue. We note several reasons for this trend. Many business and government leaders publicly proclaim the great importance of improved performance in maintaining a satisfactory standard of living without major inflation. No other system links the behaviorally intrinsic variables of employee involvement, recognition, problem identification, and accountability with the extrinsic rewards as does employee involvement gainsharing. This reward system will undoubtedly play an increasing role in helping to expand commitment to performance improvement simply because it will make more managers behaviorally attuned to the advantages of employee involvement. Managers will be more motivated because they will share the financial returns of true performance increase.

Better references on gainsharing research and practice are available today. In the past, there were few articles on gainsharing and virtually no books. Fortunately, this is no longer true. The notes at the end of each chapter indicate a vast and ever growing literature. Chapter 2 is ample proof of this fact. The nation's need to increase productivity is one reason for this growth, coupled with the expansion of principles that underlie most long-term successful applications of the various systems. Many more researchers are becoming involved in gainsharing. International exposure and application are bound to grow as other industrialized countries become aware of the fairly elaborate system that the Japanese have for sharing productivity improvements with employees. It is still perplexing to encounter a large number of managers who have not yet heard of gainsharing, considering the references that are available.

More flexible gainsharing, goalsharing, and winsharing formulas are now available. In earlier years, many managers perceived the need to establish fairly common productivity-sharing calculations. Today, calculations can suit varying conditions and most organizations custom design one to fit their own needs at a particular time. Calculations have been designed and installed for processing and job order manufacturing concerns, engineering firms, banks, hospitals, insurance companies, state and city organizations. They may be based on performance measures, such as physical measures of output and input, or on financial productivity measures, such as profit and return on investment. Some calculations approach the problem from a prospective of targeted productivity performance and are entirely based on goals. We believe that this expansion of calculations will create gainsharing applications for many more different types of organizations and sitings including even small groups.

Our gainsharing knowledge and experience have grown tremendously in recent years. It appears that more gainsharing systems have been installed during the past five years than in its entire previous history. The expansion that Joe Scanlon thought would develop in the 1950s seems to be happening 40 years later.

Organizational culture is changing fairly rapidly. Confrontational cultures within organizations are giving way to more cooperative cultures. Both unions and managements perceive much to be gained from developing a more cooperative culture because they are identifying competitors, both domestic and foreign, as the enemy rather than the forces within the organization. Management is now starting to indicate a willingness to spend the time and money to develop the employee-oriented systems that will serve to meld individual goals with corporate goals. This current emphasis is further indicative of that increased focus on the mechanisms of cooperation.

Comprehensive organizational development (OD) makes more sense today as companies become more interdependent and automated, and as they constantly change. Slow-moving organizations will be left by the wayside in the 1990s and later, and increasing numbers of managers will likely perceive the goal-oriented, employee-involvement gainsharing plans to be desirable systems toward which to move. Many firms using cross functional teams and Total Quality Management (TQM) and other systems that can evolve into gainsharing because of pressures to share the financial benefits of performance improvements. TQM, labor-management committees, and other involvement structures can be redesigned to become gainsharing involvement teams.

Aside from the trend toward high acceptance of employee involvement systems, more gainsharing systems are successes today. Plans seem to be better installed, monitored, and evaluated. Although this figure is not well substantiated, the long-term success rate is probably 65 percent. Some of the firms that drop their systems because of economic conditions would prefer to manage in a participative style and eventually reconsider this decision. Obviously, some firms do eventually drop their gainsharing plans. Most observers believe that a long-term success rate of 65 percent is outstanding considering some of the situations surrounding installation and some of the monitoring techniques used.

Richard Pascale and William Athos, in *The Art of Japanese Management*, express the belief that the superiority of Japanese management is explained by its managerial beliefs, assumptions, perceptions, style, and skill.[1] These authors maintain that involved workers are the key to high performance. In view of this assumption, if some Japanese managers can be said to be ahead of some American ones, then traditional gainsharing managers must be considered to be ahead of both these groups. New scholars also maintain that Japanese managers practice interdependence. That is, the human resource of a Japanese corporation is regarded as a collaborator—not merely an extension of a machine. Indeed, employees are not just called associates, they *are* associates. If managerial style is a functional factor in Japanese firms, then traditional gainsharing firms with high involvement reflect a kind of style that is open, oriented to problem solving, and conducive to positive working relationships in the future, with no win/lose or face-saving forms of interpersonal competition. And, over 40 million Japanese employees share the win/win concept through extensive bonus plans.

Where does this leave us? We indicated that some newer forms of gainsharing are evolving and are currently being designed. These new forms are a logical extension of the development of gainsharing since the 1930s and it is very likely that we will see examples of these new forms in the 1990s and later. The American work force is continually getting older, wiser, and more skilled. The forces that produce high-quality workers and managers will inevitably produce newer and better forms of gainsharing, with the ultimate goal perhaps being the self-directed work force.

While the practices of some gainsharing firms may foster more pseudoparticipation other than a true enhancement of the quality of work-life, a few firms are starting to adopt what might be considered new and different forms of gainsharing. Two commonly cited examples are the companies Donnelley Mirrors and Herman Miller. Both firms use innovative and advanced calculations. These companies have also had developed involvement systems and work force commitment that are likely to set the standard in the future for newer forms of gainsharing.

In 1992, the American Compensation Association (ACA) received responses on 432 performance-reward plans. Many of these plans were gainsharing plans or modified gainsharing plans. The study reveals that performance-reward plans lead organizational change as often as they lag it. Median payouts, across all plans, were a modest $867 per employee per year, or about 3 percent of base pay. These same organizations gained a median of $2,410 per employee in improved performance. Overall, the ACA study reports that performance-reward plan companies performed as well or better than their competitors for the three year study period (1989–1991). Results of a survey from 269 gainsharing firms in North America reported by Kim[2] in 1994 offer further confirmation of how employee involvement significantly impacts quality improvement. Very high levels of statistical significance were found in the association of employee involvement with improvements in product quality and improvements in production processes. Kim assessed quantitatively many of the traditional propositions discussed in this book. Perhaps his most significant finding, both statistically and substantively, is that the higher the employee understanding of the gainsharing calculation, the stronger the association with employee effort to improve quality. Thus, the benefits of gainsharing were recently documented, but what of the human side of gainsharing?

Exhibit 16.1 illustrates results collected by the U.S. General Accounting Office in a survey of gainsharing firms.[3] Of note is the fact that many gainsharing firms recognize that nonmonetary benefits are clearly associated with successful experiences. Better teamwork, increased job satisfaction, less resistance to change, and closer identification with the firm go hand in hand with the improvements in performance, as shown by the findings of the GAO survey. It is not surprising that improved labor-management relations, fewer grievances, less absenteeism, and reduced turnover are associated with gainsharing firms. The 1992 and 1994 ACA studies referred to in this book reinforce these findings.[4]

We are enthusiastic about and encouraged by recent growth in gainsharing research and application. As the General Accounting Office study concluded, "[w]e have found that when properly implemented and administered, productivity sharing plans can effectively contribute to improved productivity." We agree with this statement and believe that its future is bright. We hope this book will help those who wish to conduct research in and/or implement productivity gainsharing.

Lastly, we end this book with a list of conditions that reflect normative beliefs surrounding this important reward system. We hope that each of these can challenge policy makers within high commitment organizations to meet or exceed *optimal* conditions of gainsharing.

OPTIMAL CONDITIONS FOR GAINSHARING

1. Each plan must be custom designed to fit the specific culture, technology, and environment of each functionally autonomous organizational unit.
2. Competitive wage and fringe benefit programs should be operative *prior* to any consideration of a gainsharing plan.

Exhibit 16.1   Nonmonetary Benefits of Productivity Sharing Programs

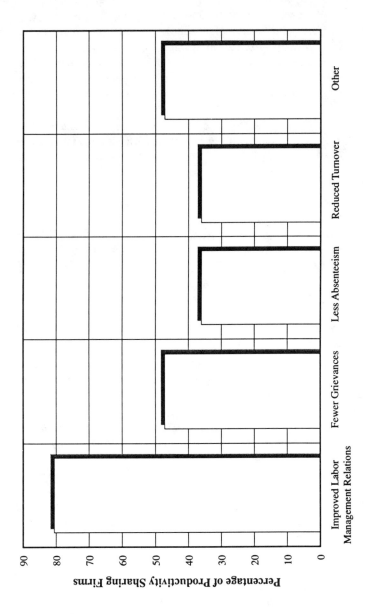

3. A gainsharing plan should not be used as a *salvage operation* but in successful and competently managed companies, although it can be useful in leading organizational change.
4. A gainsharing plan *should not* be installed along with an individual incentive system because of their competing philosophies.
5. A gainsharing plan should include *all employees at a given facility*—from the least skilled to the most skilled.
6. Gainsharing bonuses *should be paid as a percent of wages or salaries earned* during the bonus period, i.e., the actual bonus co-varies with actual earnings or at least complies with the Fair Labor Standards Act.
7. Gainsharing, because it is paid to everyone, *should not* be a part of the union contract. However, union participation in the design and implementation of gainsharing is a requirement for an acceptable plan.
8. The gainsharing plan year should be kept *out of phase* with the union contract termination date.
9. Gainsharing plan implementation *requires* an education program that enlists the great majority of employees.
10. When gainsharing replaces a previous incentive system, *special provisions for equity* and minimum levels of acceptable performance need to be secured, i.e., red-circle rates or agreements to maintain both equity and productivity need to be in place.
11. Installation of any new gainsharing plan should be subject to a *significant majority affirmative vote* of all employees.
12. The first year of gainsharing *should be a trial period* with future continuation of gainsharing after evaluation and possibly another vote.
13. Termination of gainsharing *should be subject to a 90-day notice* by management or by any significant group, such as a union.
14. Everyone involved should have *an understanding of the gainsharing formula*, at least in terms of its connection to performance.
15. The gainsharing formula *should be monitored regularly* and carefully to ensure equity to the company and to the employees and perhaps have a clause on windfalls.
16. Discussion of the labor contract and of fringe benefits *is inappropriate* in departmental and organizationwide meetings.
17. Initial gainsharing success depends on dedication, enthusiasm, and *competence of a champion*, such as the highest ranked manager at the facility.
18. The *role of catalysts* in developing, disseminating, and educating the operating facts of life are very important in the building of trust and confidence.
19. *Managerial succession requires that a thorough training and indoctrination in gainsharing principles* be conducted for any new manager taking charge of a gainsharing assignment.

20. All suggestions and minutes of the involvement system should be *open, public, and distributed* so that maximum employee recognition is achieved.

21. Quality of the *product should be improved* as part of a plan to achieve total organization performance.

22. A certain percentage of the bonus *should be reserved* to cover during deficit periods. This strategy will serve both to protect the company's interests and to encourage employees to think in the long-term.

23. The plantwide committee is a *consultative or advising body and not a decision-making one*—management manages, the committee advises.

24. *Rapid follow-up on the disposition of suggestions encourages more employees to make more suggestions.*

25. Foremen and first-line supervisors *must be involved in the plan*; otherwise they may choose to undermine it.

26. The productivity-sharing calculation, or any changes to it, must establish the bonus at a level that *does not jeopardize the company's ability to compete in the marketplace.*

27. Bonus earning should be *paid separately* from normal earnings, i.e. employees should receive a separate check.

28. Since teamwork is the key to success, *do not reward* one group of workers at the expense of other workers.

29. Employees *should be involved* in the implementation of the plan.

30. *The entire system should be reviewed in detail at least annually.*

Notes

1. R.T. Pascale and A. G. Athos, *The Art of Japanese Management* (New York: Simon and Schuster, 1981).

2. Dong-one Kim, "Factors Influencing Organizational Performance in Gainsharing Programs," Working Paper of The School for Workers and Industrial Relations Institute, The University of Wisconsin–Madison, Madison, WI, June 1994.

3. U.S. General Accounting Office, *Productivity Sharing Programs: Can They Contribute to Productivity Improvements?* AFMD-81-22 (Gaithersburg, Md.: U.S. General Accounting Office, March 3, 1981).

4. J. McAdams and E. Hawk, *Capitalizing on Human Assets: The Benchmark Study* (Scottsdale, Arizona: American Compensation Association, 1992); "Gainsharing," *ACA News,* March 1994.

Glossary of Gainsharing Terms*

Allowed Labor formula. A calculation similar to the Improshare formula. The base ratio equals the allowed labor activity multiplied by the allowed wage with a provision for all indirect labor costs.

Base Productivity Factor. The relationship in the base period between the actual hours worked by all employees and the value of the work-hours produced by these employees. This value is determined by the measurement standards used in the base period, or:

$$\text{BPF} = \frac{\text{Direct labor hours + indirect labor hours}}{\text{Total standard value hours (Improshare)}}$$

Base Ratio. The total personnel costs divided by the sales value of production (sales ± change inventory valued at cost or sales price). The original single ratio of Joseph Scanlon, often referred to as the single ratio of labor.

Bonus reserve. A portion of the gross bonus set aside to compensate for deficit months. At the end of each gainsharing year, any reserve is distributed. Any year-end deficit is absorbed by the firm.

Buy-Back principle. Workers receive a cash payment for productivity gains they achieve over established ceilings. For this bonus, management has the right to change the product standard.

Ceiling. A productivity limit. Productivity exceeding the ceiling can be banked and eventually brought back to the employees in the form of a cash payment—e.g., the buy-back.

Fixed payroll. On a current basis, the total employment costs for the human resources whose time does not vary directly with annual production volume.

Gainsharing. A generic term used to describe a broad range of sharing systems usually based on some difference between actual costs and an equitable standard.

Goalsharing. A generic term describing a broad range of sharing systems not solely based on cost. Current performance toward goals is compared to a historical standard and improvements trigger organizational bonuses.

---

*Adapted from: B. E. Moore, *Sharing the Gains of Productivity* (Scarsdale, N.Y.: Work in America Institute and Pergamon Press, 1982).

Improshare®. Invented by Mitchell Fein, the name is an acronym for *Im*proved *Pro*ductivity Through *Shar*ing. Past average productivity determines the Base Productivity Factor (BPF). The BPF is multiplied by standard hours to produce Improshare® hours. The actual hours required to produce acceptable results less the Improshare® hours can create a bonus that is split 50–50 by the company and all employees.

Incentive. Motivating action toward the expectation of a reward; inducement, influence.

Involvement system. Ranges from a type of suggestion system that emphasizes involvement to facilitate productivity-related suggestions to elaborate self-managed teams.

Memo of understanding. A document that defines the gainsharing plan— especially in regard to defining the bonus calculation and any involvement system responsibilities. While it can be used in a union environment, it is really a document that describes the plan's policies and procedures.

Multi-Cost formula. A calculation that includes some costs in addition to labor, but can include most or even all costs, which are then generally divided by the sales value of production. While based, like profit sharing, on success of the firm if most costs are included, it has many advantages over profit sharing since it is productivity related.

Multi-Pool formula. A calculation growing in popularity that establishes a series of pools, such as labor, performance, quality, and safety.

Participating payroll. Those employees sharing in the bonus payout— typically all employees (managers and workers) less the sales force and probationary employees.

Production (or departmental) committee or team. A committee composed of employee and management representatives that considers productivity-improving suggestions from its area. It refers all suggestions not within its realm of responsibility to the screening committee or larger plant board for review and, perhaps, for broader implementation.

Production value. The difference between the market value of goods and the material cost and services used in producing these goods equal to the value added by the firm.

Profit sharing. A system under which the firm pays compensation to employees in addition to their regular wages, based upon the profits of the company. While not output/input related, it is usually based on a definite formula specifying how much of the profit is to be distributed and how it is to be computed, usually at the end of the fiscal year. Some people consider profit sharing to be one form of gainsharing if paid more frequently than once a year.

Quality circles. This team-building concept involves small groups of departmental work leaders and line operators who have volunteered to spend time helping solve various departmental problems. The groups are taught problem-solving techniques and how to present their solutions to management. These circles are similar to Scanlon production committees in concept.

Rucker committee. These committees are composed of nonmanagement and management representatives whose purpose is to improve communication between workers and management about suggestions, problems, and solutions.

Rucker plan®. A productivity gainsharing program that measures economic productivity as the index of the overall effectiveness of a work group. Its goal is to maximize the output value of production (value added) for a given input value of payroll.

Rucker Standard. The percentage of the production value paid out in wages and benefits to nonexempt employees. It is calculated by dividing variable payroll costs by the production value (revenue minus outside purchases):

$$\text{Rucker Standard} = \frac{\text{Payroll costs included}}{\substack{\text{Production value} \\ \text{(revenue} - \text{outside purchases)}}}$$

If costs are less than this standard, a bonus is earned.

Sales value of production. The actual period's sales, plus or minus the inventory.

Scanlon plan. An organizationwide performance improvement plan designed to increase productivity through greater efficiency and reduced costs. The basic elements of the plan are the philosophy and practice of cooperation, the involvement system, and formulas to measure increased productivity and distribute bonuses.

Scanlon single ratio formula. One of the original productivity gainsharing formulas, the base ratio is often expressed as:

$$\frac{\text{Labor costs}}{\text{Sales value of production}} = \text{base ratio}$$

The base ratio is the expected relationship between labor costs and the sales value of production. Actual labor costs are subtracted from expected labor costs to create a bonus or deficit.

Screening committee. Composed of representatives from nonmanagement and management employees, it reviews and disposes of suggestions from the production committees, reviews bonus results, and discusses the economics of the firm. It is called a council by some firms.

Split ratio formula. A calculation composed of two or more base ratios of payroll costs divided by value of production, with each calculated for a product line to help cope with product mix issues.

Standard time. The time, usually established by a time and motion study or some other method, required for an employee to perform a specific operation without undue fatigue. Incentive earnings are gained when the worker produces in less than the standard time.

Suggestion systems. Employee involvement programs that provide employees the opportunity to give ideas to management that can increase the effectiveness and efficiency of the firm.

Value-Added formula. A formula that is similar to the Rucker formula. The value of production (sales plus changes in inventory) less outside purchases) materials, etc.) multiplied by the historically determined base ratio to equal the allowed labor cost. Then, the allowed cost minus actual cost equals the increase or decrease to productivity.

Variable payroll. Total employment costs on current basis, for people whose time input varies directly with annual production. Also, these are costs that one may want to control on a directly variable basis with current volume.

Variable purchases. Costs to procure goods and services that are consumed during production. These vary with the level of production. Management wants employees to try to conserve them by seeing their impact on the bonus; especially applicable to the Rucker Plan.

Work-Hour standard. The average number of work-hours required to produce a finished product as calculated by dividing the total work-hours by units produced. May also be based on accounting or engineered time standards.

Index

About the Authors

Brian Graham-Moore is Professor of Management at The University of Texas at Austin, where he has been since 1972. He received his B.A. (1961) from Northwestern University, his M.A. (1967) and Ph.D. (1971) from Washington University, Saint Louis. From 1964 to 1966, he was on the corporate personnel staff of Helene Curtis Industries, Chicago. From 1968 to 1972, he was on the faculty of the Graduate School of Business, The University of Chicago. Author of *Sharing the Gains of Productivity,* a monograph for Work in America, he has co-authored two previous books on Gainsharing. They are *The Scanlon Way to Improved Productivity: A Practical Guide* and *Productivity Gainsharing.* His primary research and consulting interests are reward systems, job analysis methods, and human resource information systems.

Timothy L. Ross is Partner and Director of the Ross Gainsharing Institute in Chapel Hill, North Carolina. He received his Ph.D. from Michigan State University (1969) and is a CPA. He is co-author of *The Scanlon Way to Improved Productivity: A Practical Guide,* published by John Wiley and Sons, *Productivity Gainsharing,* published by Prentice-Hall, *Gainsharing: Plans for Improving Performance,* published by BNA Books, and five manuals on gainsharing. In addition, he has written over 75 articles published by various organizations on different aspects of gainsharing. Dr. Ross also consults with organizations throughout North America, Europe, and Asia on all aspects of employee involvement gainsharing. He has worked in the area for over 25 years.

James W. Dean, Jr. is Associate Professor of Management in the College of Business Administration, University of Cincinnati. He received his Ph.D. from the Graduate School of Industrial Administration, Carnegie-Mellon University, in 1983. He conducts research on total quality management, advanced manufacturing, concurrent engineering, and strategic decision making, and has conducted collaborative research projects with many major corporations. Author of many journal articles, Professor Dean has published two books: *Deciding to Innovate: How Firms Justify Advanced Technology* (Ballinger, 1987), and *Total Quality: Management, Organization, and Strategy* (with James Evans, West Publishing, 1994).

Paul S. Goodman is professor of industrial administration and psychology in the Graduate School of Industrial Administration at Carnegie-Mellon

University, where he is also the Director of the Center for the Management of Technology and Information. He received his B.A. (1959) from Trinity College in economics, his M.B.A. (1961) from Amos Tuck School at Dartmouth College, and his Ph.D. (1966) from Cornell University in organizational psychology. His primary research interests are in the effects of technology and social systems on organizational structure and effectiveness. He is author or editor of many books on organizational behavior including *Assessing Organizational Change: The Rushton Quality of Work Experiment* (1979), *Designing Effective Work Groups* (1986), *Technology and Organizations* (1990), published by Jossey-Bass.

Larry Hatcher is an associate professor of psychology at Winthrop College, Rock Hill, South Carolina. His main areas of research include employee attitudes, participative management, and gainsharing. He received his Ph.D. in industrial and organizational psychology from Bowling Green State University. He recently completed *A Step by Step Approach to Using the SAS System* (1994), a two-volume work for SAS Institute, Inc.

James E. Jarrett is a Senior Research Scientist for the Center for Legal Studies, The University of Texas at Austin. Previously he was Director of Research at the Texas Advisory Commission on Intergovernmental Relations in Austin, Texas. Formerly he was Director of the Productivity Center at the national Council of State Governments. He holds a doctorate in political science and public administration from the University of Pennsylvania.

Ruth Ann Ross is a Partner of the Ross Gainsharing Institute, a consulting and research firm that specializes in the implementation, evaluation, and monitoring of gainsharing systems in organizations throughout North America, Europe, and Asia. She has published numerous articles on various aspects of employee involvement gainsharing and has developed extensive survey techniques and over one hundred hours of education modules.